Sean Lester

The Guardian of a Small Flickering Light

Marit Fosse and John Fox

Hamilton Books

An Imprint of
Rowman & Littlefield
Lanham • Boulder • New York • Toronto • Plymouth, UK

Copyright © 2016 by Hamilton Books
4501 Forbes Boulevard, Suite 200, Lanham, Maryland 20706
Hamilton Books Acquisitions Department (301) 459-3366

Unit A, Whitacre Mews, 26-34 Stannary Street,
London SE11 4AB, United Kingdom

All rights reserved
Printed in the United States of America
British Library Cataloguing in Publication Information Available

Library of Congress Control Number: 2015956706
ISBN: 978-0-7618-6610-7 (pbk : alk. paper)—ISBN: 978-0-7618-6611-4 (electronic)

Photo of Albert Forster © ÖNB Vienna OEGZ P 491/1
Photo of Arthur Greiser © ÖNB Vienna OEGZ P 837/1
Photo of Edward Phelan © ILO Historical Photo Archives
All other photos courtesy of the Archives of the League of Nations, Geneva.

∞™ The paper used in this publication meets the minimum requirements of American National Standard for Information Sciences Permanence of Paper for Printed Library Materials, ANSI/NISO Z39.48-1992.

Contents

Foreword — v
By Michael Møller, Director-General, United Nations Headquarters, Geneva

Introduction — 1

1 A Brief Account of Recent Irish History — 5
2 Who Was Sean Lester? — 11
3 The League of Nations — 19
4 The Manchurian Question — 27
5 Latin American Matters — 37
6 Disarmament and Finance — 43
7 Secretariat Appointments — 57
8 Minority Questions — 65
9 Appointed High Commissioner in Danzig — 73
10 Danzig in 1933 and 1934 — 91
11 Danzig 1935 — 101
12 Danzig, 1936 and Beyond — 117
13 Ethiopia/Abyssinia — 139
14 Deputy Secretary-General, 1937–1940 — 147
15 War Begins, 1939 — 159
16 The Summer of 1940 — 171
17 Becoming Secretary-General — 191
18 The End of the League — 205

Bibliography 211
Index 213

Foreword

By Michael Møller, Director-General, United Nations Headquarters, Geneva

Sean Lester was colour-blind. That is why he lost his job working as a clerk on the Northern Ireland railway system. He liked to tell his family that if it had not been for this dismissal, he would have pursued his career on the railways, probably retiring as the stationmaster of some important terminus, such as Belfast Central. Now he had to seek a new profession and started work as a journalist. The loss to the Northern Ireland railway system turned out to be the gain of the international community at a critical time in world history.

After involvement in the Irish independence movement, Lester was appointed in 1929 as the new Irish Free State's representative to the League of Nations in Geneva, and immediately recognized by his peers in Geneva as an industrious and able politician of integrity. After his first year in Geneva, the Irish Free State was elected as a member of the powerful Council of the League of Nations and Lester moved to the centre of global politics. In 1934, he was appointed as the League's High Commissioner in the Free City of Danzig, and then promoted to the second-highest post of Deputy Secretary-General in Geneva before eventually becoming the last Secretary-General of the organization, taking over from his disgraced predecessor Joseph Avenol in 1940. As Secretary-General, he found himself the "captain of a waterlogged boat", with only a skeleton crew in a deserted Palais des Nations, fighting to maintain the remaining dignity and prestige of the institution, which he eventually closed down as his final task. It was an incredible destiny for a man who always stated that he was without ambition, who had no university education and no foreign ministry experience, and yet succeeded in reaching one of the highest offices of the time through skill, intelligence and hard work.

In this book on the life of the last Secretary-General of the League of Nations, Marit Fosse and John Fox take us back to the time between the two world wars marked by a tremendous economic crisis, the rise of populist parties and fascist leaders, and a spiralling arms race that brought the world to the Second World War. Drawing on the rich material in the archives of the League of Nations, which hold Sean Lester's diary from 1934 to 1947, this volume provides a new perspective on an era that is usually seen as a failure of the multilateral system with the League of Nations unable to confront the forces that eventually led to war. As such, it is a powerful account of the events and experiences that have shaped our United Nations today, and continues to inspire our action.

Yet, Sean Lester's main legacy to us is the unwavering belief in the value of multilateral solutions and in the role of all States — large or small — in international organizations and in global politics to shape a common future. Despite his time in Danzig, witnessing some of the very worst episodes in the nazi take-over and experiencing how few were prepared to accept the gravity of the situation on which he was reporting, Lester never lost this conviction. As the last Secretary-General, he was in charge of the transfer of the assets of the League of Nations to the newly-established United Nations, demonstrating the resilience of multilateralism and its ability to be adapted to new realities based on both negative and positive lessons of the past. Above all, he showed what can be achieved through a sense of duty and respect for the rules governing our common society.

Readers will draw their own conclusions but there is no doubt that this work serves to bring much-needed attention to the continued value of multilateralism, to the need for resolute and collective action in the face of intolerance and discrimination, and to the enduring importance of an international system based on the principles of solidarity, equity and justice. It is story that deserves to be better known.

Introduction

We have previously written about the history of the League of Nations and Fridtjof Nansen, a nineteenth century explorer and the first high commissioner for refugees in the 1920s. In the present book we wanted to look into the life and achievements of a man who, as he often said himself, was without any ambition, but who nevertheless proved himself to be an outstanding diplomat—the last Secretary-General of the League of Nations, the Irishman Sean Lester.

Lester's legacy to the League and to modern times is perhaps his belief in in small states' roles in international organizations, and an outstanding witness through his personal dairies and writings to one of the most problematical but also sad chapters of European history. It is regrettable that this unassuming and courageous Irishman should remain so long forgotten and unrecognized, even in his own land.

The archives of the League of Nations in Geneva hold Sean Lester's diary from 1934 to 1947 when he served with or for the League of Nations in Geneva and Danzig, and it is on this documentation that we have largely based ourselves. We have drawn many thousands of items of information and quotations from Lester's diary. It would have been tedious to enumerate these references in endnotes, so we would recommend the interested reader to locate this material in his diary according to the chronological date of the events to which it applies. It would not be entirely correct to call it a "diary" but more something of a "scrapbook", since it contains not only his personal view of daily events but official and private letters by himself and from his correspondents that must have been retyped by his secretary, newspaper reports of events, family news, poems and even a few jokes. Although he met neither Mussolini nor Hitler, he was acquainted with hundreds of politicians, diplomats and international civil servants of the inter-war years, many of whom are referred to by their initials or nicknames—which does not always make it easy to understand to whom he is referring. His diary often reflects an Irish point of view and is not always strictly chronological. Our aim has been to give students and others interested in Lester's work and life a readable academic book and to take the readers on a historical journey through a time rich in historical events. The facts and documents described in this book have been verified through other sources in order to make it as accurate as possible, without becoming involved in the historical debate. We owe an immense debt of gratitude to the work of the authors mentioned in our reference section.

Lester kept a considerable number of letters and texts of all kinds during his life. His notes were inspired by minor and major events, the working of the League of Nations, personalities he met, political developments, some family matters . . . and fishing. They varied in length between a half-page and five pages or more, at times on a daily or twice daily basis, followed by periods of stress and imminent danger when nothing was put down and the diary hidden. A large part of the journal (1935–1941) was typed on looseleaves of paper by Lester himself or his secretary, with date and place, and often annotated "private", or "secret" or "confidential".

After his death in 1959, and several moves of house, all of these papers were mislaid and presumed to be lost. However, in 1980 an important part of his journal was found covering much of the period 1935–1941. These papers were thought to be all that had survived, and were, therefore, copied, bound under the title "Diary" together with some less interesting papers. Subsequently three more batches of papers turned up including the rest of his journal for 1934–1946, and all his other papers from 1929 to 1959.

The diary, consisting in two bound volumes, was donated to the United Nations Library in Geneva, Registry, Records and Archives Unit, by Sean Lester's daughters: Dorothy Mary Gageby, Patricia Kilroy and Ann Gorski in July 1981.

There is a great temptation to draw parallels between the epoch during which the League of Nations played its role and the world as it exists today. It is evident that there has been extraordinary progress in international affairs since the League's creation. World institutions that were being created at the time included the Permanent Court of International Justice in The Hague, the International Labour Office, the International Health Office and the High Commissioner for Refugees; all of these exist today in one form or another as the continuing legacy of the League of Nations.

A particularly interesting aspect of his diaries is his descriptions of the hundreds of people he encountered, from world-class politicians with charismatic personalities to nazi thugs of unspeakable arrogance. In between we meet all shades of politicians with different levels of morality from the almost saintly to the incompetent, career civil servants often of profound competence and integrity, and a range of other colourful characters ranging from adventurers to zealots. Apart from national leaders such as Churchill, Hitler, Mussolini, Roosevelt and Stalin, we also encounter people in this book whose principles of civilized behaviour fall well below acceptable standards. Some of the people you are going to meet were executed by hanging for war crimes and some others were found guilty of treason and died by firing squad. There are also people who lived lives of virtuous modesty and yet whose determination, clarity of vision and perseverance at key moments changed the face of the world forever—and perhaps Lester can be counted among them (except that he would have said "stubbornness" instead of "perseverance").

Through Lester's life and writings we will reconstruct a period of time that can in many aspects be compared to our own. Lester was worked for many years as a journalist, and he understood the importance of what was going on around him during a troubled time. We would like to draw attention to the similarities with our present day and age, and make students in particular aware that what happened in the 1930s could happen again. The facts are there and we would ignore them at our peril.

When Sean Lester was a young man, Ireland passed through a number of major historical events and he knew personally several of the key players. To understand Irish history during the early part of the twentieth century it is necessary to go back to the beginning of the nineteenth century, when Ireland was part of the British Empire. However, nationalism was beginning to emerge in many countries, and particularly in Ireland. It is therefore first necessary to describe some of the episodes that made it possible for this man, who had no formal higher education, to come to the fore.

We wish to thank David Chikvaidze, Chef de Cabinet of the Director-General and former Director of the United Nations Library in Geneva, for the support, encouragement and invaluable help he gave to us at each stage of this project. We are also deeply indebted to Jacques Orbeson and Lee Robinson for their valuable help and assistance. Alongside David Chikvaidze, we wish to thank the Archives Team of the League of Nations, especially Mrs Blandine Blukacz-Louisfert, without forgetting the kindness and support of the entire staff of the United Nations Library in Geneva – Carla Bellota, Pablo Bosch, Adriano Goncalves e Silva, Christina Girdano, Salvatore Leggio an Sdebastian Vernay – who were of the greatest help to us.

Chapter One

A Brief Account of Recent Irish History

The name Ireland refers to the entire thirty-two-county island, but since 1922 the country has been divided into the twenty-six counties which are now called Éire or Ireland and the six counties of Northern Ireland—also known as Ulster—forming part of the United Kingdom.

Among the early leaders in favour of Irish independence were Wolfe Tone,[1] Robert Emmett[2] and Daniel O'Connell.[3] Irish Gaelic had been the predominant language of the Irish people for most of their recorded history, but since the seventeenth century an increasing proportion of the population spoke English. The Acts of Union of 1800 brought the Kingdom of Great Britain and the Kingdom of Ireland into an arrangement known as the United Kingdom of Great Britain and Ireland, abolishing the Irish Parliament and giving Ireland representation in the British Parliament at Westminster. Up until the middle of the twentieth century Northern Ireland was dominated by the Protestant form of Christianity with the population speaking English. The political leaders of this community were known as Unionists, because they strongly favoured union with the United Kingdom—England, Scotland and Wales also being largely Protestant. On the other hand, Southern Ireland was almost entirely faithful to the Roman Catholic form of Christianity and their most radical political leaders were known as Nationalists since they sought independence for their country, which they believed was involved in a union dominated by outsiders.

In Ireland between 1845 and 1852 there was a Great Famine, sometimes referred to as the Irish Potato Famine. A large part of the population subsisted on the potato and when the crop was destroyed by potato blight their source of food disappeared. The country was capable of feeding itself, but the total failure of the British Government to grasp the dimensions of the disaster and to come to the aid of the starving population by redistributing food meant that the Great Famine today is viewed as a form of genocide. Approximately 1 million people died while at least another million emigrated, causing the island's population to fall by between 20 and 25%; Gaelic-speaking areas were hit especially hard. The famine was a watershed in the history of Ireland. Its effects permanently changed the demographic, political and cultural landscape and became a rallying point for subsequent political movements.

Throughout the nineteenth century opposition to the union with Britain began to take root. In the 1880s and 1890s the Irish politician Charles Stewart Parnell,[4] seeking some form of self-government, succeeded in introducing two Home Rule bills in the British Parliament: the first of 1886 was defeated in the House of Commons, while the second of 1893 was passed by the Commons but rejected by the House of Lords. Younger and more radical nationalists then turned toward more extreme forms of separatism. The concept of a Gaelic nation, completely independent from the United Kingdom, was accompanied by a cultural revival lead by the poet W.B. Yeats[5] and Lady Augusta Gregory.[6] However, these movements only represented a minority of the Irish population. Innovatory political thinking by Arthur Griffith[7] gave rise to a new image of the Irish people entitled *Sinn Féin* [ourselves alone], a nationalist political movement founded in 1905 favouring total separation from the United Kingdom.

During the first decade of the twentieth century, Irish politics became increasingly militarized. In order to defuse this situation, a Third Home Rule Bill was introduced by British Prime Minister H.H. Asquith[8] in 1912. The Ulster Unionists (that is to say the Northern Irish Protestants), led by Sir Edward Carson,[9] opposed home rule because they feared that they, in their turn, would then be dominated by a Roman Catholic government in Dublin. Following a series of delays, the bill was never implemented before the First World War broke out.

During the war, large numbers of Irishmen willingly joined the British Army and sacrificed their lives on the Western Front. However, the British Government insisted that, in return for post-war negotiations about Irish independence, it would expect to conscript Irishmen to fight in the trenches. This was unacceptable to the Irish Republican Brotherhood, which met on 5 September 1914, a month after the British Government had declared war on Germany. They decided to stage an armed uprising before the war ended and to accept whatever help Germany might offer. Among the plans was the landing of a German expeditionary force on the west coast of Ireland, while a simultaneous revolt in Dublin would divert the British forces allowing the Germans to get a foothold. Sometime in 1915 Joseph Plunkett[10] joined the Irish Republican Brotherhood and soon after was sent to Germany to meet with Sir Roger Casement,[11] who was negotiating with the German Government on behalf of the rebels, They expected that Germany would win the

First World War and that a rising of at least three days would allow Ireland to take a seat at the peace conference. Though declaring an Irish Republic in 1916, they even considered inviting the Kaiser's youngest son Joachim to reign over a Kingdom of Ireland after the war, where Irish Gaelic would again become the national language. Various groups of armed citizens agreed to act together at Easter 1916. The Germans, who were skeptical of Casement, but nonetheless aware of the military advantage they could gain from an uprising in Ireland, offered the Irish 20,000 old rifles, ten machine guns and accompanying ammunition, a fraction of the quantity of the arms Casement had hoped for. The German weapons were never landed in Ireland. The ship transporting them, a German cargo vessel called *Libau* disguised as a Norwegian vessel, was intercepted by the British and scuttled.

At about 11 a.m. on Easter Monday 1916 armed men occupied a number of important buildings in the inner city of Dublin, which the rebels immediately set about making defensible. The General Post Office (GPO) served as their headquarters. Their intention was to establish an independent state and they proclaimed that the leaders of the rebellion would serve as the "Provisional Government of the Irish Republic" until it became possible to elect a national parliament. The whole project was far-fetched. The British authorities reacted with extraordinary vigour and, after six days of heavy fighting, the insurgent leaders were obliged to accept unconditional surrender. In a series of courts martial ninety people were sentenced to death, of whom fifteen were actually executed by firing squad. The most prominent leader to escape execution was Éamon de Valera,[12] who did so partly due to his American birth. At the time that it occurred, the rebellion enjoyed little support from the Irish general public, but the brutal reaction of the British military to end the revolt convinced a large section of previously hesitant Irish public opinion that they should support it.

The principal beneficiary of the 1916 Easter Rising was *Sinn Féin*, which became the leading political party promoting independence. In the British general elections of 1918 it won seventy-three of Ireland's 105 seats, but the successful candidates refused to attend the London Parliament, forming instead a separate legislature in Dublin. Among the successful candidates was Éamon de Valera, who had fought in 1916, and was now re-arrested by the British alongside many other Irish politicians. On 21 January 1919 twenty-five of the remaining elected members met in Dublin as *Dáil Éireann* [The Assembly of Ireland] and adopted a Declaration of Irish Independence committing themselves to the republic that had previously been declared in 1916. With the help of Michael Collins,[13] in April 1919 de Valera escaped from prison and was made Prime Minister of the new Irish Republic.

The Irish War of Independence that followed was a guerrilla war fought by the Irish Republican Army (IRA) against the British Government and its forces in Ireland. The volunteers armed themselves through attacks on police barracks and army depots, of which hundreds were destroyed. The principal leader on the Irish side was Michael Collins, who as a young man had also fought at the GPO in 1916. Collins built up a formidable intelligence network, together with a special squad which assassinated British intelligence officers and key Irish detectives. In 1920 the British Government reinforced the Irish police with some particularly ruthless ex-soldiers known as Black and Tans leading to the committing of atrocities by both sides. As the fighting became more and more ruthless, Collins assumed greater responsibility.

The Irish combatants were on the point of collapse when, in 1920, the British Government, led by David Lloyd George,[14] offered de Valera negotiations on the future of Ireland and the two sides agreed to a truce on 11 July 1921. The British sought a compromise that would keep Ireland within the British Empire while making concessions in favour of Irish independence. A new Government of Ireland Act was agreed providing a measure of home rule. After difficult negotiations, the Act divided Ireland into two parts: the six north-eastern counties—part of Ulster—were to form "Northern Ireland", while the larger southern part of the country was to form the "Irish Free State". However, both areas were to continue as a part of the United Kingdom. On 6 December 1921, a treaty was signed creating the Irish Free State consisting of the twenty-six counties of Southern Ireland, and allowing the six counties of Northern Ireland to choose to remain as an integral part of the United Kingdom, since this is what the majority of the population there wanted.

The treaty was extremely controversial in Ireland where politicians were split about accepting the separation of the country into two parts. The inauguration of the Irish Free State was followed by a civil war in Southern Ireland between those who accepted the treaty and those who did not. Finally, the anti-treaty republicans conceded defeat in May 1923. Significantly, during the civil war, Michael Collins was shot dead in an ambush at Béal na Bláth, County Cork, on 22 August 1922. As Chairman of the Irish Provisional Government (or Prime Minister), Collins was succeeded from August to December 1922 by W.T. Cosgrave.[15] Subsequently, Cosgrave served as the first President of the Executive Council of the Irish Free State from 1922 to 1932. After the civil war, Éamon de Valera and his supporters seceded from *Sinn Féin* and founded *Fianna Fáil* [known in English as the Republican Party]. In the 1930s, de Valera became the head of government on three occasions and was elected President of Ireland between 1959 and 1973.

The dissolution of further links with the United Kingdom culminated in 1937 in the adoption, by plebiscite, of a new constitution, which gave the Irish Free State full sovereignty within the British Commonwealth of Nations. Subsequently, formal ties with the British Commonwealth were cut in 1949 when the country, calling itself Éire or in the English language Ireland, declared itself an independent republic.

As regards the six counties of Northern Ireland, the recent decades of violence between elements of the Irish and/or Roman Catholic community and its British and/or Protestant community fall outside the scope of this book.

NOTES

1. Theobald Wolfe Tone (1763–1798) is regarded as the father of Irish republicanism. He was captured by British forces for his involvement in the 1798 Irish Rebellion. Before being executed, it is believed that he attempted suicide and died from mortal wounds some days later.
2. Robert Emmet (1778–1803) was an Irish nationalist and Republican, orator and rebel leader. He led an abortive rebellion against British rule in 1803 and was captured, tried and executed for high treason.
3. Daniel O'Connell (1775–1847), often referred to as The Liberator or The Emancipator, was an Irish political leader in the first half of the nineteenth century. He campaigned for Catholic Emancipation—including the right for Catholics to sit in the Westminster Parliament, denied for over 100 years—and repeal of the Act of Union which viewed Great Britain and Ireland as one country.
4. Charles Stewart Parnell (1846–1891), the founder and leader of the Irish Parliamentary Party, was a member of the British Parliament and one of the most important figures in the nineteenth century United Kingdom. Parnell represented nationalism in Ireland between 1875 until his death in 1891.
5. William Butler Yeats (1865–1939) was an Irish poet and one of the foremost figures of twentieth century English literature, a driving force behind the Irish Literary Revival and co-founder of the Abbey Theatre. In 1923 he was awarded the Nobel Prize for Literature, the first Irishman so honoured.
6. Born into a class that identified closely with British rule, Isabella Augusta, Lady Gregory (1852–1932), was an Irish dramatist, folklorist and theatre manager. With Yeats and Edward Martyn she participated in the Irish Literary Revival and co-founded the Irish Literary Theatre and the Abbey Theatre.
7. Arthur Griffith (1872–1922) was an Irish politician and writer. He served as President of Dáil Éireann from January to August 1922, and was head of the Irish delegation at the negotiations in London that produced the Anglo-Irish Treaty of 1921.
8. H.H. Asquith (1852–1928), a Liberal prime minister of the United Kingdom from 1908 to 1916, was responsible for the Parliament Act of 1911 limiting the power of the House of Lords. He led the country during the first two years of the First World War.
9. Sir Edward Henry Carson (1854–1935) was an Irish politician, barrister and judge. He gained a reputation for fearsome advocacy, supreme legal ability and was regarded as a brilliant barrister through his wit and oratory. He was leader of the Irish Unionist Alliance and Ulster Unionist Party between 1910 and 1921 and held numerous positions in the British Cabinet. It is widely understood that Northern Ireland is Carson's creation.
10. Joseph Mary Plunkett (1887–1916) was an Irish nationalist, poet and journalist, responsible for planning the Easter Rising. Following the surrender, Plunkett was held in Kilmainham Gaol and tried by court martial. Seven hours before his execution by firing squad at the age of 28, he was married in the prison chapel to his sweetheart Grace Gifford, a Protestant converted to Catholicism.
11. Sir Roger Casement (1864–1916) was an Irish nationalist, activist, patriot and poet. A British consul by profession, Casement became famous for his reports against human rights abuses in the Congo and Peru. He was arrested for treason before the Easter Uprising and taken to the Tower of London. He was stripped of his knighthood shortly before being hanged for treason.
12. The political career of Éamon de Valera (1882 – 1975) lasted from 1917 to 1973, serving multiple terms as head of the Irish Government and head of state. De Valera was born in New York City in 1882 to an Irish mother, Catherine Coll, and Juan Vivión de Valera, a

Cuban sculptor of Spanish descent. After the death of his father, Éamon was taken to Ireland by his Uncle Ned at the age of 2 and reared by his grandmother Elizabeth Coll in County Limerick.

13. Michael Collins (1890–1922) was an Irish revolutionary leader, Director of Intelligence for the Irish Republican Army, and member of the Irish delegation during the Anglo-Irish Treaty negotiations. Subsequently, he was both Chairman of the Provisional Government and Commander-in-Chief of the National Army.

14. David Lloyd George (1863–1945) is best known as the highly energetic British Prime Minister (1916–22) who guided the country to victory in the First World War. He was a major player at the Paris Peace Conference of 1919 and is regarded as the founder of the British welfare state. He oversaw the partition of Ireland between an independent Republic of Ireland and Northern Ireland. He is the only British Prime Minister who was Welsh and spoke English as a second language.

15. William Thomas "W.T." Cosgrave (1880–1965), was an Irish politician who succeeded Michael Collins as Chairman of the Irish Provisional Government from August to December 1922. He served as the first President of the Executive Council of the Irish Free State from 1922 to 1932. Once a close friend of de Valera, they split over the Government of Ireland Act in 1921.

Chapter Two

Who Was Sean Lester?

Sean Lester came from a background which was unusual among Irish diplomats and this situation was to be even more unusual in the world of delegates and officials at the League of Nations in Geneva. Born in 1888 in the village of Woodburn on the outskirts of Carrickfergus, a large coastal town in Ulster, he began life as John Ernest Lester. His father Robert ran a grocery shop and subsequently moved with his family to another shop on the Ormeau Road in the city of Belfast. John Lester went to school at the Methodist College which, despite its name, was an interdenominational and co-educational school. In the Irish context it is significant that Lester was brought up as a Methodist (i.e. a Northern Irish Protestant Christian), and his formal education ended—as was usual at that time for working-class boys—when he was 14 years old. With such a background he would normally have been loyal to the British Crown but, during the early years of the twentieth century, Lester discovered the cause of Irish independence and became interested in Irish history and the Irish language.[1]

He first worked as a railway clerk until it was discovered that he was colour-blind and he soon found himself out of a job. A meeting with another young Ulsterman, Ernest Blythe,[2] convinced him that the world had more to offer.[3] Blythe was a journalist and Lester accompanied him on cycle rides as he reported on meetings, court proceedings and markets in the region for local newspapers. Lester became a journalist himself working for a number of northern Irish newspapers—the *Portadown Express,* the *Armagh Guardian* and the *County Down Spectator*—signing his articles "Sean Mac Leastair". Throughout his life, most people knew him by the name of "Sean", but others continued to use his original name "John", while some of his close friends and family members often called him "Jack", which is a common diminutive of John. All of these names occur in his diary.

But Blythe and Lester had more in common than journalism. A broad intellectual movement calling itself the Gaelic Revival, appeared in the late nineteenth century with a commitment to the Irish Gaelic language and furthering Ireland's individual culture, religion and sports. Lester joined the Gaelic League, an inspirational cultural organization, and also the Dungannon Clubs, a young revolutionary group that sought to unite Protestant and Catholic Irish men and women with a view to achieving the country's independence. In 1908 he became a member of the Irish Republican Brotherhood and thus favoured an independent Irish State. Only a few Ulster Protestants belonged to this movement consisting of people who had the romantic notion of recreating the ancient nation of Ireland. Many years later, Lester wrote that he was looking for "Irish freedom and happiness and development, while believing that only on the basis of Irish liberty could the two islands [Great Britain and Ireland] become friends." While calling for Irish independence, the manifesto of the Dungannon Clubs also recommended abstinence from alcohol and Lester respected this directive for many years. He believed in the cause of Irish nationalism, although the Gaelic League did not commit itself entirely to this movement until 1915. It was through the League that many future political leaders and rebels first came to the fore.

As a young journalist Lester worked for several different newspapers. There was a sharp and bitter political divide in northern Ireland between Protestant Unionists and Catholic Nationalists, and both sides were extremely apprehensive of anyone who did not clearly belong to their camp. Since the economy was controlled by the Protestants, they were in a strong position to impose their attitudes on their workers. Lester's allegiance to Irish nationalism was specifically referred to by one newspaper proprietor in writing a reference for him. While it may be understood that changing job was a way of learning as much as possible about journalism and advancing his career, it could also be inferred that once his Unionist superiors learned of his enthusiasm for the Gaelic League, they were anxious that he should move on. His employers referred to his intellect, humour, reserve and capacity for untiring industry. It was also noted that he was a firm believer in the rule of law and that he was able to remain calm in the most intimidating circumstances. Firsthand knowledge about political, racial and religious tension would provide a firm foundation for his time as High Commissioner in Danzig. In 1913 Lester moved to the *Connacht Tribune* in Galway, where his nationalist views were probably more welcome and which would sow the seeds for a lifelong love for the west coast of Ireland.[4]

Lester subsequently progressed to Dublin to work for the *Daily Express* and the *Dublin Evening Mail* for which he became chief reporter in 1915. Because he had been born a Protestant and a Unionist and now clearly belonged to the opposition Nationalist movement *Sinn Féin,* he was viewed with suspicion by the (pro-British) government authorities in Dublin who at one stage tried to have him dismissed from his job.

Although he had received military training as an officer in the Irish Volunteers, on Easter Monday 1916 Lester was one of those who, due to confusion over instructions, did not become involved in the rebellion. On that day he was with Eoin MacNeill,[5] commander-in-chief of the Irish Volunteers, who issued an order that the uprising should not take place—but his order was ignored by other extremists. It is possible that Lester's abilities as a journalist and propagandist were recognized as of greater value to the nationalist cause than as a combatant. He was detained in prison overnight as a republican suspect, but the owner of the newspaper where he worked, Henry Doig,[6] required him to be released. Otherwise he continued to work normally, although doing so had become increasingly difficult. His last journalistic post was as news editor at the moderate *Freeman's Journal* between 1916 and 1922, the organ of the old Irish Nationalist Party. This newspaper was raided repeatedly by the British Army, by the Black and Tans and later by *Sinn Féin*—that is to say by military groups of all political creeds. Just for good measure, in 1922 the printing presses were blown up by a branch of the Irish Republican Army opposed to the Anglo-Irish Treaty.[7]

With Ernest Blythe as best man, in 1920 Lester had married Elizabeth Ruth Tyrrell, known as "Elsie", the daughter of a wealthy Belfast merchant. She was to be a dynamic element in Lester's future career and he never ceased to sing her praises in his diary. They would have three daughters together: Dorothy Mary (known as D.M.), Ann and Patricia.

After the Irish War of Independence, Lester found himself on the winning side, with a number of his friends joining the new government of the Irish Free State. After fifteen years in journalism, now aged 31 and with the responsibilities of marriage, Lester sought and was offered the post of Government Press Officer in Dublin. He was a firm believer in truthfulness and the freedom of the press. Through his friendship with Ernest Blythe, his post was transferred to the Department of External Affairs when the latter was set up in 1923 and he was subsequently made responsible for the modest League of Nations section. Another former journalist friend, Desmond Fitzgerald,[8] became the Minister of External Affairs. Lester's position was seen as a means of supplying Irish representatives abroad with reliable information to counteract anti-Irish propaganda inspired by the British Government. As things turned out however, the Publicity Department was to be more concerned with counteracting propaganda by de Valera and other politicians opposed to the government of the Irish Free State and its Prime Minister W.T. Cosgrave. Lester's department was looked on with considerable suspicion during a *Dáil* debate in late 1923. It was even proposed to abolish it as dangerous and unconstitutional.

Lester was made Director of Publicity in 1925 and continued in this line of work for four years. Much of it was routine forwarding of information from representatives abroad to the relevant home departments. He was also concerned with passports and other more formal diplomatic matters.

In 1929 there was an economy drive affecting several government departments and the Department of External Affairs—the value of whose existence had often been challenged—came under examination. Because Lester had entered the department in his mid-30s in an essentially non-diplomatic capacity, he was not considered as a regular civil servant and was likely to lose his post. Patrick McGilligan,[9] then a government minister, liked and respected Lester and was reluctant to see him faced with dismissal. The Irish Free State's Permanent Representative at the League of Nations in Geneva, Michael MacWhite,[10] had occupied this post for six years and was about to be appointed Irish ambassador to the United States of America. It was decided to replace him in Geneva with Lester who, by going abroad and learning languages, could thus become an established civil servant. MacWhite was an experienced and multilingual diplomat, and initially his replacement by the monolingual and untried Lester had a negative impact on Ireland's position in Geneva.

Lester had, at first, been reluctant to go abroad. Neither he nor his wife had ever been outside the British Isles before; neither spoke any continental languages. His experience as a journalist may well have been irrelevant to the work required by the League of Nations and now aged 40 the upheaval would be considerable for him and his family. Nevertheless, he accepted the offer and in April 1929 arrived in Geneva accredited to Sir Eric Drummond, the Secretary-General of the League, as the representative of the Irish Free State. As we shall see, in many ways he had now found his true vocation. Although it was supposed to be subordinate to the British Government, the Irish Free State pursued its own objectives in its foreign policy. Lester found that he was not required to be subservient to London and did not receive any instructions from Dublin. He thus found himself free to act in the meeting rooms of the League according to the dictates of his conscience as a fair-minded, diligent and determined diplomat who respected the Covenant of the League of Nations, and particularly distinguished himself by drawing attention to the hypocrisy of the Great Powers. It is interesting to observe that Poland's membership of the League of Nations often resulted in bitterness and frustration as it sought to be taken seriously as a Great Power, whereas Lester representing Ireland achieved a great deal by simply pursuing realistic ambitions.

He had been closely associated with the Cosgrave administration, had been an official spokesman for the government and had entered the Department of External Affairs by the back door through his acquaintance with leading political figures. He was thus more directly linked with a political party than many permanent representatives at the League of Nations and quickly demonstrated considerable political skill.

Lester obviously considered himself as a civil servant, and would serve both the Cosgrave and de Valera administrations with equal loyalty. As part of his new functions in Geneva he made the League of Nations and its activities known in Ireland, as formerly he had publicized Ireland and the Cosgrave government to the world. After elections in Ireland, Éamon de Valera became President of the Executive Council on 1 March 1932 and made several trips to Geneva to address the League of Nations.

We may note that Lester had acquired wide general, as opposed to the diplomatic, experience. He knew the political parties of his own country well; he had worked for newspapers of widely differing viewpoints; and he had participated in a nationalist freedom movement. He himself believed that, to be a good internationalist, one must first be a good nationalist. Certainly his political background had helped him to appreciate the outlook of the numerous newly established small states created by the Treaty of Versailles. His personal background, by contrast, gave him an understanding of being in a minority and of holding minority views—problems which Lester later had to deal with in Geneva and Danzig.

He was subsequently seconded to the service of the League of Nations in 1934 as High Commissioner in the League-controlled Free City of Danzig.[11] He sought a compromise between the German majority and the Polish minority, and endeavoured to protect the city against nazism, becoming the subject of a harsh intimidation campaign orchestrated by Hitler's government in Berlin. His courageous stance in Danzig is remembered in Poland to this day. He resigned as High Commissioner in 1936 and found no encouragement to return to his former post in Dublin. His integrity and political skills were recognized by the League of Nations and he was promoted to the post of Deputy Secretary-General in the Secretariat in Geneva.

At the height of the Danzig crisis, when there were widespread fears for Lester's safety, Tadeusz Gwiadoski,[12] an official at the Polish Foreign Ministry in Warsaw, had this to say about Lester:

> He is a man with a very dignified character, down-to-earth, honest, possessing a deep sense of his responsibility and a lot of civil courage. In the present situation, which has been very difficult for him, he has behaved in an exemplary fashion.[13]

During the 1930s the League was rapidly losing its power and prestige. Following the start of the Second World War in 1939, the French Secretary-General Joseph Avenol wanted to cooperate with the Axis forces whom he secretly admired and considered as inevitably the victors. Lester and his colleagues clashed with Avenol over his infidelity to the principles of the

League and, after a long and agonizing period of turmoil during the summer of 1940, which further damaged the League's image, Avenol resigned.[14] This resulted in Lester becoming Acting Secretary-General in September 1940. Keeping the League going until the post-war period with only a skeleton staff was a thankless task, which he considered as the hardest time of his life. He was under considerable strain at work, separated from his entourage of international civil servants, the diplomatic community and his family in Ireland. In April 1946 he presided over the final Assembly of the League, working on its administrative liquidation until August 1947, when he left Geneva. He was retrospectively made Secretary-General of the League from 1940 to 1947.[15]

Sean Lester retired to Connemara in Ireland to fish in the local rivers and lakes and tend his garden. He received an honorary degree from Trinity College, Dublin, in 1947 and another from the National University of Ireland in 1948.

Although the League of Nations failed in its ambition to prevent further world conflict, in his work for the League Sean Lester embodied the best ideals of an international civil servant. For his distinguished service in maintaining the League during the war, in 1945 he received the Woodrow Wilson Foundation award. He died in hospital in Galway on 13 June 1959 and is buried in the Church of Ireland graveyard in the town of Clifden.

NOTES

1. McNamara, P. *Sean Lester, Poland and the Nazi Takeover of Danzig*, p. 52. Dublin: Irish Academic Press, 2009.

2. Ernest Blythe (1889–1975) was an Irish language and Protestant activist. He joined Irish nationalist movements, which led to years of arrests, imprisonment and hunger strikes. He spent the Easter Rising of 1916 in prison. From 1918 until 1922 he served as Minister for Trade and Commerce. He supported the Anglo-Irish Treaty and in 1923 he became Minister for Finance in Cosgrave's first government. Later managing director of the Abbey Theatre in Dublin.

3. Gageby, D. *The Last Secretary-General: Sean Lester and the League of Nations*, pp.1–7. Dublin: Town House, 1999.

4. Gageby, pp. 8–11.

5. Eoin MacNeill (1867–1945) was an Irish scholar, nationalist, revolutionary and politician, described as "the father of the modern study of early Irish medieval history." In 1913 he established the Irish Volunteers and served as its chief-of-staff. After the Easter Rising he was arrested and sentenced to life imprisonment, although he had taken no part in the insurrection. Released in 1917. Later he became a minister in the Irish Government.

6. Henry Stuart Doig (1874–1931) was a director of the *Freeman's Journal* and editor of the *Daily Express* and *Irish Daily Mail*, an Irish unionist newspaper published from 1851 until June 1921. In its heyday, it had the highest circulation in Ireland.

7. Gageby, p.14; McNamara, p. 53.

8. Desmond FitzGerald (1888–1947), an Irish revolutionary, poet, journalist and politician, was born in London of Irish parents. He took part in the Easter Rising of 1916 and supported the Anglo-Irish Treaty, becoming the first Minister for External Affairs of the Irish Free State.

He represented the new state at the League of Nations. In 1927 he became Minister for Defense.

9. Patrick McGilligan (1889–1979) was an Irish lawyer and politician. Between 1924 and 1932 he served as Minister of both External Affairs and Industry and Commerce, in the latter capacity pushing through the Shannon Hydroelectric Scheme, then the largest hydroelectricity project in the world. In 1927 he set up the Electricity Supply Board (ESB) and the Agricultural Credit Corporation.

10. Michael MacWhite (1883–1958) was born in a remote farm in County Cork. He travelled extensively as a teacher and journalist in Europe, and fought for Bulgaria in 1912. A born adventurer, he joined the French Foreign Legion in 1913 and saw action in France, Gallipoli and Macedonia, receiving the Croix de Guerre three times for valour. In 1919, he was secretary to the Irish Legation at the Paris Peace Conference. In 1923, he became Irish permanent delegate to the League of Nations and Ambassador to the United States in 1929.

11. Fosdick, R.B. *The League and the United Nations after Fifty Years: The Six Secretaries-General*, pp. 49–8. Newtown, CT: 1972; Gageby, pp. 93–148

12. Tadeusz Gwiazdoski (1889–1950). Polish diplomat who worked in the Ministry of Foreign Affairs from 1918, becoming deputy head of its Political Department in 1934. Ambassador to France, 1939–1940; Secretary-General of the Ministry of Foreign Affairs of the Polish Government in exile in London 1941–47. Died in London.

13. McNamara, p.172.

14. Letter from Lester to the President of the Assembly League of Nations, Box A.17, League of Nations Archives.

15. 28 March 1947, Box A.17, League of Nations Archives.

Chapter Three

The League of Nations

At the end of the First World War General Smuts[1] of South Africa declared: "I believe the world is now ready for the greatest advance in human government in the history of mankind." The founding of the League of Nations in 1919 marked this great stride towards the peaceful solution of international problems. The League's major goals included the building of a lasting peace through cooperation among nations. In signing the Covenant of the League countries agreed to impose economic sanctions on any country that attacked another, thus making war unattractive for the aggressor. It was also anticipated that the League would tackle other political situations, such as providing encouragement for people striving for independence and defending the interests of national minorities. There were wider interests too. States were often overwhelmed by epidemics, economic crises and technological change which needed to be tackled at the international level. The League was also required to assume responsibility for a number of what were called "technical" problems involving the global economy, the traffic in women and children, the rights of workers and refugees, the repatriation of prisoners-of-war, the opium trade, etc.[2]

Already in the nineteenth century the need for international cooperation had been recognized on some administrative, non-political matters such as the post and telegraph system, leading to the setting up of the first international institutions. There had also been progress in the humanitarian field with the founding of the International Committee of the Red Cross. However, each country still considered itself the best guardian of its own interests, which meant that international agreements should not appear to interfere with national sovereignty. States could enter into agreements but, because of the principles of non-intervention and sovereignty, a country that violated its undertakings was not likely to be punished by sanctions imposed by the international community. The sovereignty of states was enshrined in the Covenant of the League of Nations, as also was unanimity among its members as a precondition for action.

The First World War had an enormous impact on international cooperation. When the causes of the war were examined, it was noted that the governments of countries often entered into secret treaties and declared war on their neighbours without consulting their people. In 1914, as a result of a tragic series of blunders following a relatively minor incident, an unstoppable train of events had been set in motion resulting in "a war by accident". President Woodrow Wilson of the United States felt that imperialism and militarism were dangerous tools in the hands of reckless leaders. He proposed the founding of an organization based on cooperation and openness, on international law, on trade and freedom of the seas, and on self-determination for colonial peoples. For the first time in history, the League of Nations provided a forum where European and non-European states were treated as equals, could discuss their concerns and defend their interests. However, it was not going to be easy for Wilson's concepts of international relations to exist alongside the bad old habits of European diplomacy. What made his proposals attractive to the Allied Powers meeting in Versailles in 1919 was that they were given a permanent seat on the Council of the League of Nations and, since unanimity was required in any voting procedure, this was equivalent to a veto in everything but name.

The founding of the League of Nations sought to put an end to secret diplomacy by establishing transparency in international, particularly bilateral, relations. If international agreements could be made an open book for all the world to read, if misunderstanding, distrust and even deliberate falsehood could be abolished, future wars might be prevented. Of all the questions before the League, this one allowed people to form a balanced opinion about the big issues of the world which may involve them in heavier taxes or military service.

This is not as simple as it appears. The forces of secrecy and silence are much more powerful than supposed. There may be great and unseen economic interests to be served. Moreover, there are moments of national emergency when secrecy seems almost essential. Nevertheless, while self-seeking interests may be threatened by transparency, openness also requires a moral courage and fearlessness which only a few possess. Although nothing in his previous career would suggest it, Sean Lester could be counted among these resolute people.

The Irish Free State had been admitted to the League in September 1923.[3] Lester's international vocation began when he was sent to Geneva as the permanent representative in 1929. It could be said that at this time the League of Nations was at the height of its prestige. However, the 1930s would produce a devastating series of blows that would bring the reputation of the

League of Nations to ruin and the world to a new conflagration. The League would be weakened by fear of another war and thus member states adopted an attitude of appeasement to aggressive acts while avoiding any strong military action. Although the League is said to have failed, it was in fact the actions of governments that would completely undermine any authority that the League of Nations possessed.

The Geneva that Lester discovered in 1929 was the diplomatic centre of the world with the League holding conferences and hosting committees dealing with every question of international interest (economic, financial, social, political, health, etc.). The quarterly Council sessions of the League were the highest diplomatic authority in the world, while delegates attending the annual Assembly filled the meeting rooms and all of the city's hotels. The Assembly allowed even small countries to have a say in world affairs, although the Great Powers were not entirely happy about this since it meant that they were not always able to control the outcome.[4] And the opposite situation also applied: the small countries were not able to halt what the Great Powers decided to do or—during the 1930s—what they ought to have done, but did not.

Very soon, Lester showed himself to be a person who was ready to place Ireland on the international stage. He put himself forward as an independent broker of sound judgement not connected with any power bloc. Within a year the Irish Free State was voted a seat on the powerful Council as an independent voice defending the mandate of the League of Nations.

Lester's lack of formal education and diplomatic training might have been a great disadvantage in a setting where most of his colleagues were university graduates and where proceedings were conducted jointly in English and French. Although he learned to speak French, Lester's strong Northern Irish accent sometimes caused amusement—even to himself. Later, after being transferred to Danzig, he also acquired a working knowledge of German. Nevertheless, his initial lack of diplomatic experience may account for the relatively modest scale of his activities in his first year in Geneva. On the other hand, Lester had more than compensated for this omission by being self-educated in the "University of Life".

Lester, his wife and three daughters installed themselves at a choice address in Geneva at 43, Quai Wilson, overlooking the lake and with a view of Mont Blanc. The Irish Free State delegation did not have any other premises so, as well as being a home, one room in the apartment became an office, while other private rooms became reception areas. Lester complained to Dublin that his salary and expenses did not allow sufficient money for entertaining other delegations. His predecessor, Michael MacWhite, had already pointed out to the authorities in Dublin that he had been unable to return acts of courtesy.

Another Irishman who had already spent some time in Geneva was Edward Phelan,[5] a member of the British delegation at the Versailles Conference and who had helped create the International Labour Office. The Lesters and the Phelans became close friends, meeting weekly to play bridge and tasting different wines. Lester, who had never consumed alcohol before the age of 30, became an amateur devotee of wine while living in Geneva. The Lester family soon adopted the other leisure habits of international staff in Geneva: walking in the Swiss and French Alps in the autumn, skiing in the winter and holidaying on the Mediterranean in the summer.

The Secretariat of the League of Nations was divided into twelve departments of which the most important were the Political, Central, Legal and Information Sections. Other significant sections dealt with Mandates, Minorities, Health, Opium, Disarmament and Intellectual Cooperation. Another department dealt at various times and under various names and organizational arrangements with Economics, Finance, Communications and Transit. Two semi-independent organizations were the Permanent Court of International Justice in The Hague and the International Labour Office, which was located in its own building in Geneva.[6]

Although he had very little relevant prior experience, during the next five years Lester became deeply involved in the League's activities. After spending a year or two finding his feet and learning French, he began to participate in the debates. He adapted to the world of international politics very quickly and learned that "modern diplomatic life can only mean hard work." He was called upon to act as chairman of some of the League's committees, as rapporteur to the Council and at times served as acting-president of the Council and the Assembly. Lester was able, through his enterprise and freedom of action, to play a significant role in League affairs and even earned the title of "the shrewdest face in all Geneva".[7]

At the League's annual Assembly, the Fourth Committee was often considered as the most import one since it was concerned with financial matters and the newly formed International Labour Organization.[8] On this committee, Lester became close friends with the Norwegian delegate Carl Hambro,[9] who he considered to be a good and courageous speaker. "Hambro is a fighter, a good speaker (uses English as a rule) and his courage is beyond question. Stoutly built, with a round, clean-shaven face, blue Norwegian eyes." In some later reflections, Lester wrote in his personal diary that Hambro was one of his best friends in League circles. "I worked with him for years in the Fourth Committee of the Assembly. We fought together—it was rarely wrong to follow his lead—against bigger and less altruistic interests, and often in a small but never hopeless minority." During the Second World War, Hambro and Lester were to become the two leading personalities of the League of Nations.

The third member of the team was Salvador de Madariaga,[10] the Spanish delegate, who was one of the most ardent supporters of the League. Lester described de Madariaga as one of the quickest and most brilliant minds he had ever met, a clever speaker and an amusing conversationalist. His bald head and bird-like features were not unlike those of Lester himself and they were often mistaken for each other. These three combined their forces to fight for questions of principle in the committees' decisions leading to big political clashes when they tried to thwart the Great Powers' monopoly about the future policies of the organization.

One of the greatest characters in the meetings of the League of Nations was the French politician Aristide Briand.[11] As French governments rose and fell during the Third Republic, Briand remained Minister of Foreign Affairs. In the aftermath of the First World War, he sought reconciliation with Germany, but was faced with strong internal opposition. Briand told Lester that he believed the origin of his family name was of Irish ancestry—possibly O'Brien. He was often President of the Council and Lester says that he was "the greatest of them all"—he was also, like Lester, an angler.

Lester tells an amusing story concerning the Frenchman. Briand never took much interest in his appearance which was often dishevelled. One day he had gone fishing in Switzerland and aroused the attention of two passers-by. They asked him who he was and, although he looked like a tramp, he replied: "I am the President of the Council of the League of Nations." He was immediately taken to the local police station and arrested for impertinence. There it was established by telephone that he was indeed who he said he was, and the three protagonists retired to the nearest bar.

Another person who he met frequently in Geneva and London was the British politician Anthony Eden[12] who became a close friend. Lester admired Eden's honesty and sincerity, and the fact that he did not display the superiority complex typical of Englishmen abroad. Eden would eventually become the British Foreign Secretary and was to be an important ally of Lester during the Second World War. Eden described Lester as an "Irishman with gentle manners but a firm will".

When working on the minorities committees, Lester had come into contact with another French politician Henry Bérenger,[13] who was as despicable as Briand and Eden were admirable. Lester was disgusted with the "intolerable humbug" of this man who, he says, was "contemptuous of the League". A supporter of slavery, Bérenger nevertheless spoke nauseatingly about "liberty, equality and fraternity". No doubt aware of the contempt in which he was held, Bérenger arranged for an attack in the French press on Lester and another of his Norwegian allies, Dr Christian Lange,[14] to which Lester remarked: "it is a compliment that my name should be associated with that of a man whose honour and integrity made him an ornament of the League of Nations".

While Lester often complained that he did not receive answers when he consulted Dublin about political questions, there was one topic which always drew an immediate response—birth control. As a profoundly Catholic country, the Irish Free State had decided that the only form of birth control allowed was abstention from "conjugal relations". The dilemma was that, whenever the subject came up in the documents of the League of Nations, any attempt by the Catholics to oppose birth control was likely to provoke a wide-ranging public debate and keen interest from journalists, which the Irish Government wanted to avoid at all costs.

By reason of his interventions in the affairs of the League of Nations, Lester became well known both to national delegates and to Secretariat officials as a man of sincerity and moral courage. He often represented Ireland at the quarterly Council meetings, standing in for the Minister for External Affairs and/or Éamon de Valera, who was not always able to attend. Except on the matter of birth control, he did not often receive any guidance from his government on which of the League's policies he should support. He was therefore able to follow the dictates of his own conscience and Lester's activities as permanent delegate drew the envy and admiration of his colleagues. At one stage he protested loudly to Dublin: "I cannot help taking my job seriously even if nobody else does." His main interest was to defend the reputation of the League of Nations, and by his action he became known for independence of judgement and strength of character, gaining considerable prestige in diplomatic circles. In August 1931 Lester had been provided with an assistant, Thomas J. Coyne, who presumably relieved him of some of the more routine work.

The precise degree of independence of the Irish Free State with regard to the United Kingdom was never clearly stated nor fully understood. For instance, Irish diplomats appointed to foreign countries were still expected and required to present credentials bearing the signature of King George V of the United Kingdom. The Imperial Conference of 1930 resulted in the 1931 Statute of Westminster which stated that the laws adopted by the British Parliament did not necessarily apply to its dominions. The policies pursued in Geneva made it clear that the Irish Free State was prepared to assume its independence to a degree that, for example, Australia, Canada and New Zealand were not. The Irish delegation was prepared not only to show that it was independent of the United Kingdom, but that it was ready to assume its role in world politics. The League of Nations gave the Irish Free State an opportunity to act as a completely autonomous nation.

Ireland's three-year term on the Council from 1930 to 1933 was the beginning of a period of turmoil within the League of Nations. There was a series of initial problems: discrimination against minorities living in Upper Silesia; the failure of the Disarmament Conference; bitter relations between the Germans and the Poles over the Free City of Danzig; and the Manchurian

Crisis. During this time Lester distinguished himself in carrying out the League's work, particularly in its attempts to bring a resolution to two wars in South America.

By 1933, Lester had acquired a reputation as an astute, fair-minded, diligent and determined person, who championed the rights of small nations and who defended the Covenant of the League of Nations. With his close colleagues among the lesser powers, he showed that the small nations were perfectly aware of the hypocrisy guiding the policies of the Great Powers. His experience in the field of mediation had grown considerably as chairman of committees dealing with conflicts in Latin America. The Free City of Danzig (now Gdańsk in Poland) was the scene of an emerging international crisis between nazi Germany and the international community over the issue of the "Polish Corridor" and the Free City's relationship with Hitler's Third Reich. By 1933, the Secretariat of the League of Nations was desperately seeking a new High Commissioner for the city.

NOTES

1. Jan Christiaan Smuts (1870–1950) was Prime Minister of South Africa from 1919 until 1924 and from 1939 until 1948. Leader of the Boers in the Second Boer War (1899–1902). During the First World War, he commanded the British Army in East Africa. From 1917 to 1919, he was a member of the British War Cabinet and helped found the Royal Air Force. He became a field marshal in the British Army in 1941, and served in the Imperial War Cabinet under Churchill. He was the only person to sign the peace treaties of both the First and Second World Wars.

2. Fosse, M.; Fox, J. *The League of Nations: From Collective Security to Global Rearmament*, pp. 49–60. New York, NY: United Nations, 2012.

3. *Essential Facts about the League of Nations*, p. 39. Geneva, Switzerland: League of Nations, 1936.

4. De Azcárate, P., ed. *William Martin: Un Grand Journaliste à Genève*, p. 204. Geneva, Switzerland: Centre européen de la Dotation Carnegie pour la paix internationale, 1970.

5. Edward J. Phelan (1888–1967) dedicated his life to social justice and guided the work of the ILO for nearly three decades. He helped map out the design of the ILO in the Treaty of Versailles in 1919 and was one of the principal authors of the ILO Constitution. He became the ILO's fourth Director-General in 1941 until his retirement in 1948.

6. Fosse & Fox, pp. 14–33. A good description of the League of Nations can also be found in: Myers, D.P. *Handbook of the League of Nations since 1920*. Boston, MA: World Peace Foundation, 1930.

7. Gageby, D. *The Last Secretary-General: Sean Lester and the League of Nations*, p. 47. Dublin: Town House, 1999.

8. *Essential Facts about the League of Nations*, p. 26.

9. Carl Joachim "C.J." Hambro (1885–1964) was a Norwegian journalist, author, philologist and leading politician, serving as President of the national Parliament for twenty years. He was actively engaged in international affairs, including the League of Nations (President of the Assembly, 1939–1946), delegate to the UN General Assembly (1945–1956) and member of the Norwegian Nobel Committee (1940–1963). In Lester's correspondence he is referred to as "The Northerner".

10. Salvador de Madariaga y Rojo (1886–1978) was a Spanish diplomat, writer, historian and pacifist. Joined the Secretariat of the League of Nations and was appointed chief of the Disarmament Section in 1922. In 1928, became Professor of Spanish at Oxford University.

Later, ambassador to the United States of America and France, and permanent delegate to the League of Nations. From 1933 served as both Spanish Minister for Education and Minister for Justice. In July 1936, he sought exile in England.

11. Aristide Briand (1862–1932) was a legendary French statesman who served eleven terms as Prime Minister of France during the French Third Republic and was a co-laureate of the Nobel Peace Prize in 1926.

12. Robert Anthony Eden, 1st Earl of Avon (1897–1977), was an English Conservative politician who was Foreign Secretary for three periods between 1935 and 1955. An outspoken opponent to appeasement in the 1930s. He became British Prime Minister in 1955, but the second year of his premiership was overshadowed by the Suez Crisis when the United States refused to support the UK and France.

13. Henry Bérenger (1867–1952) was a French writer and politician who was an influential Senator from 1912 until 1945, sitting on committees on finance and foreign affairs. He was France's ambassador to the United States from 1926 to 1927.

14. Christian Louis Lange (1869–1938) was one of the world's foremost exponents of the theory and practice of internationalism. His long association with the Interparliamentary Union was coupled with being Norway's permanent delegate to the League of Nations. He was awarded the Nobel Peace Prize in 1921.

Chapter Four

The Manchurian Question

A sequel to the First World War was that China had at last begun to come out of centuries of isolation. Lacking a central government after 1916, it was torn by civil war which encouraged the birth of a movement opposed to "unequal treaties"; in other words, treaties in which China paid for one modest advantage by awarding a considerable political, territorial or economic advantage to a foreign power—the foreign power dismissively claiming that the primary objective was to contribute to the economic, financial or technical reconstruction of the country.

It was in 1925 that the League of Nations began to provide China with technical assistance and this would continue up until the early years of the Second World War. At the time of the creation of the Republic of China, the Chinese Government requested that the technical bodies of the League of Nations should be involved in the economic reconstruction of the country following the civil wars. This collaboration became more complex in 1930 with the involvement of the Health Section and concerned all of the League's technical bodies after 1931. The general liaison of these units with the Chinese Government was at first ensured by sending various directors from technical sections of the Secretariat to visit China.

For instance, the Under Secretary-General Joseph Avenol visited China in December 1928. The objective of the Avenol Mission, which was received warmly in Nanking, Canton and Mukden, was to strengthen relations between China and the League of Nations. In July 1933, the Council installed a committee to guarantee and co-ordinate this liaison, and placed Dr Ludwik Rajchman[1] from Poland in charge, director of the League's Health Section, whose mandate lasted until August 1934. Subsequently, this collaboration was ensured by Robert Haas,[2] secretary to this committee. In fact, Rajchman, the right-hand man of Sir Eric Drummond, continued to be the main agent of the League of Nations' activities in China. During his numerous missions to China he even became adviser to the ministers of health and finance in Nanking, where the government of Jiang Jieshi (Chiang Kai-Shek)[3] was located.

The League of Nations' missions were always provided following a precise request from the Chinese Government. The technical units of the League would send a delegation of experts to China for brief visits that, in some cases, would result in a report submitted to the Chinese authorities on technical measures to be adopted. The Health Section collaborated mainly on the development of a central office of applied hygiene and carried out health and veterinary projects in some of the interior provinces. The Organisation for Communications and Transportation directed its activities towards collaboration with the road and canal services of the Chinese National Economic Council. The Economic Relations Section identified experts who reviewed agricultural and, more particularly, forestry problems. In 1931, the Organisation for Intellectual Co-operation sent a mission that produced a report on all of the problems affecting education. It proposed to support the intellectual training offices that the Chinese Government had decided to set up in Nanking, as well as helping Chinese students in the west to adapt to the technical training provided in Europe and the United States. A technical delegate of the Council, in his report dated May 1934, noted that, with the exception of some specialized branches, the number of Chinese students participating in the reconstruction of their country never ceased increasing. In order to speed up the process, the technical organizations of the League of Nations provided their support so that the Chinese authorities could benefit from the experience of similar administrations and institutions existing in other countries.

In September 1931 the Japanese invasion of Manchuria brought the League face-to-face with its first major crisis. Manchuria was essentially a part of China but through remoteness—it lay beyond the wall—and the increasing weakness of the central government, had become semi-autonomous and was in fact carrying out direct negotiations with Japan. Japanese settlers had for a long time been moving into Manchuria. However, their proportion of the population was small as a result of large-scale Chinese emigration encouraged by the Nanking Government. Japan had also substantial investments in the area. For instance, Japan controlled the railway and its accompanying strip of territory running from the sea into the interior. It had 10,000 soldiers stationed to protect the railway line, as well as consular police exercising jurisdiction over Japanese nationals settled in Manchuria. The Japanese had concluded treaties with China and the USSR guaranteeing them the right to administer the zone served by the south Manchurian railway and to maintain garrisons there.

By signing the nine-power treaty in 1922, Japan had also agreed to respect the territorial integrity of China. This commitment was valid when the

Japanese liberals were in power. However, the economic crisis after 1929 completely upset the parameters of the situation by bringing the question of access to the exterior to the fore and by weakening the liberals in favour of the conservatives and military nationalists. Little by little, Japan sought to extend its influence over Manchuria. On the night of 18 September 1931, the Japanese engineered an incident in the Mukden region of Manchuria when they alleged that Chinese bandits had sabotaged the railway. The Japanese reaction was suspiciously prompt and well-orchestrated. The Japanese Army bombarded several towns in the region and then systematically occupied them. By the beginning of 1932, the conquest of Manchuria was complete and the area was renamed Manchukuo, an ideal jumping-off point for Japanese expansion on the mainland of Asia. The Chinese delegate to the League of Nations, Yen Wei-Ching Williams,[4] tried in vain to draw the League's attention to the significance of what was happening in the Far East.

Finally, on 21 September 1931, the Manchurian Affair was brought before the Council of the League of Nations by the Kuomintang, the ruling political party in the Republic of China, making reference to Article 11 of the Covenant which states that: "Any war or threat of war, whether immediately affecting any of the Members of the League or not, is hereby declared a matter of concern to the whole League . . . ." With the signing of the Covenant of the League of Nations fifty-seven nations had entered into a solemn agreement that aggression towards another member state was amoral. Thus, every League member was required to come to the assistance of China, particularly since China had requested them to do so. Japan, however, had a permanent seat on the Council and stated that it preferred direct negotiations. During the 1930s, this was to become, in its endless variations, a well-trodden path for the guilty party to avoid taking the blame for aggression. While the smaller states expected action, for various reasons, France, Germany and the United Kingdom did not want to risk military intervention. The British military advisor remarked, without wishing to be sarcastic, that the small powers' "moral fervour and determination to carry the Covenant out to the letter, varied noticeably in proportion to their geographical proximity to the scene of action."

Prompted by the American Secretary of State, Ernest Hutchinson,[5] the League of Nations ordered Japan to withdraw its troops from the Chinese territories it had invaded by 16 December 1931. This date passed without anything happening, except an accelerated thrust by the Japanese troops into north-west China and sly protestations of innocence from Tokyo, arguing that the army was only defending itself from provocative attacks by Chinese patriots.

The Chinese Government appealed again to the League of Nations by letter, dated 29 January 1932, with reference to breaches of Articles 10 and 15 of the Covenant, and by another letter of 12 February 1932 in which it requested that the matter should be placed before the annual Assembly. It was in vain that Aristide Briand used his prestige as Chairman of the Council of the League of Nations to call a halt to hostilities and for the withdrawal of Japanese troops. Paralysed by the rule of unanimity—its Achilles' heel—the Council was adjourned on numerous occasions after having adopted ineffective resolutions. These successive obstacles gave time for Japan to complete its conquest of the desired territory. The Council accepted to set up an international commission, frequently called the Lytton Commission, responsible for carrying out an inquiry in the field.

Unanimity was required for the decisions of both the Assembly and the Council, except in matters of procedure and some other specific cases, such as the admission of new members. As stated earlier, this general regulation concerning unanimity was designed to be a condition recognizing national sovereignty. The League sought solution by consent and not by dictation. If a dispute was referred to the Assembly, a decision required the consent of the majority, but had to include all the members of the Council.

The Lytton Report was commissioned by the League of Nations in December 1931 to try to determine the causes of the Mukden Incident, which had resulted in Japan's seizure of Manchuria. The Lytton Commission was headed by the Earl of Lytton[6] of the United Kingdom, and included representatives of the United States, Germany, Italy and France. The group spent six weeks in Manchuria in the spring of 1932 on a fact-finding mission, after meeting with government leaders in the Republic of China and in Japan. It was hoped that the report generated by the Commission would help defuse the growing hostilities between Japan and China and maintain peace and stability in the Far East.

In spite of care to preserve impartiality between the conflicting views of China and Japan, the effect of the report was regarded as a substantial vindication of the Chinese case. In particular, the Lytton Commission stated that the operations of the Japanese Army could not be regarded as legitimate self-defence. Regarding Manchukuo, the report concluded that the new state could not have been formed without the presence of Japanese troops; that it had no general Chinese support; and that it was not part of a genuine and spontaneous independence movement.

The Lytton Report was transmitted to the Assembly in October 1932. At the time, it caused a sensation for, even if it did not specifically name Japan as the aggressor, its conclusions in this direction were unambiguous. The compromise that it put forward consisted of making Manchuria administratively independent, while maintaining it within the framework of the Chinese State, it being understood that the legitimate rights of Japan would be recognized in a bilateral agreement concluded between the two parties concerned.

Fatefully, the Lytton Report highlighted the weaknesses of the League of Nations and its inability to enforce its decisions. Collective security had proved to be a sham. By the time the Lytton Commission had prepared its report, Japan had established the puppet government of Manchukuo and rejected the condemnation of the League with impunity. China realized that it had little to gain from the Council and referred the matter to the Assembly.

The first Shanghai Incident took place in January 1932 when five Japanese Buddhist monks were attacked in Shanghai by agitated Chinese civilians. Over the next few hours, a riot broke out and a factory was burnt down. Once again it has been suggested that, due to the well-rehearsed character of these incidents, this was orchestrated by Japanese agents. There was an upsurge in anti-Japanese protests in the city with Chinese residents of Shanghai marching through the streets and calling for a boycott of Japanese-made goods.

The situation continued to deteriorate. By 27 January, the Japanese military had already concentrated a large force around the shoreline of Shanghai on the pretext that it had to defend its concession and citizens. The Japanese demanded public condemnation and monetary compensation for any damage to Japanese property. They required the Chinese Government to take active steps to suppress further anti-Japanese protests in the city. To everyone's surprise, an irregular Chinese Army had been massing outside the city and posing as great a danger to Shanghai as the Japanese military. In the end, the Shanghai authorities bribed the Chinese Army hoping that it would go away and not incite a Japanese attack. However, at midnight on 28 January, Japanese carrier aircraft bombed Shanghai and 3,000 Japanese troops attacked. The irregular Chinese Army, which had been expected to leave, put up a fierce resistance. Both the Chinese and Japanese poured troops into Shanghai but by 2 March the Japanese had overrun the city.

Manchuria was the League's first major defeat. This reverse reveals perhaps better than any other event during Secretary-General Drummond's administration that the high purposes of the League were confronted with political realities. There had been prior difficulties, but somehow the League had been able to overcome them, not always gloriously but with a reasonable degree of pragmatic success. It was the misfortune of the League that the Manchurian Crisis in the autumn of 1931 occurred during the financial panic sweeping the world. Another misfortune was that it came at the same time that the League was planning for the final session of its Disarmament Conference.[7]

Some people were appalled at the number of documents and resolutions issued by the League of Nations in favour of China and the lack of any impact on the ground. The European press began printing articles and cartoons satirising the League's inability to stem the Japanese advance. On 14 March, representatives from the League of Nations arrived in Shanghai to force the Japanese to negotiate. While meetings were going on, intermittent fighting continued in both outlying areas and in the city itself, which Japan had refused to evacuate. On 5 May, China and Japan signed the Shanghai Ceasefire Agreement making Shanghai a demilitarized zone and forbidding China to garrison troops there, while allowing the presence of a few Japanese units in the city. China was allowed to keep only a small police force within the city.

An extraordinary session of the Council had taken place in December 1932 devoted to the situation in Manchuria. The Chinese unilaterally agreed to stop fighting, although the Japanese rejected the ceasefire and persisted with their aggression. Then Yosuke Matsuoka[8] was drawn into the arena of foreign affairs to head Japan's delegation to the League of Nations. On 24 February 1933, an extraordinary session of the Assembly unanimously voted a resolution based largely on the findings of the Lytton Report. The report, recommending that Japan withdraw her troops occupying Manchuria and restore it to Chinese sovereignty, was adopted by 42 to 1—only Japan voting against it. The Assembly decided not to recognize Manchukuo and demanded the withdrawal of Japanese troops. It was pointed out that Japan, up until this time a model member of the League, was flagrantly ignoring Articles 12 and 15 of the Covenant of the League of Nations which concerned arbitration, while disregarding embarrassing reports about its activities. Among the "The Six Brothers of Tokyo" who were involved, amongst others, in the Geneva negotiations, was General Matsui Iwane.[9] Matsuoka gained international notoriety for his defiant speech condemning the League of Nations and announcing Japan's withdrawal, leading the Japanese delegation out of the League's Assembly Hall with the statement: "We are not coming back". On 27 March 1933 the Japanese Government announced its decision to leave the League of Nations due to "irreconcilable differences of view" that divided it on the "fundamental principles to be followed in establishing a lasting peace in the Far East". The withdrawal of Japan from the League of Nations came into effect in 1935 according to the terms laid down in the Covenant.

In complete contrast to the drama of the Japanese withdrawal, Lester had quietly led the minor powers in the Assembly who were in favour of sanctions against Japan. While other diplomats only took action as a result of instructions from their governments, Lester's situation was unique in that he was free to act as he saw fit. He was responsible for the clear-cut condemnation of Japan and reaffirmation of the Stimson[10] Doctrine that denied the recognition of international territorial changes executed by force. Lester pointed out that the Covenant of the League of Nations had been "a solemn contract between Japan and fifty-six other nations."

For Lester, the Manchurian Crisis was an opportunity to put into practice some of what he had learned since arriving in Geneva: the need for prompt action; for small power initiatives where Great Power initiative was impotent; and for scrupulous adherence to the Covenant when invoked. He said that "the Covenant must be applied as completely and as firmly against a powerful aggressor as against any small state which takes the law into its own hands." Lester stood out as a man of great sincerity and courage with a clear idea of morality, and he was earmarked for future great responsibility within the League of Nations.

Much of his action must have been on his own initiative. National elections in Ireland with accompanying instability and fear of violence leading to a change of government made it unlikely that he received any detailed instructions from home in late 1931 and early 1932. Until September 1932 he was the Irish Free State's first and only delegate to both to the Council sessions and the Assembly. If Lester saw the Manchurian Crisis as important, there were others who considered the part he played in the crisis to be equally significant. He was invited to lecture on the subject at the Royal Institute of International Affairs in London in 1933, and a number of writers at or near the time singled him out as having assumed a major role in the debates.

For a number of reasons, the reaction of the powers on the Council to the situation in China was feeble. It was clear that collective security only worked when all the Great Powers opposed a common enemy. The system did not work when that enemy was a member of the big power club. In fact, in these situations it seemed easier to apply sanctions to the victim than to the aggressor. According to the American historian William Keylor, the American Department of State "continued to discourage American trade and investment with the remainder of China under the control of the Kuomintang. The export of American strategic materials to Japan continued without interruption throughout the 1930s." What the United Kingdom did was also shameful. "Great Britain was even less inclined to take the risk of annoying Japan by forcing it to leave a region where it had no particular national interests . . . . Throughout the long Manchurian episode, British policy towards East Asia was dominated by the ambition to divide the region into spheres of commercial or strategic influence to the mutual satisfaction of Japan and England." In later years, Lord Robert Cecil[11] suggested that the British Government felt powerless to coerce the Japanese aggression in the absence of support from France and the United States, although Lester says that he felt the British were the most reluctant to get involved. It was also felt that the imposition of economic sanctions on Japan would immediately provoke military action that would fall on the British possessions and drive them out of the Far East.

In the autumn of 1937, the Chinese Government requested the assistance of the League of Nations in organizing a campaign to combat epidemics that were, in its opinion, out of control due to the Sino-Japanese Conflict. Three medical units were created and medical equipment was sent to China. These units worked in close collaboration with the Chinese health authorities, which placed medical staff at their disposal. The campaign, which started at the beginning of 1938, continued until February 1939. At this time, the Chinese authorities asked for changes to be made in order to confront new circumstances. During 1938, the League became particularly concerned about taking preventive measures against typhus and smallpox. It also had to confront serious epidemics of cholera and malaria, which had been triggered by vast population movements as people fled before the invading Japanese armies.

For the League, the Manchurian Crisis and its sequels were a complete disaster. It showed that the League was helpless to provide its members with the protection foreseen by Article 16 of the Covenant. Rather than fearing strong economic reprisals on the part of the other member states, it was demonstrated throughout the 1930s that a Great Power could commit any act of aggression without risking any form of sanction other than expressions of disapproval, which themselves were sometime false. The dispute between China and Japan over Manchuria was the first time the League had been called upon to deal with a conflict between two of its members and involving a large disputed territory. Both countries were at the time members of the Council. The League's slowness in dealing with the dispute and ultimate failure to take effective action exposed its fundamental weaknesses and was the first step in its progressive political eclipse in the 1930s.

Due to feuds within Chiang Kai-Shek's Nationalist Party, China was at this time in a state of almost continuous disorder and civil war to which the disastrous floods of 1931 merely gave added impact. The government did not try to stop popular hostility shown towards the Japanese, which manifested itself in attacks on individual Japanese and in boycotts and destruction of Japanese goods. Japan, on the other hand, overpopulated, powerful and united, was increasingly falling under the control of militaristic politicians and industrialists anxious to take advantage of their neighbour's weakness and seize territory once and for all. To show their intent, in March 1935 the Japanese military began assassinating cabinet ministers.

NOTES

1. Ludwik J. Rajchman (1881–1965) was a Polish bacteriologist. He was the son of Aleksander Rajchman, founder and first director of the Warsaw Philharmonic. After working in London, he set up the Polish Central Institute of Epidemiology and in 1921 became Director of the League of Nations Health Organisation. He was one of the founders of UNICEF, and served as its first Chairman from 1946 to 1950. See also Chapter 17 in this book.
2. Robert Haas (1891–1936) was the French Director of the Communications and Transportation Section of the League of Nations.
3. Chiang Kai-shek (1887–1975) was a twentieth-century Chinese political and military leader. He was an influential member of the Kuomintang, the Chinese Nationalist Party, and was a close ally of Sun Yat-sen. When Sun died in 1925 Chiang took his place as leader. He served as Chairman of the National Military Council of the Nationalist Government of the Republic of China from 1928 to 1948.

4. Yen Wei-Ching Williams (1877–1950) was a Chinese writer, politician and diplomat from Shanghai. A graduate of the University of Virginia, he was also China's first ambassador to the USSR and a delegate to the League of Nations.

5. Ernest N. Hutchinson (1864–1938) was an American Democratic politician. After being a ranch hand and a stage-coach driver, he studied at the University of Chicago and became a veterinary officer. His political life began when President Cleveland (1837–1908) appointed him as meat inspector in San Francisco. He was United States Secretary of State from 1932 until his sudden death in 1938.

6. Victor Alexander George Robert Bulwer-Lytton, 2nd Earl of Lytton (1876–1947), was a British politician and colonial administrator. He served as Governor of Bengal between 1922 and 1927 and was Acting Viceroy of India for a short period in 1926.

7. Fosdick, R.B. *The League and the United Nations after Fifty Years: The Six Secretaries-General*, pp. 38–9. Newtown, CT: 1972.

8. Yōsuke Matsuoka (1880–1946) was a Japanese diplomat and Minister of Foreign Affairs during the early stages of the Second World War. He was also one of the architects of the Tripartite Pact, between Japan, nazi Germany and fascist Italy, and the Japanese–Soviet Neutrality Pact in 1941. Following the surrender of Japan, he was arrested, but died in prison in 1946.

9. Matsui Iwane (1878–1948) was a general in the Imperial Japanese Army and the commander of the expeditionary forces sent to China in the Second World War. He was responsible for "The Rape of Nanking" in 1937 resulting in more than 200,000 victims. Convicted of war crimes by the International Military Tribunal for the Far East, he was sentenced to death by hanging.

10. Henry Lewis Stimson (1867–1950) was an American statesman, lawyer and Republican Party politician. He served as Secretary of State (1929–1933) under President Hoover and articulated American opposition to Japanese expansion in Asia. He served as Secretary of War (1940–1945) and took personal control of building the atomic bomb.

11. Edgar Algernon Robert Gascoyne-Cecil (1864–1958), known as Lord Robert Cecil, was a British lawyer, politician and diplomat. He was one of the architects of the League of Nations, whose service to the organization saw him awarded the Nobel Peace Prize in 1937.

Chapter Five

Latin American Matters

As the dispute over Manchuria faded into a futile discussion and an acceptance of a *fait accompli*, Lester's attention was becoming increasingly absorbed by two other questions. There was firstly the on-going Chaco Boreal War between Bolivia and Paraguay which had erupted again in 1932 and was finally settled—though not by the League—in 1938; and secondly the Leticia Dispute between Peru and Colombia which arose in September 1932 and was in effect ended by May 1933, although the final treaty came a year later. In the Chaco War there was a considerable loss of life. The same might have been true in Leticia had not the League managed to bring about a settlement.

Neither of these disputes concerned major states nor indeed, viewed objectively, were they major international issues. Yet in each case the participants were League members, though none were on the Council and three were in serious arrears with their contributions. However, they were willing to place their case before the League. In both cases the League's reputation in Latin America as a peace-keeping force was involved, more particularly since two other bodies—the United States-dominated Pan-American Union and the Washington Commission of Neutrals, an association of South American states—were also involved.

As has already been noted, Ireland was elected as a member of the Council of the League for a three-year term in 1930, while Éamon de Valera was elected President of the Executive Council of the Irish Free State in March 1932. De Valera took charge of Ireland's foreign policy while acting as his own Minister for External Affairs. In that capacity, on his first appearance at Geneva he was elected President of the Council of the League from September 1932 to January 1933.[1] In a speech that made a worldwide impression, he appealed for genuine adherence by its members to the principles of the Covenant of the League. When de Valera was not present, Lester took his place on the rostrum.

In September 1932 the Council appointed a Committee of Three, including the President and two others, to keep an eye on the renewed Chaco confrontation.[2] This committee consisted of Lester (Irish Free State), Salvador de Madariaga (Spain) and José Matos[3] (Guatemala). The League could not actually intervene in either the Chaco or the Leticia Disputes without being called upon to do so by a member state. The Bolivian delegate to the League was Adolfo Costa du Rels,[4] who was to play a significant role in the League's affairs during the Second World War as acting Chairman of the Assembly. His Paraguayan counterpart was Ramón Cabellero de Bedoya.[5]

The Gran Chaco area had an ill-defined border and there had been a series of skirmishes between Bolivia and Paraguay going back to the nineteenth century. When prospectors from two different companies believed that they had discovered oil in the area, a bloody border dispute broke out in July 1932 lasting three years leading to the deaths of an estimated 130,000 combatants. The fighting took place in the form of modern warfare and involved tanks, fighter and bomber aircraft, and naval warships. In fact, neither Lester's committee nor any of the subsequent committees found a solution to the crisis; it was only the physical exhaustion of the two belligerents that brought this war to an end. The absurdity of the conflict became evident when the oil companies announced that there was nothing of commercial interest under the Gran Chaco.

As the dispute between Bolivia and Paraguay became more severe, efforts to find a solution undertaken by neighbouring countries failed, such as the so-called "Mendoza Plan" put forward by Argentina, Brazil, Chile and Peru. Then, the Bolivian Minister for Foreign Affairs sent a telegram to the President of the Council of the League of Nations stating that Paraguay had actually declared war upon his country. The Committee of Three proposed to restore peace through arbitration.

The Commission of Neutrals in Washington and Lester's group in Geneva made several attempts to try to settle the Bolivia/Paraguay Dispute. In September 1932 the League's Council expressed the opinion that it was preferable for the Commission of Neutrals to find a solution. When this Commission gave up the task in February 1933, the way was clear for the Council to declare an arms embargo. In May, the Council decided that, before taking any action, it must send an on-the-spot commission to find out what was going on. After some delay caused by the two countries temporarily accepting arbitration, the commission arrived in February 1934. By this time, Lester had ceded his place on the Committee of Three to Édvard Beneš[6] of Czechoslovakia and his presidency of the Council to Francisco Castillo Nájera (Mexico).[7] In its report the commission found both parties responsible and encouraged new efforts in favour of an embargo. Thus, the

Committee of Three called for such an arms embargo concerning Bolivia and Paraguay, and addressed a letter to the Secretary-General asking him to prevent weapons and war material reaching these two countries. There were difficulties regarding control, although many neighbouring countries did cooperate. The Argentine Government proposed that the embargo should also include provisions for troops and all forms of motor transport. The embargo came into force in the summer of 1934, and included the participation of the United States. At its meeting in November, the Assembly adopted the text of a treaty which Bolivia accepted, but Paraguay did not. Finally, in June 1935 Bolivia and Paraguay agreed to stop fighting.[8]

Elsewhere in Latin America, the Salomón-Lozano Treaty had been signed in Lima in 1922 in order to give Colombia access to the headwaters of the Amazon River. A "trapeze" of land was ceded by Peru to Colombia at the point where the borders of Colombia, Brazil and Peru met in an area called "Tres Fronteras", including the river port of Leticia which was now transferred from Peru to Colombia. Despite the treaty's ratification in 1928, the agreement proved to be unpopular with local people because it had been signed in secret and it awarded Colombia a region that had a large Peruvian population. On 1 September 1932 a group of armed Peruvian civilians seized Leticia in a demonstration against the treaty and expelled the Colombian representatives. After some days of hesitation, President Luis Miguel Sánchez[9] of Peru despatched military forces to support the rebels in Leticia and also in a nearby town called Tarapacá, both settlements located in the Amazonas Department of present-day southern Colombia.

Since there were few roads, no Colombian military presence in the area and Colombia did not possess a proper navy that could sail up the Amazon, President Sánchez believed that there was little chance of a counter-attack being launched. However, within ninety days Colombia had organized a respectable military reaction to the Peruvian invasion by capturing the Peruvian settlements of Puerto Arturo and Güeppí, located some distance away on the Upper Putumayo River near the border with Ecuador. The Colombian General Alfredo Vásquez Cobo[10] managed to assemble a flotilla of old ships that he had acquired in Europe. It was not until December that his fleet reached the mouth of the Amazon River setting off alarm signals in Peru. He sailed the 2,500 kilometres up the river to the town of Tarapacá, which was quickly recaptured in a bloodless attack since no Peruvian troops were present at that time. On the same day, the Colombian president Enrique Olaya[11] broke off all relations with the Peruvian Government due to an aerial attack on the Colombian ships. He ordered the town of Leticia to be attacked, but the Peruvian troops could not been forced out.

In January 1933, the "undeclared war" between Colombia and Peru called for urgent attention by the League of Nations because Colombia had appealed to the Council citing Article 15 of the Covenant. In February, the case was brought before the Council, which expressed its opinion that Colombia had been the victim of an aggression and required Peru to withdraw its forces before negotiations could begin. The Council's draft report stated the facts of the dispute and its recommendations. García Calderón,[12] the Peruvian delegate, walked out of the room when the Council stated that Peru had illegally occupied Colombian territory. However, this gesture did not mean that Peru had actually withdrawn from the League of Nations.

Lester was acting President in Office of the Council and on 18 March the Committee of Three, including the same members as the Gran Chaco affair, was asked to take responsibility for the Leticia Dispute. Lester reminded the two countries of their responsibilities as members of the League of Nations. His first action was to request Peru to refrain from any intervention by force on Colombian territory and to request Colombian authorities to limit their action strictly to the preservation of order in their own territory. Lester had exchanges with Eduardo Santos,[13] the Colombian representative, and also with the Peruvian representative, García Calderón. It is interesting to note that both García Calderón of Peru and Costa du Rels of Bolivia would later become trusted allies of Lester in his future career in the League.

On 3 February 1933 Brazil announced that, because Colombia had decided to place the affair before the Council of the League of Nations, it would abandon its mediation in the dispute. There was then a British proposal that Brazilian troops should remain in the border area until the completion of the negotiations. Colombia asked for the terms of existing treaties to be respected and the Committee of Three appealed to the two parties to show a spirit of conciliation, while deeply deploring the absence of the Peruvian representative. The Committee's report was accepted by Colombia, but not by Peru. The Peruvian Government made counter-proposals which attempted to explain that Leticia's cession to Colombia under the 1922 treaty had been a mistake.

The first meeting of the Conciliation Committee of Three, under Lester's presidency, examined the question of the evacuation of Leticia by Peruvian troops and made reference to Brazilian mediation. Lester proposed a draft agreement between Colombia and Peru based upon the acceptance by the two parties of the Council's recommendations.

It was learned that a Peruvian cruiser and two submarines (!), part of Peru's Pacific fleet, were passing eastward through the Panama Canal on their way to the Amazon. The Peruvians explained that their warships were intended merely to support their army for defensive purposes. Lester's Committee considered it desirable that Peru should abstain from sending these vessels towards the Amazon Basin. The Colombian Government then requested permission for its military aircraft to refuel on the territory belonging to other governments. The dispute was likely to escalate.

Lester wrote to the delegate of Peru pointing out the difficulties in reaching an agreement to settle the dispute and answered the questions raised by the Peruvian Government. The Council suggested that an international authority should be formed on a temporary basis to ensure the security of the disputed territory. Lester also tried to establish an arms embargo against Peru if its government continued to pursue unreasonable demands.

On 30 April 1933, while at Santa Beatriz racetrack reviewing 20,000 young recruits for Peru's undeclared war with Colombia, President Sánchez was shot in the chest by a member of a suppressed political party. Although transported to hospital, he died three days later. This brought about a fundamental change in the situation and, fifteen days later, the new Peruvian president, Óscar Benavides,[14] adopted an accommodating attitude towards the crisis in order to bring it rapidly to an end. He had a meeting with his friend and head of the Colombian Liberal Party, Alfonso López Pumarejo,[15] where it was suggested that the situation could be defused by handing the administration of Leticia temporarily over to a League of Nations' commission. This commission took up its functions in June. A so-called "international force" took possession of Leticia, but it consisted mainly of Colombian soldiers wearing "SdN" armbands (Sociedad de las Nationes). The flag of the League of Nations flew over Leticia for a whole year before the cessation of all hostilities.

Later, Colombia and Peru signed an agreement to begin negotiations on the lines recommended by the League of Nations. The towns of Güeppí and Puerto Arturo would be evacuated by the Colombians and Leticia would be evacuated by the Peruvians. The signature on 24 May 1934 in Rio de Janeiro of a treaty between Peru and Colombia agreed that Leticia finally belonged to Colombia. In the Rio de Janeiro Protocol, as it was called, Peru stated that: "We sincerely deplore the events that occurred starting September, 1932. Specifically those that damaged our relationship with Colombia." The Salomón-Lozano Treaty was also reaffirmed as the document governing ownership of the Leticia Trapeze.

The Leticia settlement was one of the League's very few successes in the 1930s and can be compared in importance with such earlier settlements as that between Greece and Bulgaria in 1925. Lester used his position on these committees to show that the League's machinery could be used efficiently and without unnecessary delay to achieve results. He acted with the greatest possible speed and authority as chairman of the committee which found a swift and equitable solution. The whole affair took place within five months and did not involve the annual Assembly. It also established Lester's personal reputation in the Council independent of his position as his country's representative, and this contributed to his appointment to Danzig late in 1933. His efforts brought him to the attention of the League Secretariat and began his transformation from national to international civil servant.

NOTES

1. *Essential Facts about the League of Nations*, p. 85. Geneva, Switzerland: League of Nations, 1936.
2. Minutes of the sixty-eighth session of the Council of the League of Nations, *Journal officiel*, September 1932, pp. 1573–86; and *Journal officiel*, November 1932, Annexe 1388, pp. 1760–1.
3. José Matos was the permanent delegate of Guatemala to the League of Nations in the 1930s and later became Minister of Foreign Affairs and of Armaments for Guatemala.
4. Adolfo Costa du Rels (1891–1980) was a Bolivian writer and diplomat who became the last President of the Council of the League of Nations. He was the author of many plays, novels and other writings, mostly in French, and received several literary awards.
5. Ramón V. Caballero de Bedoya (1880–1979) was the Paraguayan permanent delegate to the League of Nations and successively from 1923 to 1939 Ambassador to France, Belgium and Switzerland, and later delegate to UNESCO.
6. Édvard Beneš (1884–1948) was a leader of the Czechoslovak independence movement. From 1918–1935, Beneš was the first and longest serving Foreign Minister of Czechoslovakia, holding the post through ten successive governments, one of which he headed himself. President of Czechoslovakia from 1935 to 1938 and again from 1940 to 1948. A skilled diplomat, between 1923 and 1927 he was a renowned and influential figure at international conferences.
7. Francisco Castillo Nájera (1886–1954) was a Mexican diplomat and politician. He was president of the Assembly of the League of Nations from 1934 to 1935, Ambassador to China and the United States, and Secretary of Foreign Affairs from 1945 to 1946.
8. *Essential Facts about the League of Nations*, pp. 172–5.
9. Luis Miguel Sánchez Cerro (1889–1933) was a high-ranking Peruvian army officer and President of Peru from 1931 to 1933. On 22 August 1930, as a lieutenant-colonel, he overturned the eleven-year dictatorship of Augusto B. Leguía after a coup d'état in Arequipa.
10. Alfredo Vásquez Cobo (1869–1941) was a Colombian politician and soldier. In 1932, he was given the task by President Olaya of liberating Leticia. In 1933, upon his retirement he was considered a national hero. The airport in Leticia bears his name.
11. Enrique Alfredo Olaya Herrera (1880–1937) was a Colombian journalist and politician, President of Colombia from 1930 to 1934 representing the Colombian Liberal Party. Later appointed Minister of Foreign Relations and ambassador to the Vatican, where he died suddenly on 18 February 1937.
12. Francisco García Calderón Rey (1883–1953) was a Peruvian writer who also became the Peruvian Minister to Belgium. He was born into a wealthy and politically prominent family in Valparaiso, Chile. His father was the President of Peru for a short time during the Chilean occupation of Peru.
13. Eduardo Santos Montejo (1888–1974) was a leading Colombian publisher and politician, active in the Colombian Liberal Party. He owned the prominent Bogotá newspaper *El Tiempo*. He served as President of Colombia from 1938 to 1942, having been elected without opposition.
14. Óscar Raimundo Benavides Larrea (1876–1945) was a Peruvian soldier and politician. Acting President of Peru on two occasions, 1914–1915 and 1933–1939. In 1940, he was awarded the title of Grand Marshal.
15. Alfonso López Pumarejo (1886–1959) was a political figure for the Colombian Liberal Party and twice Colombian president—between 1934 and 1938 and again between 1942 and 1945.

Chapter Six

Disarmament and Finance

The Council of the League of Nations began in 1920 with four permanent members (France, Italy, Japan and the United Kingdom) and four non-permanent members who were elected by the Assembly for a three-year period. The number of non-permanent members was increased from four to six by an Assembly resolution of 25 September 1922. In 1926 the membership was further increased to nine and, in 1933, it was provisionally increased to ten. A further increase to eleven was approved by the Assembly in 1936. The League sought the solution to disputes by consent and not by dictation. Unanimity was required for the decisions of both the Assembly and the Council, except in matters of procedure and some other specific cases, such as the admission of new members. This general regulation concerning unanimity was the recognition of national sovereignty, but usually resulted in great slowness and fragility in taking decisions and particularly in requiring compliance with these decisions.

From September 1930 to September 1933 the Irish Free State was voted as a non-permanent member of the Council and therefore Lester became involved in the big political issues. Much of his time in 1932 and 1933 was occupied with disarmament and finance. There were, however, many other aspects of the League's activity in which he was actively engaged. Lester represented Ireland at virtually all the Council meetings except the sixty-eighth (September 1932) and seventy-seventh (January 1933) sessions when, since it was the Irish Free State's turn to provide the president, de Valera came over to Geneva in person.

Some of the work was routine, such as even the most inactive Council member could hardly avoid. Lester as Rapporteur presented the Council with a series of reports on health, child welfare and the drug problem. Furthermore, food and epidemic relief in China, the welfare of blind, illegitimate and delinquent children, and the putting into effect of the 1931 Drug Convention were other matters in reports edited by Lester and presented at the appropriate time to the Council.

A dispute between the United Kingdom and Persia over an oil company arose when Lester was acting President of the Council in December 1932. Lester accepted a request for delay from the Persian delegate. Later he recommended the Council to postpone consideration of the question until January 1933, meanwhile urging both governments to refrain from any action aggravating or extending the dispute and reminding them that placing it before the Council did not preclude them from arriving at a bilateral agreement themselves. This was, in fact, the eventual outcome. Council presidency also gave Lester such formal tasks as swearing in a new Under Secretary-General, the Italian Massimo Pilotti,[1] with whom he was later to be joint Deputy Secretary-General for a brief time.

As an ordinary Council member, we find Lester withdrawing a suggestion that the president should attend the funeral of Paul Doumer,[2] the assassinated French President, which was taking place at the same time as that of Albert Thomas, the ILO's first Director-General. The point was raised that attending the funeral of the French Head of State would set a precedent for the Secretary-General to attend the funerals of all other Heads of State.

Lester was one of those who welcomed Turkey in July 1932 as an Assembly member, remarking how Ireland remembered that during the Irish Potato Famine in the nineteenth century Turkey had sent food from 2,000 miles away to help. A year later, when the ending of the British mandate enabled Iraq to join the League, he welcomed this ancient people into the circle of modern states.

In March 1933, he spoke on a Danzig-Poland clash (the Westerplatte Incident), commending the Poles for withdrawing the increased harbour guard which had been at the origin of the dispute, and mentioning the High Commissioner who represented the authority of the League of Nations in Danzig. Just over eight months later he was to take over that same position.

There were, however, four fields of activity in which Lester, by chance or inclination took a particular interest during his last two years as Irish Permanent Delegate. These were the Disarmament Conference, the League's internal and external financial policy, the controversy over higher Secretariat appointments and the minority questions.

The League of Nations had been set up to prevent war through collective security and the settling of disputes between countries through negotiation. All the major powers, except the United States, had committed themselves to disarmament in both the Treaty of Versailles and the Covenant of the League of Nations. Thus, the Assembly of the League of Nations asked the Council set up a Preparatory Commission in 1925 with a view to holding a conference at some time in the future on disarmament. The commission consisted of representatives of all members of the Council and six other members of the League of Nations, as well as Germany, the United States and the USSR, all three of whom were (at that time) non-members. Chaired by Jonkheer Loudon,[3] former Minister of Foreign Affairs for the Netherlands, the commission's more notable members included Lord Robert Cecil (United Kingdom), Joseph Paul-Boncour[4] (France), Louis de Brouckère[5] (Belgium), Count Bernstorff[6] (Germany) and Hugh Gibson[7] (United States of America). The Preparatory Commission met six times before finally being dissolved on 9 December 1930, having prepared a draft convention on armaments reduction as well as a final report, which were presented to the Disarmament Conference itself when it convened in February 1932.

When the League of Nations had been set up in 1919, Germany had not been asked to join. Following the Locarno Accords of 1926, Germany had provided guarantees concerning its western frontiers and was therefore allowed to become a member state of the League with a permanent seat on the Council. From 3 to 20 January 1930, the second Reparations Conference had been held at The Hague concerning the final settlement of the matter of payments by Germany to the Allies after the First World War. The German Government accepted to pay 38 billion gold marks over fifty-nine years. Acceptance implied that Allied troops stationed in the Rhineland would leave five years earlier than the date foreseen in the Treaty of Versailles. However, the economic crisis that struck Germany in 1931 completely eclipsed any chance of this payment being made. This conference led to the creation of the Bank of International Settlements (BIS) in Basle, which was responsible for managing the German reparations. The end of reparations was decided during the International Conference of Lausanne in June 1932, but did not lead to the demise of the BIS. The Austrian Chancellor Johannes Schober[8] — former head of the Viennese police—obtained the suspension of Austrian reparations.

The Conference for the Reduction and the Limitation of Armaments (known as the Disarmament Conference) opened in Geneva on 2 February 1932, under the chairmanship of Arthur Henderson,[9] the former British Foreign Secretary. Sixty-one countries were represented at the Conference; in other words, almost all the countries that existed in the world at that time. Henderson called for an international treaty to be concluded to guarantee disarmament in all countries. Significantly, the German delegates requested equal treatment (*Gleichberechtigung*) as the foundation for their participation in any treaty. Eyebrows were raised at the Japanese delegation which consisted of nearly forty senior naval officers!

Awaited expectantly for many years, the Disarmament Conference took place in a troubled international atmosphere: there was the conflict in the Far East between China and Japan which had entered its most critical phase; there was growing nationalism in Germany causing alarm in France, Poland

and other countries; finally, there was the economic crisis that had overwhelmed the world since 1929.

The opening of the conference aroused immense enthusiasm everywhere and the local journalist Jean Martin put it this way: "This special meeting goes beyond the significance of a major conference."[10] Numerous trade union, religious and women's organizations came to Geneva bringing petitions signed by millions of people enthusiastically imploring rapid and universal disarmament. The petitions and the enthusiasm would all be tragically betrayed—there would be no disarmament.

The conference set up two main bodies: the General Commission and the Bureau. The Bureau was made up of the chairman of the conference, the honorary chairman Giuseppe Motta,[11] fourteen vice-chairmen and the chairmen of the four commissions on land armament, naval armament, air armament and national defence.

Lester, who had participated in the last few meetings of the Preparatory Commission, now headed an Irish delegation of four. The seventeen plenary meetings taking place in February 1932 were mostly taken up with a long general discussion in which Lester was one of the few delegates who did not speak, although he was on a procedure committee. The General Commission (confined to heads of delegations) held twenty-seven meetings up to June 1932, and a further fifty-one between December 1932 and June 1933. It resumed the following October but by then there was little hope of any useful outcome.

The story of the conference is one of naivety and bitter disappointment. The draft convention that had been laboriously drawn up by the preparatory commission for the conference over a period of five years was immediately thrown out. It was then the major powers who, one after another, placed various plans or compromise proposals on the desk of Chairman Henderson, which were then discussed by the other delegations. Unanimity was required and this was impossible.

Lester entered the discussions in April 1932. He said the Irish Free State was not committed to either the quantitative or qualitative limitation of armaments. He hoped both would be possible, and that a degree of internationalization might also guide the Conference. Though he did not despair because the ponderous machinery of the Conference moved so slowly, he thought it was time that a formal declaration could be made in favour of one principle, even if details of application would be left aside for the moment. On the understanding that it did not prevent the Conference from adopting other measures, he supported the British proposal for qualitative disarmament. In a similar hope of reaching some agreement, in July 1932 Lester was one of forty-one delegates who supported Henderson in his request for a positive vote on the final resolution—however imperfect.

The talks were beset by a number of difficulties from the outset. Among these were disagreements over what constituted "offensive" and "defensive" weapons. Obviously, the military hierarchy was strongly opposed to the principle of disarmament and was uneasy about the details of national defence being discussed in public. The central problem of disarmament was essentially a Franco-German affair. The increasingly military-minded German governments could see no reason why their country could not enjoy the same level of armaments as other powers, especially France. The problem was how to reconcile German military ambition with France's fear of its neighbour. In the German view, the disarmament of vanquished countries should only be a prelude to general disarmament and it referred to the Treaty of Versailles to support its arguments. France retorted that there could be no worthwhile discussion of a formula for disarmament until a concrete and precise system of verification had been implemented. On 14 September 1932 the German delegation decided that it would no longer participate in the Disarmament Conference until the principle of equality as a right for every state had been accepted.

Various plans had previously been proposed by different countries, some of which were far-fetched (the Patagon Plan and the Poldève Plan). In June 1932 the conference was presented with a series of proposals from the American President Hoover[12] and, for some days, it appeared as if progress would be achieved. These proposals were based on the principle that arms should only be used in self-defence and, as a result, the solution was to increase this type of weapon and to reduce offensive arms. Nevertheless, even these modest proposals did not receive a favourable reception. Édouard Herriot[13] (France) felt that they did not provide a guarantee of security against an aggressor. Had not the League been incapable of protecting China against the territorial ambitions of Japan? The British Government declared itself in favour of the principle, but expressed reservations about the list of arms that had to be reduced. By now, it was obvious that Japan and Italy had no intention whatsoever of disarming.

Lester realized that the work of experts had to be followed up by willingness to cooperate at a political level. He seems to have combined a realistic view of small power limitations in this field with an impartial attitude towards the great powers. His advocacy of a healing policy towards Germany is illustrated in his account of a conversation with Édvard Beneš of Czechoslovakia in early 1933.

> I said to him that no peace could be built in Europe on a Germany which was kept in a conditions of inequality and under the heel. . . . I said that it had often seemed to me that the geographical frontiers had been drawn not so much to help new states but to weaken Germany. Beneš agreed and told me how in

1919 he had asked the great powers to take away a million of the Germans who were to be included in Czechoslovakia, but this had been refused.

Here we can plainly see that the seeds of the Second World War had been sown during the Versailles Conference. Lester also has this to say about Beneš:

> He has occupied a big place in international affairs—which is a synonym in recent years for League affairs. Small, unimpressive in appearance, friendly and intelligent . . . A university professor of humble origin, a patriot who joined Masaryck's little revolutionary committee in Paris when the [First World] war broke out, the guide to a country in a most difficult political and geographical situation, he has evoked not only admiration, but also one might also say affection.

On 11 December 1932, the representatives of the United Kingdom, the United States, France, Italy and Germany recognized the principle of equality of rights for all nations. Germany had therefore won a considerable victory and took up again its place at the conference table three days later. After one year's work, the Disarmament Conference could be said to have reached the point where it might reasonably have been expected to begin.

On 14 December 1932, Lester was among those who welcomed the German representative, saying he believed his presence essential. He was, however, doubtful about the legality of the procedure, and welcomed the British and French assurances that it would rarely be used and always with the consent of the Conference. In this case he felt the end justified the means. He had always thought that the progress of the Conference would depend to an overwhelming extent upon agreement between the major armed powers. His delegation's main preoccupation was that agreement should represent the very greatest possible degree of disarmament, and now that the Great Powers had come back ready to reach an agreement the Conference might be able to persuade them to go further. However, he supported the view that, though Great Powers were important, it was for all states of the world to draw up a convention.

In an attempt to break the deadlock, in March 1933 the British politician Ramsay MacDonald[14] put forward a plan allowing Germany to reach equality on arms within five years. He also proposed international control through a permanent commission and foresaw regional pacts of mutual assistance. According to this approach, the paramilitary groups at the base of the nazi regime would have to be counted as part of the army. Faced with the disturbing and barbarous attitude adopted by the nazi regime within its borders, the Great Powers wrapped the MacDonald Plan in safeguards, among which—before any kind of disarmament—was a "trial period".

Lester thought that concessions should have been made to the German demand for a certain number of tanks, anti-aircraft guns and heavy artillery. When the request was first made there was a reasonably democratic government in Germany. A few months later, France and the United Kingdom would have been delighted had they been able to agree on such equitable terms. On 30 January 1933 Adolf Hitler came to power in Germany and the whole purpose of the conference became null and void. Hitler's intention was to equip Germany with a powerful army, navy and air force as soon as possible. He saw the League of Nations as the embodiment of the German humiliation in the Treaty of Versailles and seized this opportunity to wash his hands of the obligations of the Disarmament Conference. On 14 October 1933 the nazi government announced its withdrawal from both the conference and from the League of Nations; it had no intention of giving the regulatory two years' notice before pulling out. All German nationals, official delegates and international civil servants were instructed to leave the services of the League of Nations at once. Germany placed the entire responsibility for its withdrawal on the Western powers who, it was said, had no real wish to disarm or to allow Germany to become a leading player on the world stage. By 1937 both Germany and Italy possessed huge armed forces and a tremendous quantity of armaments.

The departure of the German delegation was a mortal blow for the Disarmament Conference, which frittered away in pointless discussions for another three years. Even though it was never officially closed, it no longer served any purpose. The League of Nations was unable to admit the fact that a meeting on which the world had placed so much hope had been a fiasco. In the eyes of the general public, the failure of the Disarmament Conference was synonymous with the failure of the League of Nations. The conference sessions subsequently became very irregular and the last one was held in the spring of 1937, when the armaments race that would result in the Second World War was in full swing. As a newspaper cartoon at that time expressed it: "A candle goes out." The League proved incapable of preventing aggression by the Axis Powers in the 1930s. The absence of the United States from the organization, its reliance upon unanimous decisions, the lack of an armed force to impose its decisions and the continued self-interest of its leading members meant that this failure was inevitable.

But other factors were also contributing to failure of the disarmament process. As Hugh Gibson himself would put it ten years later:

> Through all the years of discussion in Geneva it was demonstrated that the direct approach to the reduction of arms was merely an attempt to deal with the symptoms rather than with the disease. [...] It soon became clear that no important results were to be achieved through negotiations limited to men and ships and guns. There were various attempts to find other approaches [...]

these approaches had their merits, but they [...] ignored a fundamental problem. Over a long period a number of Great Powers had built up a whole system of national life and national economy based on huge military establishments. These had come to be a recognized way of dealing with the problem of unemployment. To begin with, there were large numbers of men absorbed into the military forces. To supplement these were government arsenals with another army of workmen, with a still larger number employed in providing supplies, food, clothing, and transportation. No government living under this system could undertake drastic reduction of armaments without disrupting the whole national economy. We may as well recognize the fact that there can be no more than fragmentary and regional reductions until the nations are prepared to grapple with this fundamental difficulty.[15]

Lester in general supported British proposals mainly because they alone seemed likely to produce a result, and also partly perhaps from respect for Arthur Henderson's personal dedication to disarmament. Henderson, who chaired the Disarmament Conference during the first two years of its existence, was awarded the 1934 Nobel Peace Prize, but all efforts to bring the Conference to a successful conclusion were undermined by fear, distrust, hatred, inequality, jealousy and power. In his personal diary in October 1935, Lester wrote:

> Sorry to hear of Arthur Henderson's death. We knew him and his wife, a sweet and unpretentious little woman, quite well and I'll miss Uncle Arthur's cheery greeting in the Geneva lobbies.
>
> His presidency of that Conference saved his life three years ago. The collapse of the Labour Government, his defeat in his own constituency when, in 1931 (Oct. 2), Labour was overwhelmed (devaluation of the pound), led to a break-down, and when he came back to Geneva as the President of the Disarmament Conference he shocked us all with the appearance of a broken and dying man.
>
> But the new duties kept him in affairs—big affairs—and he slowly reconstructed his ego(!). He certainly "won merit" by his impartiality and energy in endeavouring to bring peace to a peaceless Europe. Henderson had two aides in his disarmament work. One was Philip Noel-Baker[16] (Univ. professor—Labour) who has published a book on Inter Commonwealth relations. Baker had, for some time, been helping Nansen in, I think, his Russian refugee work, and is a humanitarian and a good European. A.H. must have owed much to him during the first strenuous year of the Conference.
>
> And then Zilliacus[17] —Zilly to all the world—a member of the Information Section of the Secretariat, but a man of character and opinions. Regarded as radical, Zilly is strongly Labour in politics and international in outlook. A British subject of Finnish origin and married to a fascinating Pole. We worked together to some extent for the Sino-Japanese question on which our views coincided.
>
> Bernard Shaw[18] went to Geneva once and apparently Zilly had been in touch with him about the arrangements. He met Shaw at the railway station

and introduced himself. "Zilliacus?" said Shaw, "Why, I always thought it was a telegraphic address."

But on a grander scale, did the League of Nations have a role to play in facilitating global economic and financial relations? It was suspected that financial shocks and economic melt-downs were as disastrous for the world economy as wars. When it was first set up it was anticipated that the League would steer clear of economic and financial affairs. However, this situation changed quite quickly.[19]

Towards the end of 1919, some 150 leading economists signed a petition requesting that there should be a greater level of financial coordination at the global level. For this reason the League of Nations convoked the world's first International Financial Conference in Brussels in September/October 1920. In order to prepare for this conference, Sir Eric Drummond set up a new Economic and Financial Section under the direction of Sir Arthur Salter,[20] who was aided by Jean Monnet.[21] Alexander Loveday,[22] a 30-year-old Scottish statistician, was hired to provide as complete a picture as possible of the global economy covering currency, public finance, international trade, retail prices and coal production. Loveday established a fledgling Economic Intelligence Service and called a preliminary conference specifically to standardize national statistics that could be compared at the international level.

During the First World War countries had adopted financial practices that had set in motion inflation that continued after the war. In the eight months between the convocation of the financial conference and its opening, unemployment, poverty and hardship worsened dramatically throughout Europe, so that the necessity of the conference was clear to all those concerned. The Brussels Conference did not result in general agreement on measures to be adopted, and galloping inflation continued in Central and Eastern Europe, but the role of the League of Nations in economic and financial relations was clearly established.

By 1924 the League had set up its Economic and Financial Organisation (EFO). It consisted of three elements; those responsible for naming these three units seemed to have suffered from extreme caution in their vocabulary—or a lack of imagination. While the names of the different units must have been clear to those involved, they do not appear to have contemplated the possibility of confusion. The secretariat of the EFO was called the Economic and Financial Section, while its two technical units were named as the Economic Section and the Financial Section. Their work was overseen by an Economic Committee and a Financial Committee. By 1930, the Economic Section was under the direction of the Italian Pietro Stoppani, while the Financial Section was headed by Alexander Loveday. The latter remained responsible for the Economic Intelligence Unit. Drummond placed Joseph Avenol as overall coordinator of the EFO, but Stoppani and Loveday, while occasionally disagreeing, were able to work together satisfactorily and Avenol was rarely called upon to intervene. These various sections, units and committees performed a Herculean task in advancing our understanding of the way the economy works. During the Second World War the EFO was considered to be of sufficient value to be evacuated to Princeton University in the United States and continued providing valuable services until the demise of the League in 1946.

While the Disarmament Conference was going nowhere, representatives of sixty-six nations met for the London Economic Conference from 12 June to 27 July 1933, with the purpose of reaching agreement on measures to fight global depression, revive international trade and stabilize currency exchange rates. Like the Disarmament Conference, the Economic Conference collapsed without producing any concrete outcomes. The United States' President Roosevelt denounced currency stabilization. He issued a message to the Conference condemning its efforts at stabilization when "broader problems" existed, asserting that the exchange rate of a nation's currency was less important than other economic values.

The Disarmament Conference had been a victim of the repercussions of the Wall Street collapse of 24 November 1929 in the United States and the ensuing depression which had by 1931 affected nearly every League member and, of course, international co-operation in general. In the depths of the Great Depression in November 1932, Franklin Delano Roosevelt defeated incumbent Republican President of the United States, Herbert Hoover. Roosevelt, with his New Deal economic policy, encouraged economic self-sufficiency. States everywhere adopted the same policy and assumed freedom of action, each one acting in its own best interests, leading to a rise in economic nationalism. To cut costs and to absorb unemployment, many of them began to construct major armaments industries. With their gaze firmly fixed on Germany and Italy, France and the United Kingdom began to rearm in earnest.

According to the French author Pierre Gerbet, the economic crisis hastened the rise of nazism in Germany, strengthened Japan's expansionist tendency and encouraged hard-line fascism in Italy.[23] The League of Nations thus witnessed three major powers leave the fold one after another, commit repeated acts of aggression and band together in an attempt to bring the League down by any means possible. The League now had to decide what its responsibility was in the economic crisis and how it was to continue functioning with the rapid decline in contributions from member states.

In truth, the major powers had never accepted the League of Nations' role as an international forum and had no faith in its virtues, except when it corresponded to their own interests. Thus, during the course of the 1930s, there was a return to old-style bilateral and secret diplomacy—the very ills that Woodrow Wilson had identified as the root cause of wars. Most of the time, the French and British democracies only used the League to support the decisions that they had already taken far away from Geneva or to submit issues that could not be resolved through other diplomatic channels.[24] The most damaging example is the Ethiopian Conflict, during which the British and French held secret negotiations with the Italians, instead of insisting that the issue should be resolved by the League of Nations.

However, the arrival of new member states, such as Mexico in 1931, Turkey and Iraq in 1932, the USSR, Afghanistan and Ecuador in 1934 and Egypt in 1937 could have raised the hope that the prestige of the League of Nations might be consolidated.[25] Nevertheless, this increase in universality could not compensate for the loss of Japan, Germany and Italy.

In September 1933 Lester, who was for the fifth consecutive year the Irish representative in the Assembly's Fourth Committee, was appointed Rapporteur to the Assembly and his subsequent report at the Plenary meeting includes this aspect of his work. Remarking that the Fourth Committee is notorious in being the last to finish its work, he went on to say that this year they had fewer of the more political questions and so his report was ready on time. Nearly every year, the Fourth Committee was the scene of big political clashes between the major powers and the lesser powers on questions of principle which seemed important for the future of the organization.

In a less dramatic way Lester's involvement in the League's finances showed he had a sound grasp of the essentials. Faced with a rapidly dropping income, many delegates could only think of reducing staff salaries and curtailing activity. Lester took the line that a certain minimum of money had to be found and put forward suggestions to this end. To him, economy could be positive, making better use of existing resources and avoiding overlapping.

NOTES

1. Massimo Pilotti (1879–1962) was an Italian jurist and judge. Pilotti was the first President of the European Court of Justice in Luxembourg from 1952 to 1958.

2. Joseph Athanase Gaston Paul Doumer, commonly known as Paul Doumer (1857–1932), was a French professor, journalist, politician and diplomat. He was elected President of France in June 1931, defeating the better known Aristide Briand, until his assassination in May 1932.

3. Jonkheer John Loudon (1866–1955) was a senior Dutch diplomat and politician who had been Minister of Foreign Affairs for the Netherlands during the First World War.

4. Augustin Alfred Joseph Paul-Boncour (1873–1972) was a French politician of the Third Republic. He was the Permanent Delegate to the League of Nations from 1932 to 1936, Minister of War in 1932, Premier from December 1932 to January 1933, and Foreign Minister on three separate occasions.

5. Louis De Brouckère (1870–1951) was a Belgian socialist politician. He represented Belgium at numerous League of Nations conferences. He was a professor at the Free University of Brussels and member of the Académie Royale (1934). He was appointed minister of State in 1945.

6. Johann Heinrich Graf von Bernstorff (1862–1939) was a German politician. Ambassador to the United States and Mexico from 1908 to 1917. A founding member of the German Democratic Party and a member of the German Parliament 1921–1928. He was a member of

every German delegation to the League of Nations. Bernstorff left Germany in 1933 after the nazis took power and moved to Geneva.

7. Hugh Simons Gibson (1883–1954) was an American diplomat, an ardent supporter of the League of Nations and the International Court of Justice. He was renowned for his sense of humour, which never diminished his professionalism.

8. Johann Schober (1874–1932) was an Austrian police official who served three times as Chancellor of the country. He is also known as the Father of Interpol—the International Criminal Police Commission.

9. Arthur Henderson (1863–1935) was a British politician and trade unionist, the illegitimate son of a domestic servant. He was the first Labour cabinet minister, the 1934 Nobel Peace Prize Laureate and served three terms as the Leader of the Labour Party. To his colleagues, due to his integrity, devotion to the cause and imperturbability, he was known as "Uncle Arthur".

10. De Azcárate, P., ed. *William Martin: Un Grand Journaliste à Genève*. Geneva, Switzerland: Centre europeen de la Dotation Carnegie pour la paix internationale, 1970.

11. Giuseppe Motta (1871–1940) was a Swiss politician. He was a member of the Swiss Federal Council (1911–1940), elected to the year-long post of President of the Confederation five times. He was also President of the League of Nations Assembly (1924–1925).

12. Herbert Clark Hoover (1874–1964) was the thirty-first President of the United States (1929–1933). Hoover, born to a Quaker family, became a self-made man as a professional mining engineer. He achieved American and international prominence by providing humanitarian relief efforts in Belgium and in the famine-stricken USSR during and after the First World War.

13. Édouard Marie Herriot (1872–1957) was a French Radical politician of the Third Republic who served three times as Prime Minister and for many years as President of the Chamber of Deputies.

14. James Ramsay MacDonald (1866–1937) was a British statesman, a powerful orator, much admired for his pacifism. He was the first ever Labour Party Prime Minister of the United Kingdom, leading a Labour Government in 1924, and from 1929 to 1931, and a National Government from 1931 to 1935.

15. Gibson, H. *The Road to Foreign Policy*, p. 105. New York, NY: Doubleday, Doran, 1944.

16. Philip John Noel-Baker (1889–1982) was a British politician, diplomat, academic, an outstanding amateur athlete, and renowned campaigner for disarmament. He is the only person to have won an Olympic medal (1920) and received a Nobel Prize (1959). He was a Labour member of parliament from 1929 to 1931 and then from 1936 to 1970, serving in several ministerial offices.

17. Konni Zilliacus (1894–1967) was a left-wing politician in the United Kingdom. Of Finnish and American parentage, he spoke nine languages fluently. Between the wars he was an official of the League of Nations, and after the Second World War a Labour member of the British Parliament.

18. George Bernard Shaw (1856–1950) was an Irish journalist and playwright, an accomplished orator and a co-founder of the London School of Economics. An ardent socialist, he opposed the exploitation of the working class. He was an outspoken vegetarian who condoned the rise of dictatorships during the 1930s.

19. Clavin, P. *Securing the World Economy: The Reinvention of the League of Nations, 1920—1946*. Oxford, UK: Oxford University Press, 2013.

20. James Arthur Salter (1881–1975) was a British politician and academic. He joined the British civil service and during the First World War was a colleague of Jean Monnet. In 1919 he was appointed secretary of the Supreme Economic Council in Paris and then worked for the League of Nations. Later he became a professor at Oxford University, a member of Parliament and held government posts.

21. Salter, J.A. *Geneva and the League of Nations*. London: Faber & Faber, 1961.

22. Alexander Loveday (1888–1962) was a British economist, who worked for the League of Nations before serving as Warden of Nuffield College, Oxford from 1950 to 1954. He was evacuated from Geneva to Princeton during the Second World War.

23. Gerbet, P. *Société des Nations et Organisation des Nations Unies*, p. 77. Paris: Éditions Richelieu, 1973.
24. Yearwood, P. Guarantee of Peace: *The League of Nations in British Policy, 1914–1924*. Oxford, UK: Oxford University Press, 2009.
25. *Essential Facts about the League of Nations*, pp. 38–40. Geneva, Switzerland: League of Nations, 1936.

Chapter Seven

Secretariat Appointments

Many political clashes referred to by Lester centred on the question of appointments to the higher positions in the Secretariat. Essentially, there were two grievances voiced by Lester and other small-power delegates. Firstly, the top three ranks—the Under Secretaries-General; the Deputy Secretary-General and the Secretary-General himself—were in practice monopolized by the Great Powers. Secondly, the Under Secretaries-General had no specific duties and did not fit into the League hierarchy. It was evident that their real function was simply to keep their home governments informed about the League's activities. This, it was argued, was bad in principle and also financially wasteful.

On 9 December 1932 Lester presided over a secret Council meeting which approved the appointments of the German Ernst Trendelenburg[1] and the Italian Massimo Pilotti as Under-Secretaries-General—the latter presumably on a temporary basis until a higher appointment became free. At the same meeting the issue arose of creating the new post of a second Deputy Secretary-General and appointing someone from a minor power to fill this post. Sir Eric Drummond, the Secretary-General, wanted the Council's unofficial approval for a nomination so as to put an end to speculation, but was induced to postpone this by Lester and Hambro, the former saying that he hoped the Secretary-General would "bear in mind the views of member states and not only the needs of the service and personal considerations." Eventually, the Spaniard Pablo de Azcárate[2] was appointed as the second Deputy Secretary-General at the May 1933 Council session representing the minor powers. But was Spain really a minor power? Azcárate "interpreted his appointment not as a homage to Spain but as a gesture aimed at giving the smaller powers a stronger voice and more importance within the Secretariat." The question of two Deputy Secretaries-General—one from a major power and one from a minor power—would not be resolved satisfactorily until Lester's appointment in 1937.

A similar pattern of discussion can be seen over the appointment of a successor to the Secretary-General. In January 1932 Sir Eric Drummond, who had been Secretary-General of the League of Nations since its inception in 1919, signified his desire to resign before the end of the year. It was his intention to return to the British diplomatic service and he hoped to become ambassador with some prestigious appointment—the United States of America, for example. He gave a number of reasons for wishing to resign, but he had already been Secretary-General for thirteen years and felt that this was quite long enough.[3]

Eric Drummond was born in 1876 and educated at Eton. He began his Foreign Office career in 1900 and in 1906 became private secretary to Lord Edmond Fitzmaurice, the Parliamentary Under-Secretary. He came into contact with Sir Edward Grey,[4] the British Foreign Secretary, and up to 1919 developed close friendships with many of his superiors. From 1912 to 1915 he was private secretary to Herbert Asquith, the Prime Minister, and then to the succession of foreign secretaries from 1915 to 1919—Grey, Arthur Balfour[5] and George Curzon.[6] He was so highly regarded that when a candidate was needed for the position of Secretary-General of the League of Nations, Balfour immediately nominated Drummond. When the Paris Peace Conference had first begun to consider the governance of the League of Nations, the delegates had thought that it should be headed by someone who would be equivalent to some kind of world governor bearing the title of "Chancellor" and who would be empowered to call meetings upon his own initiative. They wanted a great statesman and their gaze was directed towards the Greek Prime Minister, Eleftherios Venizelos. When Venizelos refused, it was decided that it would be better if meetings were called upon the initiative of member states and thus the organization could be headed by a senior civil servant. The choice then fell on Drummond.[7]

His nomination was acceptable to Georges Clemenceau of France and Woodrow Wilson of the United States. During his ultimately fourteen-year tenure, he set up the Secretariat to provide a body of expert opinion on technical matters and to permit the delegates to concentrate on settling controversial political issues. Drummond was particularly active on the disarmament question, the Manchurian Crisis, the repatriation of prisoners-of-war and refugees. He was very concerned that Germany should join the League as soon as possible and played a major role in the negotiations for its admission.[8]

To the announcement of his resignation Drummond attached a note in which he gave his personal views about how his successor should be appointed. In recent years tension had arisen between the League's Council and its Assembly due to jealousy about the influence that different Great Powers exercised in meetings and among the members of the Secretariat. Evidently, if the Secretary-General was a national of a Great Power, the government in question had a great deal of influence over the League's policies. As soon as a representative of one Great Power was awarded a hierarchical position, the other Great Powers claimed similar privileges. The same situation applied among the small powers. Drummond proposed that this situation could be avoided if the next Secretary-General came from a lesser and neutral power. Sir Eric's choice therefore fell upon a Dutch jurist working at the Permanent Court of International Justice, Willem Jan Marie Van Eysinga[9] —but, when approached, Eysinga declined the position. It was also possible that a candidate from a small power could meet with strong opposition, while a majority of member states might prefer another Englishman to be appointed. If this were to be the case, the choice would fall on Sir Alexander Cadogan.[10]

Drummond remarked that "it may seem odd that I do not recommend the present Deputy Secretary-General, M. Avenol". He observed that from a personal point of view he did not consider Joseph Avenol's appointment "altogether justified" and there was likely to be opposition from Germany and Italy over choosing a French national.

In the end, Drummond's considerations proved irrelevant since already in 1919 an understanding had been reached that the first Secretary-General of the League of Nations would be an Englishman and the second one a Frenchman. In this same line of logic, the first Director of the International Labour Organization (ILO) had been a Frenchman, Albert Thomas,[11] and when he died in May 1932 it was proposed that his place would be taken by an Englishman, Harold B. Butler.[12] The British Foreign Office realised that if France supported Butler's appointment to the ILO, Paris was likely to expect London to support Avenol for the post at the League of Nations. Furthermore, Avenol had been loyal to the League and to Drummond, was considered an Anglophile and was the "obvious" candidate.

Meanwhile, Germany let it be known that it would support a British candidate both for the League of Nations and also for the International Labour Organization, and was opposed to the candidature of Avenol. However, the British Foreign Office replied to the German ambassador in London that, because of Butler's appointment at the ILO, it was unlikely that a British candidate would be put forward for the post of Secretary-General. The small powers obtained some support from Germany, then under-represented among higher posts in the Secretariat. To avoid Avenol's appointment as Secretary-General being vetoed in the Council, an unofficial compromise was reached by which the Germans would receive one Under Secretary-General post, while two posts of Deputy Secretary-General would now be established. One of these would go to Italy (in return for its support for Avenol) and the other to one of the smaller powers—as we have just seen, to Spain, which was at that time considered as a minor power.

At a secret Council meeting in May 1932 Lester outlined some of the difficulties which followed a change of Secretary-General and asked if Drummond would postpone his departure from March 1933 until after the Assembly held in the autumn. In September 1932 the Irish and Norwegian delegates—Lester and Hambro—were pressing for a delay in making the appointment as a committee was discussing the reorganization of the high direction of the Secretariat and this might affect the voting. In October 1932 Hambro and Lester continued their efforts to delay a pre-arranged appointment. On the 15 October Hambro thought the Council should take no decision until the Assembly had discussed and voted upon the Fourth Committee's resolutions (which Lester and Hambro had done much to shape) concerning the principal officers of the Secretariat. Nevertheless, a vote was taken on the new Secretary-General and Avenol was chosen unanimously, although as a concession it was agreed not to make a formal announcement until immediately after the next Assembly.[13]

The Assembly ratified this decision on 9 December 1932 and Avenol took up the position of Secretary-General on 1 July 1933. He named Drummond's Chef de Cabinet, Frank Walters,[14] as Under Secretary-General and Director of the Secretariat's Political Section. Walters served as Avenol's main channel of communications with the British Government.[15]

Joseph Louis Anne Marie Charles Avenol was born 9 June 1879 in Melle, Deux-Sèvres, France. He was the son of Ernest Joseph Marie Avenol, a member of the Pope's Swiss Guard and a solicitor, and Marie Françoise Renée Dehansy. In his youth Avenol had wanted to become a monk, but on 4 September 1901 he married Jeanne Maurel. At 17 he began his studies in law at the University of Poitiers and continued his law and political science studies at the University of Paris. His religious and traditionalist background made him a devout, but non-practising, Roman Catholic. When his secretary Vera Blanche Lever, who he had known since 1917, became Avenol's companion and long-time confidante, he did not divorce his wife as this would have meant excommunication from the Roman Catholic Church. This private situation produced protocol problems in his later diplomatic career in Geneva, where Vera Lever served as hostess at the lunches and dinners he gave.

In 1905 he was appointed to the coveted post of inspector of finances and was promoted to the post of inspector-general in 1910, later becoming an international financial expert in the French Ministry of Finance. From 1916 to 1923 he was a financial delegate to the French Embassy in London and in 1921 was made an honorary Knight Commander of the Order of the British Empire (OBE).

In 1922 the French Ministry sent Avenol to Geneva to handle the League's finances. In February 1923 he was named Deputy Secretary-General, replacing Jean Monnet,[16] who resigned in December 1922 to return to Cognac to save his father's firm. Avenol became responsible for the

League's coordination of post-war financial reconstruction, particularly in Central Europe. In this capacity he devised financial solutions for countries in need, such as Austria, Bulgaria, Estonia, Greece, Hungary and also China, where he was sent on a League mission in 1929. His financial expertise was appreciated.

Avenol concerned himself less with administration than Drummond, who had reorganized the Secretariat before resigning. The administrative alterations that Avenol did initiate brought the League's Secretariat closer to French bureaucratic procedures (more top down, with a new Central Section for coordination purposes). Passing on to his subordinates all matters that he considered of secondary importance, Avenol concentrated on political and technical affairs.

It has been said that Avenol was "neither a diplomat nor a politician", being a financial and economic expert. He spoke badly in public, with words that were "dull, embarrassed, without warmth, often inaccurate and obscure" and, compared to Drummond, it was said more than once that he was "lazy". It is not surprising that he had few close colleagues among the Secretariat or among the politicians who attended the meetings of the League. He was a person of the extreme right, thinking little of the League's ideology, of democracy or of public opinion. This goes a long way to explaining his passive acceptance of the events leading up to the Second World War. Towards the end of his period in office it was said that he found it difficult to take any decisions, and when he did it was the wrong one.

The seven years he served as Secretary-General was a time of increasing tension and instability on the international stage—and failure on the part of the League of Nations. Avenol took office shortly after Japan had left the League and in the same year Germany also departed. Italy followed in December 1937. Avenol favoured the Hoare-Laval Pact—a clumsy attempt to gain Mussolini's support by recognizing some of his claims on Ethiopia while preserving some of the African nation's independence. He worked behind the scenes to weaken his own organization's sanctions against Italy. After Ethiopian Emperor Haile Selassie fled his country, Avenol tried to arrange—unsuccessfully—for Ethiopia's membership of the League to be rescinded. He had seriously misjudged the attitude of member states.

Weakened by the Ethiopian fiasco, the League had to watch helplessly as the Free City of Danzig was taken over by the German Nazi Party between 1934 and 1936. The League's only response to the unification of Germany and Austria in 1938 was to drop Austria from the dues list. The League was a mere onlooker to signing of the Munich Agreement in September 1939, permitting Hitler to take over the Sudetenland of Czechoslovakia. Spain's foreign minister fell out with Avenol over German and Italian intervention in his nation's civil war. Avenol brushed aside Albania's appeal for an emergency meeting as Italy invaded that country in April 1939. And Germany's

1939 invasion of Poland never even came up on the Geneva agenda. Respect for the League had fallen so far that the Gestapo invaded the home of the League's High Commissioner in Danzig the night before the war began—even though he had had tea with Hitler ten days previously! Avenol worked to prevent action or criticism of those countries in an effort to appease them and lure them back to the League, at the same time as sacrificing more docile member states. By the summer of 1940, Avenol's behaviour had become a severe embarrassment to the League in general and to Lester in particular.

Sir Eric Drummond did not become the British Ambassador to Washington, being appointed to Mussolini's Rome instead. Upon the death of his brother in 1937, he became the seventh Earl of Perth. His period in Rome was a disastrous time as a close alliance developed between the two right-wing regimes of Germany and Italy, and Italian military ambitions escalated in Africa and Europe, ultimately concluding in the outbreak of the Second World War.

NOTES

1. Ernst Paul Archibald Trendelenburg (1882–1945) was a German lawyer, civil servant and politician. He and his wife committed suicide in 1945 after the rape of their daughter.
2. Pablo de Azcárate y Flórez (1890–1971) was a Spanish diplomat born in Madrid. During the 1920s he worked in the Minorities Section of the League of Nations Secretariat. During the subsequent Spanish Civil War, Azcárate served as Ambassador of the Spanish Republican Government to London.
3. Fosdick, R.B. *The League and the United Nations after Fifty Years: The Six Secretaries-General*, pp. 19–46. Newtown, CT: 1972.
4. Sir Edward Grey (1862–1933) served twice as British Foreign Secretary, firstly from 1892 to 1895 and then from 1905 to 1916. It is argued that had Grey clearly stated in July 1914 that Britain either would—or would not—support France in the event of war, the First World War could have been avoided. In 1914, Grey issued his famous warning: "The lamps are going out all over Europe; we shall not see them lit again in our lifetime."
5. Arthur James Balfour (1848–1930) was a British Conservative politician who served as Prime Minister from 1902 to 1905. He was one of the wealthiest young men in the United Kingdom. He oversaw the Entente Cordiale, an agreement with France that influenced Britain's decision to enter the First World War. The declaration of 1917 promising the Jews "a national home" in Palestine bore his name.
6. George Nathaniel Curzon (1859–1925), known as Lord Curzon, was a British Conservative statesman who had been Viceroy of India and was appointed Foreign Secretary in October 1919, but who was passed over as Prime Minister in 1923 in favour of Stanley Baldwin.
7. Ellis, C.H., ed. *The Origin, Structure and Working of the League of Nations*, p. 163. London: Allen & Unwin, 1928.
8. Fosdick, pp. 43–52.
9. Willem Jan Marie van Eysinga (1878–1961) was a Dutch lawyer and diplomat. From 1908 to 1912 he was professor of civil law at Groningen University and later of international law at Leiden University. From 1931 to 1946 he was a judge at the Permanent Court of International Justice in The Hague.
10. Sir Alexander Cadogan (1884–1968) was a British diplomat and civil servant. He was Permanent Under-Secretary for Foreign Affairs from 1938 to 1946. His long tenure in this

office makes him one of the central figures of British policy before and during the Second World War.

11. Albert Thomas (1878–1932) was a charismatic French socialist politician and the first Minister of Armament for the French Third Republic during the First World War. Following the Treaty of Versailles, he was nominated as the first Director-General of the ILO, a position he held until his death in 1932.

12. Harold Beresford Butler (1883–1951) was trained in the British Ministry of Labour. He prepared the first draft of the Preamble to the ILO Constitution in 1919. Butler took over as ILO Director from 1932 to 1938 during increasing social turmoil resulting from the economic crisis. During his time as Director, the United States of America joined the ILO.

13. Fosdick, pp. 71–5.

14. Francis "Frank" P. Walters (1888–1976), Under-Secretary General and later Deputy Secretary-General of the League of Nations. Author of *A History of the League of Nations*.

15. Fosdick, pp. 47–50.

16. Jean Omer Marie Gabriel Monnet (1888–1979) was a French political economist and diplomat. He is regarded by many as a chief architect of European unity and one of the founding fathers of the European Union. Never elected to public office, Monnet worked behind the scenes of American and European governments.

Chapter Eight

Minority Questions

Up until the First World War, European politics had been dominated by two matters: the claims of persecuted national minorities in Europe and colonial expansion in Africa and Asia. Of these two potential sources of conflict, the first one was the most serious, because it was this that had triggered the Sarajevo Incident leading to the outbreak of the First World War. One of the first tasks facing the League of Nations was, therefore, precisely the question of minorities.

Among the outcomes of the war was the collapse of four great empires: the Ottoman, the Austro-Hungarian, the Russian and the German. As could have been anticipated, the new territorial division of Europe took place at the expense of the defeated nations (particularly Germany and Austria-Hungary) and to the advantage of the victorious countries, such as France, the United Kingdom, Italy and Belgium. All the new states created following the First World War were obliged to sign minority rights' treaties as a precondition for diplomatic recognition. Treaties were signed between the League of Nations and some of the newly established nations: Czechoslovakia, Poland, Romania and Yugoslavia. Similar treaties were also imposed on some of the nations defeated in the First World War: Austria, Bulgaria, Hungary and Turkey. At the same time, Albania, Greece, Lithuania, Estonia, Latvia and, outside Europe, Iraq were persuaded to accept minority obligations as a condition for being admitted to the League of Nations. When Iraq achieved independence in 1930, it was granted membership of the League on condition that it protected minorities and foreigners. Iraq agreed to provide these guarantees—but the promise turned out to be worthless. In December 1933 Lester was presiding over the Council when it discussed the petitions from Assyrian communities living in Iraq.

Some countries reacted negatively to these treaties believing that their sovereignty was being restricted and their right for self-determination infringed. They felt that the League was influencing their national, religious and educational policy, signifying that they were not masters of their own affairs. As a result, the League was burdened with resolving a number of minority questions which tended to conflict with the territorial integrity guaranteed by the Covenant. These new nations also noted with displeasure that minority treaties had not been drawn up for France, Germany, Italy, the United Kingdom and Russia—they only applied to the minor or vanquished nations other than Germany. Another problem was that minorities who had no foreign state to support their claims were relatively disadvantaged when compared to ones backed up by a powerful army or group of interests in a neighbouring country.

Even if these measures multiplied the number of borders, and thus customs barriers, they enabled the number of national minorities to be reduced from about 60 million to some 20 million people, which, from the political and national points of view, represented considerable progress. In this way, the League of Nations intervened. "The protection of minorities should be conceived as one of the means that the treaties have provided to the League of Nations to carry out its work, which is to safeguard peace."

The minority rights contained in the treaties covered the protection of people's life and liberty, as well as freedom of worship. They also envisaged acquiring the nationality of the country in question, equality before the law and enjoyment of equal civil rights, particularly in being allowed to assume public office. Freedom to use the mother-tongue was also guaranteed. On the contrary, the minorities also had certain responsibilities. The Assembly of the League of Nations defined them in its resolution of 21 September 1922, which stated that people belonging to racial, religious or linguistic minorities were required to co-operate as loyal citizens with the nation to which they belonged.

> By means of this guarantee, any member of the League of Nations has the right to draw the Council's attention to any violation or risk of violation of any of the obligations. Respect of minority rights is possible thanks to the right of intervention. Indeed, the League of Nations is empowered to intervene in the internal affairs of a State if the right of minorities is not respected. Any person, association or State may send information concerning the situation of a minority to the League of Nations. It is also possible to communicate complaints in the form of petitions.
>
> To make this guarantee effective, the Council has introduced a procedure according to which any petition considered receivable shall be communicated to the concerned government with any observations, then together with the latter submitted for examination by a Committee consisting of three or exceptionally five members of the Council who are responsible for deciding if the

matter shall or shall not be drawn to the attention of the Council. If, after any negotiations with the concerned governments, the Committee succeeds in obtaining from it reasonable concessions, it may decide to call the matter closed. In the opposite case, the Committee will request that the matter is placed on the agenda of the Council, which will examine it during its regular sessions.[1]

The vast majority of these petitions came from German and Hungarian minorities. They complained about the loss of private property and the lack of opportunity to express their particular culture.

Towards the end of his time as Permanent Delegate of the Irish Free State and before becoming High Commissioner for Danzig, Lester was concerned with the question of minorities. This often involved the grievances of persecuted groups and even of individuals. Among the numerous conflicts that the League of Nations had to resolve in this area was that of the German minority in Czechoslovakia complaining about agrarian reform, German minorities in Poland, the confiscation of the property of the former Hungarian regiment of frontier guards in Romania, and the matter of schooling in Upper Silesia. Since the separation of Ireland into two parts, any Irishman was likely to take an interest in minorities. In Northern Ireland there was a large Roman Catholic minority who favoured a united Ireland and had reason to feel discriminated against. In the Irish Free State less than 5% of the population was Protestant. As a Northern Irish Protestant with nationalist leanings, Lester belonged to a political minority in the north and a religious one in the south. Lester's concern with minorities in the League of Nations came about partly by chance. In March 1933, Japan left the League and the position of Council Rapporteur on Minorities thus became vacant. The Irish representative was asked to take on this task in addition to his Health, Drugs and Child Welfare responsibilities. Prior to this Lester had made only a few small contributions on minority questions.

The international community had been aware of the need to protect religious and minority rights since the seventeenth century. At the Versailles Peace Conference in 1919 the Supreme Council established "The Committee on New States and for The Protection of Minorities". From now on the protection of minorities and the recognition of human rights were subjects of international concern. It was recognized that there were people who required their elementary rights to be guaranteed by an external international body as individual governments would not necessarily be able to do so. This was a considerable improvement compared to earlier periods, since minorities could now expect protection, the rule of law and the absence of discrimination. They were also guaranteed the use of their own languages.

Even before Adolf Hitler came to power in Germany in 1933, problems with the minority treaties were evident. When Germany obtained a permanent seat on the Council of the League, the protection of Eastern European minorities became a problem. Various European governments continued to abuse minorities, many of whom protested loudly to the League of Nations. However, the League interfered as little as possible. The system suffered an apparent death blow with Poland rejecting its minority treaty in 1934.

The area that concerned Lester most was Eastern Europe and in particular Silesia which, after the First World War, was disputed by Poland and Germany. Upper Silesia was a source for coal and iron ore, as well as lead, copper, silver, gold, zinc, cadmium, arsenic and uranium. Particularly, Lower Silesia was the site of large copper mining operations. The region was also known for stone quarrying to produce limestone, marble and basalt. Since the Second World War, Silesia lies principally within Poland.

In 1921 a League of Nations commission issued a decision about how the area would be divided. The result was that some Germans minorities found themselves in Polish Silesia and some Polish minorities in German Silesia. There were a number of additional circumstances making the situation particularly complicated: the Germans were mainly Protestant and the Poles mainly Roman Catholic; the Poles possessed one-third of the territory but two-thirds of the minerals; while the Poles were mainly working class, the landowners, businessmen, factory owners, local government officials, police and even the Catholic clergy were German. Numerous petitions were sent to the League based either on Article 147 of the Covenant or under the sometimes ambiguous terms of the Silesian Minorities Treaty. Even though Germany had signed a treaty in 1922 to protect minorities in Upper Silesia, specifically mentioning the Jews, it was clearly adopting discriminatory measures against them. The Germany of 1933 was a very different place from that of 1922. The French member of the Council, Paul-Boncour, was able to remind the German delegation that they themselves had insisted that they would respect the rights of minorities on their territory. The Jewish community drew world attention to the anti-Jewish legislation of nazi Germany and the resulting persecution, and sought to have its policies condemned. Germany and Poland both questioned the League's right to examine the petitions, with Germany already adopting the extreme position that the Jews did not constitute a national minority.

An interesting case arose when the nazis came to power in Germany in January 1933. A Jewish warehouse employee in Upper Silesia was dismissed from work as a result of racial discrimination. In his petition he complained that the anti-Jewish legislation of the Third Reich was also being applied to Upper Silesia, in violation of the German-Polish Convention of 1922, which guaranteed all minorities in Upper Silesia equal civil and political rights. The petition requested the League to state that all the anti-Jewish measures, if and when applied in Upper Silesia, infringed the convention and were therefore null and void, and that the rights of Upper Silesian Jews be reinstated and that they receive compensation. The German delegation was under the strictest instructions from Berlin to avoid a discussion of the matter and the German representative, Friedrich von Keller,[2] lodged an objection, but his plea was rejected by an ad hoc committee of jurists.

On 24 May 1933 Lester presented to the Council a report from a committee of three jurists who had been asked to give an opinion on the first of these objections. After further German obstruction about procedures, Lester insisted that he could not accept any suggestion that the Council was not doing its duty. While the German views were treated with "every possible courtesy and consideration", he pointed out that the German delegation often expressed itself in an emotional manner. The protection of minorities was a sacred duty and the Council would faithfully carry it out. He insisted in going through the report paragraph by paragraph to find out why the Germans objected to it. The report was passed (the German representative abstaining) and Lester concluded by saying that he had not the slightest doubt the matter would not have to be discussed again as he was sure the German Government was determined to carry out its international obligations. He was wrong; the League was now dealing with a nazi regime that played according to its own rules. On 23 March 1933, the German *Reichstag* adopted the Enabling Act which effectively made it into an agency for rubber-stamping Hitler's dictatorship. On 2 May trade unions were forbidden in Germany and all political parties except the nazis were banned.

Four days later von Keller tried to avoid a general debate on the petition, but these tactics failed too, and in two public sessions (30 May and 6 June 1933) the persecution of Jews in Germany was fully discussed. Many of the speakers severely censured Germany for the treatment of its Jews and demanded that they be accorded minimum human rights. Paul-Boncour reminded the Germans that a very large population of German speakers was protected in Poland by the same treaties. In a unanimous decision—Germany and Italy abstaining—the Council adopted a resolution noting the German Government's declaration and requesting it to furnish the Council with information on further developments.

Lester seems to have put a good deal of effort into following up these cases and getting them discussed without undue delay. His reputation for independence and courage was confirmed by these negotiations. Even the Italian Government reported to Berlin that the pursuit of its anti-Jewish policies was creating a very bad impression in Geneva. Some years later Lester wrote that the League's protest against German policies in Silesia in May 1933 had been the first move to protect the Jews from what later became "a series of unparalleled horrors". He also pointed out that the Poles had every reason to be pleased with the Council's verdict, which would give them confidence when dealing with the Germans.

Without actually admitting its errors, on 30 September 1933, the German Government submitted a letter stating that the rights of the Jews of Upper

Silesia had now been restored. However, from now no one could have any confidence when the nazi regime claimed to have "fulfilled its obligations". The discussions in the Council brought the situation of the Jews in Upper Silesia and the struggle for their rights on to the international agenda, but no substantial improvement was achieved—rather the opposite. Those Jews who protested about discrimination in Upper Silesia were unlawfully arrested or driven out of the country. Forged lists of communist workers were drawn up who were then sacked without compensation. Jewish doctors, lawyers, judges, dentists and civil servants were boycotted or dismissed. Loans to Jewish people were called in. Eventually, a whole mass of Jewish traders, artisans, shopkeepers and workers were deprived of the ability to earn a living.[3]

As in the case of disarmament, Lester was at this stage in favour of a conciliatory policy (later he opposed appeasement). In his diary in 1935 he recalls the events of 1933. At the Assembly, Henry Bérenger of France was on the Sixth Committee, and a subcommittee was formed to discuss drafts of a resolution which, while not mentioning Germany, were designed to condemn her publicly—not on the legal grounds of the Silesian Treaty, but on general grounds, the rights of man. Bérenger led the attack, ably assisted by William Ormsby-Gore,[4] a British Cabinet Minister. Lester had an extremely poor opinion of Bérenger and his principles, and Bérenger knew it.

> I regret now that I did not force the attack on the Bérenger proposal. I felt weakened. Naturally I had no kind of instructions from the Government . . . the fight was continued on other lines . . . but I yielded to the general view of the Committee. Germany had left the League within one month, and I firmly believe her decision was partly due to the impression carried away by Goebbels of this experience in the French-dominated Assembly as well to the position created in the disarmament.

With the decline of the League of Nations' prestige in the 1930s, the minority treaties were increasingly considered unenforceable and useless. The League's Council, charged with enforcing the various treaties, often failed to act upon complaints from minorities. There was an unwritten rule that state policies aimed at the cultural assimilation of minorities should be ignored as the "minor evil" with regard to the rights enshrined in the minority treaties when those policies were seen as guaranteeing the internal stability of the state concerned.

When the Council did review cases, the discussions were commonly dominated by the countries whose ethnic groups were affected and who tried not only to resolve the problem of mistreatment of their minorities but also score other political goals on the international scene, sometimes even sacrificing the very minority in question (the German and Hungarian governments are recognized as having abused the system the most). Also, of course, the

League, lacking its own army or police force, had no power to oblige any state to adhere to its recommendations. Its only real weapon was the force of public opinion engineered by the press. In order to diminish the pressure of public opinion, the Council often resorted to postponing decisions or issuing non-committal resolutions.

NOTES

1. League of Nations. *Essential facts about the League of Nations*, pp. 200–8. Geneva, Switzerland: League of Nations, 1936.
2. August Friedrich Wilhelm Keller (1873–1960) was a German diplomat. He served as ambassador in Belgrade, Brussels, Buenos Aires and Ankara, and represented Germany at the Geneva Disarmament Conference in 1933.
3. Gageby, D. *The Last Secretary-General: Sean Lester and the League of Nations*, p. 42. Dublin: Town House, 1999.
4. William George Arthur Ormsby-Gore (1885–1964) was a British Conservative politician and banker. He had been a British representative to the League of Nations since 1921.

Chapter Nine

Appointed High Commissioner in Danzig

Following its defeat in the First World War, Germany was forced to cede large parts of its territory to its neighbours, among them Poland. After more than 100 years during which the Polish state had not really existed, having been partitioned by Prussia (later Germany), Russia and the Austro-Hungarian Empire, Poland was re-established as an independent country in November 1918. However, the area occupied by the Polish-speaking population was largely land-locked. Giving Poland access to the sea was the penultimate proposition by American President Woodrow Wilson in his Fourteen Points Speech of January 1918. The Poles held the view that without direct access to the Baltic Sea their economic independence would be illusory. When Poland was reconstituted under the Treaty of Versailles, the country was ensured a free and secure access to the sea by what is known as the Polish or Danzig Corridor. Unfortunately, the population of this corridor, and particularly that of the city of Danzig, was predominantly German.

In 1919, the Allies attempted to resolve all the world's problems with the Treaty of Versailles. Many tasks under the peace treaties were assigned to the League, for instance the Saar and Danzig agreements, as well as duties concerning the protection of minorities.[1] There were inevitably solutions that were less successful than others, but none more so than Danzig. A compromise was agreed to relieve the city of Danzig of its German sovereignty in order to make it a special territory providing Poland with a port on the Baltic Sea. It was a flawed concept that satisfied nobody. Under articles 100 to 108 of the Treaty of Versailles and the subsequent Conventions of Paris and Warsaw, the Free City of Danzig was established on 10 January 1920. The "free city" was placed under the political protection of the newly created League of Nations. What this meant was that, while it provided Poland with a port, Danzig did not actually form part of either Poland or Germany but was governed by the League. The basic idea was that both the Poles and the Danzigers would have an important economic interest in making a success of the free city, but this did not happen. The city was a desirable possession for both Poland and Germany, leading to two decades of conflict between the local German and Polish populations, the Danzig, German and Polish Governments, and the League of Nations. During the period 1934 to 1936, the Free City of Danzig would become a hornet's nest—precisely those years when Sean Lester was the High Commissioner.

France was keen to have a strong Poland as a future ally whose border with Germany would provide an obstacle to its expansion in an eastward direction. The British Prime Minister, David Lloyd George, was opposed to the idea of Polish independence since "the new Poland owed its existence entirely to the efforts of the Allies." He added prophetically that if the Poles were given access to sea via Danzig, it would be the starting point for a second world war.

Why, if Danzig was supposed to be Poland's outlet to the world, was the city not simply incorporated into Poland? Why did it sit deliberately outside the frontiers of Poland? Like many of Wilson's Fourteen Points, the thirteenth granting Poland "access to the sea" was open to different interpretations. During the Paris Peace Conference the Cambon Commission was created to deliberate on the matter of Danzig and on 12 March 1919 awarded the city to Poland. When the British Prime Minister, David Lloyd George, rejected this decision, the commission refused to alter its judgement. Over the following weeks, Lloyd George persuaded Wilson that Poland was incapable of administering a city populated by people of a different ethnicity and religion. He believed that the day would soon come when Danzig would be handed back to the Germans and the Allies would be making future difficulties for themselves if the city became an integral part of Poland. Thus, the "Free City of Danzig" was created and administered by the League of Nations in the belief that mutual economic interest would lead the Poles and the Danzigers to work together. Nevertheless, the Poles felt cheated, particularly as the League's future high commissioners often obstructed the application of Polish rights within the city.

A convention between Poland and the Free City of Danzig was signed in Paris on 9 November 1920, stating that Danzig was placed within the customs zone of Poland. It granted Poles particular privileges in the fields of maritime transport, customs, railways, diplomacy, etc. Another agreement, the Warsaw Convention between Poland and Danzig, was signed on 24 October 1921. Poland's interests in Danzig were both economic and political since the Versailles Treaty gave Poland responsibility for the foreign affairs of the Free City. In its weakened position at the end of the First World War Germany was helpless to oppose these arrangements, but since the majority of the city's inhabitants were German it was obvious that the situation was not and could not remain stable. Furthermore, this strip of territory cut East Prussia off from the rest of Germany—an arrangement bitterly resented by the Germans, who spent vast amounts of money on propaganda drawing attention to the injustice of the Versailles Treaty and the Polish Corridor. Anybody trying to access East Prussia by land would now have to cross Polish soil. Ominously, the National Socialist German Workers' Party (*Nationalsozialistische Deutsche Arbeiterpartei—NSDAP*), commonly known as the Nazi Party, stated that redressing this situation was one of its priorities.

Thus, while the Polish authorities were keen to make sure that they had unhindered access to the Baltic Sea via Danzig for their foreign trade, Germany wanted guaranteed access by road and rail across the same piece of land to East Prussia. The Polish Government started a process of ethnic cleansing in the area that provided access to Danzig and the coast by encouraging the German-speaking population to leave.

Even before the Secretariat of the League of Nations was fully organized, Secretary-General Drummond attempted to tackle some of the enormous problems resulting from the First World War, especially those matters which directly or indirectly involved the League and resulted from the peace settlement. Of particular importance were the questions of Danzig and the Saar, which affected Germany's relationship with the League as well as with France and Poland. Drummond's approach was for the League to take charge of its responsibilities in these two areas as quickly as possible in the hope that nothing would occur to make the already strained relations worse between France and Poland on one side and Germany on the other.[2]

In mid-July 1919 Drummond raised with Arthur Balfour, a member of the British Cabinet, whether the proposal to appoint General Sir Richard Haking,[3] the Allied commander in Danzig, as provisional administrator and potentially as the first High Commissioner might not be an error. Drummond argued that General Haking was probably the best man in a difficult situation where military knowledge was required. However, the duties of High Commissioner surely required different qualifications. For instance, he would be required to draw up a Constitution for the Free City. Drummond was hoping that the League of Nations would be allowed to function as stipulated in the Versailles Treaty, fearing that the Council was being used purely as an instrument to execute the policies of the Allied and Associated Powers. At the end of October 1919 Drummond decided to support General Haking as provisional High Commissioner until the Treaty between Danzig and Poland had been ratified and the Free City's Constitution had come into force, despite the need to differentiate between what was done in the name of the League and what was done in the name of the Allied powers.[4] The period during which Haking administrated Danzig on behalf of the Allies would give a good indication of his qualifications to be the permanent High Commissioner. General Haking did eventually become the fourth High Commissioner from 1921 to 1923.[5]

In conformity with the Treaty of Versailles, a High Commission of the League of Nations was set up in Danzig and a High Commissioner appointed for periods of about three years to ensure that the Constitution was observed. While he could use his veto on the city's international affairs, his powers over the internal administration of the city were less clear. For instance, during the 1920s and 1930s his position was not supported by any military authority, while the police force remained in the hands of the city's government. This was to prove a fatal flaw. His principal function was to regulate any dispute between Danzig and Poland before, if necessary, passing it on to the Council of the League of Nations. Poland and Danzig could (and often did) make an appeal against his verdict to the Council, whose decision was final. He had supervisory rights over Danzig's armaments, foreign loans and foreign policy. Finally, individuals or groups had the right of petition allowing them to approach the League of Nations directly as long as their request was channelled through the city's Senate. This too was to become a fatal flaw. The High Commissioner's only weapons were the sending of reports to the Council in Geneva, usually on an annual basis, calling emergency meetings and then implementing the instructions of the Council.

The Council designated Sir Reginald Tower[6] as the first official High Commissioner of the League of Nations in Danzig on 13 February 1920. Tower and the three British High Commissioners who followed him—Lieutenant-Colonel E.L. Strutt,[7] General Haking and M.S. McDonnell[8]—strongly favoured the city's interests over those of Poland, which concluded that membership of the League of Nations had done it more harm than good. The city was supervised by a People's Assembly or *Volkstag,* and governed by a twelve-man Senate with executive power. The Free City had a democratic Constitution drawn up by representatives of all political parties—and the High Commissioner. The adopted Constitution was accepted by the Council of the League of Nations on 17 November 1920. It is important to note that a two-thirds majority of the Senate was required to amend the Constitution, with the amendment then being submitted to the League's Council for "approval". If the Senate ever achieved this two-thirds majority, the League may in fact have been helpless to prevent it from assuming some form of independence. Apart from expressing its opinion, exactly what the Council could do if it disagreed with the Senate remained unclear—yet another flaw.

However, during the first ten years of the Free City's existence this arrangement worked quite well. But relations between Danzig and Poland began to deteriorate when, with amazing imprudence, the Danzig port authorities began to impose restrictions and extra charges on Polish imports—their principal source of revenue. They chose to concentrate on their trade with

Germany and to avoid dealing with Poland. The Poles, with incredible energy and speed, then built a modern trade and naval port at Gdynia, immediately to the north of Danzig. This new port created unemployment in Danzig, since, by May 1932, the total exports and imports of Gdynia surpassed those of Danzig.

The short-lived Polish-Soviet War had erupted in 1920 in the aftermath of the First World War. This was basically a border dispute that was settled largely in Poland's favour in March 1921 and the new eastern frontier would remain in place until 1939. During the hostilities, local German dockworkers in Danzig went on strike and refused to unload ammunition supplies for the Polish Army. While the ammunition was finally unloaded by British troops, the Poles learned an important lesson. They established a permanent ammunition depot with a military garrison at Westerplatte on the eastern bank of the Vistula River opposite the city. It was following this episode and following the same logic that the Poles had begun to construct the port of Gdynia. In December 1925, the Council of the League of Nations accepted the establishment of a permanent Polish military guard of eighty-eight men at Westerplatte to protect the war material placed there. At dawn on 1 September 1939 Westerplatte was to play a significant role in world history.

Until 1933, the successive High Commissioners were mainly occupied with Danzig/Poland disputes. Although he supervised the Constitution of Danzig, the High Commissioner's position was vague on internal politics. It was strengthened in 1920 by a Council decision that in an emergency he could request Polish troops to keep order in Danzig; this decision was reconfirmed in 1936. The details of exactly what Poland was entitled to do in the Free City soon became a permanent matter of dispute between local politicians and the Polish Government. While the German-speaking representatives of Danzig tried to uphold the city's independence and sovereignty, Poland sought to extend its privileges. Nazi intrigues, therefore, found a particularly fertile terrain in the city and confrontations were frequent. Furthermore, the limited powers granted to the High Commissioner did not allow him to resolve these local problems.

There were several disputes between Danzig and Poland. The German population of the city protested against the Westerplatte depot, the placement of Polish letter boxes within the city and the presence of Polish warships in the harbour. In retaliation, the attempt of the Free City to join the International Labour Organization was rejected by the Permanent Court of International Justice at The Hague after protests by the Polish ILO delegate.

Up until 1933, the High Commissioner decided on a number of disputes between Danzig and Poland ranging from the fundamentally important to the utterly trivial; in many cases one of the parties subsequently appealed to the Permanent Court of International Justice in The Hague. However, in the summer of 1933 bilateral agreements were concluded between the Danzig

Senate and Poland in which they decided to settle all future disputes through direct negotiations and to abstain from further appeals to the High Commissioner and the International Court.

In 1925, the German Foreign Minister, Gustav Stresemann,[9] had proposed that France, Germany and Belgium should recognize as permanent the western frontiers of Germany that had been agreed at Versailles. This included the promise not to send German troops into the Rhineland and the acceptance that Alsace-Lorraine was permanently part of France. The French Foreign Minister, Aristide Briand, agreed with Stresemann's proposals. However, as Germany refused to guarantee its eastern frontiers at the same time, France sought to give Poland and Czechoslovakia the security they required by signing treaties with them. The Treaties of Locarno (or Locarno Pact), covering a wide range of European border settlements, were signed in October 1925. Because it suggested that Germany was ready to live within the borders established by the Treaty of Versailles, the Locarno Pact opened the door to Germany becoming a member of the League of Nations and obtaining a permanent seat on the Council. However, Poland was irritated that, although it considered itself to be a Great Power, it had not been and was never offered a permanent place on the Council.

During the 1920s, events in the new Polish state were a cause for concern. Although it had been set up as a parliamentary democracy, political life had been subject to corruption, incompetence and infighting resulting in instability. In 1926, the old war-horse Józef Piłsudski[10] led a *coup d'état* to restore order and clean up politics, ruling the country as a virtual dictator from 1926 to his death in 1935. Although he sought prosperity for the country, many of his followers took advantage of the situation to increase their personal wealth. His government lacked political experience and there was a remarkable lack of vision and naivety in its foreign policy. For example, Poland pursued a policy aiming at the goal of becoming a major world power. Tragically, while pursuing this unrealistic policy, it completely failed to appreciate that the ultimate purpose of Hitler's policies during the late 1930s was to maintain peace with Poland until the time came to move Germany's border eastwards.

Both Polish Foreign Minister Jósef Beck[11] and President Piłsudski believed that membership of the League of Nations had done Poland more harm than good and therefore sought good relations with Germany rather than supporting the League's policies. For instance, in order to join the League Poland had been obliged to sign a convention protecting its minorities, whereas the major powers had exempted themselves from such obligations. In Poland Jews and other minorities were treated with suspicion and faced discrimination. Anti-Semitic riots began to take place as a result of economic difficulties. For some centuries, Poland had been controlled by a landed aristocracy with middle-class Jews in charge of commerce and finance. With the setting up of the new country, the Catholic and Polish younger generation found themselves faced with barriers and competition in accessing business and the professions. The Jewish community began to feel uneasy and started placing its money abroad.

In the second volume of *Mein Kampf*, published in December 1926, Adolf Hitler wrote that it was impossible for Germany's large population to live within its boundaries. He indicated his intention of extending Germany's frontiers eastward until the nation occupied a much greater area of land. When Hitler came to power in Germany in January 1933, the Polish military immediately doubled the number of troops at the Westerplatte depot, breaking international law in order to test the reaction of the new chancellor. After international protests, the additional troops were withdrawn. However, the clumsiness of Polish policies following this and other disputes alarmed the population of Danzig and played into the hands of the local nazi politicians, giving them an absolute majority in the May 1933 *Volkstag* elections.

In the aftermath of the German-Polish Non-Aggression Pact of 1934, Danzig/Polish relations improved and Hitler instructed the local nazi government to cease anti-Polish provocation. In return, Poland did not support the actions of the anti-nazi opposition in Danzig, thus giving the nazis a free hand to intimidate socialists, Roman Catholics and Jews. Already, the Poles were being lured into a false sense of security and it was not until the summer of 1939 that they suddenly realised their predicament—by which time the trap was about to snap shut. For example, the Polish Ambassador to Germany, Józef Lipski,[12] made the following unwise statement about a meeting with Hermann Göring:

> A National Socialist Senate in Danzig is also most desirable from our point of view, since it brought about a rapprochement between the Free City and Poland. I would like to remind him that we have always kept aloof from internal Danzig problems. In spite of approaches repeatedly made by the opposition parties, we rejected any attempt to draw us into action against the Senate. I mentioned quite confidentially that the Polish minority in Danzig was advised not to join forces with the opposition at the time of elections.

A succession of officials of varying nationalities and professions held the High Commissioner's post for periods ranging from a few months to a few years. However, in September 1932 a problem arose when the Italian Count Manfredi Gravina[13] died suddenly in Danzig after a surgical operation. As a temporary measure Dr Helmer Rosting,[14] a Danish official of the League of Nations who was an expert on Danzig in the Minorities Section of the Secretariat, was appointed for six months, later renewed until a permanent appointment could be made. During 1933 the problem of finding a new High Commissioner for Danzig had become increasingly urgent—and difficult. Rosting would not be relieved until January 1934. Indeed, he might never have been replaced at all if he had not been appointed Director of the Minorities Section in Geneva in October 1933, thus making it necessary to take a decision concerning his successor.

By November, High Commissioner Rosting requested a meeting of the Council (the guarantor of the Free City of Danzig) regarding breaches of the Danzig Constitution over the suppression of the press and the arrest of two Danzig newspaper editors by the emergent nazi administration. Such a meeting was not to the liking of Secretary-General Avenol, who did not want to do anything that might antagonize the Government in Berlin.

The difficulty of finding an acceptable and willing candidate for the post of High Commissioner may be explained on three grounds: the range of qualifications required; the restrictions concerning the nationality of the candidate; and the reputation of the position. Ideally, the High Commissioner should have had experience in dealing with European minority problems, experience in inter-state disputes, as well as having a knowledge of the German and, if possible, the Polish languages. It was obviously necessary to choose a High Commissioner who was acceptable to the Danzig and Polish authorities, and this ruled out French and German candidates. Considerable tact, patience and finesse were needed in coping with the legal intricacies of the situation and confronting the frequent ill-will of the parties concerned. There was a reluctance to accept a person who was the representative of a Great Power, although in fact both the United Kingdom and Italy had provided high commissioners. At the same time, a representative from a small country was felt by many to be at a political disadvantage. Finally, the difficulties of the position were well-known since unpleasant disputes in Danzig had been a regular feature of Council discussions since the founding of the League and it had become impossible to satisfy all or, indeed, any of them. With the accession to power of the German Nazi Party in 1933 there were indications of a gathering storm, thus a man of character and courage was needed.

Considering all this, it is surprising that there was one obvious candidate and that it took so long to pinpoint him. Lester had the experience of dealing with East European minority problems and with inter-state disputes. He was thoroughly familiar with the workings of the League and was now well-known to members of the Council and the Secretariat as a colleague who had resolved difficult situations through fair-mindedness, hard work and determination. He was a national of a state which had no treaty relations with Germany or Poland, and which had demonstrated that it did not readily follow British policies. It was, nonetheless, indirectly strengthened by being a member of the British Commonwealth and Lester had many acquaintances in the Foreign Office in London. Lester's ignorance of German and Polish was his only obvious handicap.

Efforts to find a new High Commissioner had been going on for some time since Rosting's temporary appointment. At a secret Council meeting held on 29 September 1933, Sir John Simon[15] who, as British representative, was Rapporteur for Danzig, stated that repeated efforts to find an acceptable candidate were being blocked by Poland insisting that this person should not be a representative of a Great Power or a Commonwealth national, thus artificially restricting the choice. The Polish delegate justified his attitude on the grounds that so far the Rapporteur had only submitted the names of British candidates, to which Simon replied that candidates from the British Dominions had been offered as well. There is no indication that Lester was being considered at this stage.

The British Foreign Office, commenting on reports of the meeting, wrote that since Italy, France and Germany were for various reasons ruled out, the United Kingdom was the only European Great Power left on the Council that could submit a candidate. "We will try a list of British Dominion and foreign names in that order and hope with German help get a British candidate accepted." But on 6 October E.H. Carr,[16] the British Council agent in Geneva, reported that all of these candidates had been rejected: "Three because they had too little experience, and then another one because he had too much experience." Carr had then considered two Norwegians, good lawyers with not too much political experience and an American: "I dislike the idea of falling back on an American." Then Lester's name came up for the first time.

> Lastly, the Secretariat suggested that we should consider Lester who had made himself a considerable reputation here and would certainly have strong support on the Council. It is a serious drawback that he knows no German, but I believe all the same he would make a very good High Commissioner and it would not be easy for either side to find good reasons for turning him down. I have today asked him, as coming entirely from myself, whether he would object to my suggesting his name [...] as a suitable candidate. He asked for time to think it over (and probably to consult his delegation), but his reaction was not altogether unfavourable.

The British Foreign Office's comment was that Lester seemed a good choice apart from not knowing German and that "perhaps too the Poles' reluctance to have a British subject will not extend to the Irish Free State." On 13 October Carr reported that the French and Spanish representatives on the Council, as well as the Danzigers, favoured Lester and that the Council discussion on the subject had been adjourned to the following day to enable the Polish Foreign Minister, Colonel Beck, to arrive from Warsaw. Beck, a tall, handsome and vain man, considered by some to be arrogant and devious, was to play a vital, but negative, role in the story of Danzig over the next seven years.

Throughout the 1920s successive Polish Governments had accepted the candidates proposed by Geneva for the post of high commissioner, often to the detriment of Polish interests. The Polish Government did not think that the post was particularly important, especially as the high commissioner had no executive power. The country also wanted to be taken seriously as a "Great Power", but its own interests were continually overshadowed by those of France, Germany and the United Kingdom. Secretary-General Avenol was sensitive to German interests in Danzig, while Poland had the impression that it was always faced with a *fait accompli* over the choice of high commissioner. Indeed, as early as July 1933, months before Germany's exit from the League, Avenol had argued that it was both unfair and dangerous for the League to allow Poland to have too much influence over the selection of Danzig's new high commissioner. The Poles wanted to lay down conditions for the high commissioner's selection in order that they might have the representative of a small power to deal with (and intimidate). In October 1933, the Poles had decided to adopt a stronger position over the choice of the next high commissioner. They insisted that the ideal candidate should not be the national of a Great Power nor of a British Commonwealth nation, which greatly restricted the choice.

When the delegates met again on 14 October, Simon was close to exasperation, emphasizing the urgency of making an appointment since Rosting's term of office expired at midnight, when also his own responsibilities for finding a High Commissioner lapsed. He drew attention to the twenty-eight names that had been considered, and how often the matter had been discussed and adjourned, and he recalled the qualities desired—character, independence, familiarity with League methods and possessing the confidence of Council members. He proposed Sean Lester as a colleague whose achievements were known to all.[17]

Colonel Beck, without giving any reason, said he could not accept this proposal and suggested instead that Rosting's term of appointment should be extended. There followed an inconclusive and at times irritable discussion. It should be remembered that it was on this same day that Germany had dramatically announced its withdrawal from both the Disarmament Conference and the League of Nations. Konstantin von Neurath's[18] telegram containing this depressing and alarming news had reached Geneva shortly before the Council met for its afternoon session and tempers were wearing thin. What this also meant is that Germany played no further role in the choice of high commissioner.

After Beck had spoken, the Spanish delegate, Salvador de Madariaga, said that he had worked closely with Lester on Latin American problems and he knew that Lester would have given great satisfaction to the Polish Government. He therefore wished the Council could have agreed on a candidate so deserving of confidence. He did not understand Poland's refusal to accept a name without giving an explanation. The French and Italian delegates also spoke warmly of Lester's experience and qualities. Simon, a man normally undisturbed by delay and indecision, now showed impatience stating that adjournments were no answer and that he would resign as Rapporteur if there was another one. He had been trying for twelve months to find a name that would be generally acceptable. He added that he did not understand, and no one else seemed to know, what possible reasons the Poles could have for objecting to Lester's candidature.

Beck now stated that he was asking for the definite re-appointment of Rosting. The President of the Danzig Senate said that a choice must be made: either Rosting should be definitely re-appointed or Lester should be chosen, whose selection he would regard with satisfaction. A discussion followed as to whether Rosting was available. As we know, he was about to re-join the Secretariat in Geneva. It transpired that he had already been asked if he would be willing to resign his new Secretariat appointment in order to stay in Danzig — but had declined. After this meeting the Council met again in private, but still failed to reach a decision and the matter was adjourned for ten days.

At this stage, Lester withdrew his candidature not wishing to accept an appointment under such circumstances. Simon reported back to London that though he would prefer a Great Power candidate, he had agreed, in view of previous Polish objections about other candidates, to support Lester. He hoped that the Council adjournment would enable the Polish Government to reconsider its attitude towards Lester, which could be attributed to insufficient knowledge in Warsaw about his qualifications. Simon would not support another candidate since he was convinced that no other such candidate possessed qualifications equal to those of Lester. If no decision was reached by 26 October, it was his intention to state publicly that it was the Polish Government's attitude that had resulted in his resignation as Rapporteur.

Beck's objection seems to have been that Lester would be a mouthpiece for British policy, though if this was the case he was woefully ill-informed about recent Anglo-Irish relations! The British Ambassador in Warsaw, William Erskine,[19] took up the question on 23 October and found Beck still harping about old grievances. Polish opinion, Beck claimed, was suspicious about the United Kingdom and still remembered the first High Commissioner Tower with disfavour. Erskine replied that the suspicion was unjust and explained the reasons for selecting a candidate who was not necessarily British. After consulting the Polish representative in Geneva by telephone, on 26 October Beck agreed on behalf of the Polish Government to accept Lester's candidature. The precise details of the arrangement were worked out over the next few days. The Council held a special final meeting on this day to make the formal appointment. The United Kingdom, Poland and the Free City of Danzig were all represented by junior delegates since agreement had in fact already been reached and the meeting was marked by a relaxed and congratulatory atmosphere.

Although Germany had now left the League, German diplomats in Dublin and London were asked to make inquiries by their government about the background of Lester and his wife, particularly to find out if they had any Jewish blood. Although they generally provided accurate information to Berlin, the embassies were responsible for two appalling errors: that Lester had attended Queen's University, Belfast; and that his wife Elsie had Jewish ancestors.[20]

The poisoned chalice of High Commissioner in Danzig benefited from a disproportionally large salary. In mid-January 1934 Lester took over for three years at an annual salary of 72,000 gold francs (equivalent to Swiss francs), including a large house, free electric light and heat, a car and chauffeur. It had originally been 80,000 but had been reduced by 10% on account of the general economic crisis, but remained extremely high by 1930's standards. As a comparison, the Irish High Commissioner in London, one of the top two posts in the Department of External Affairs, received about 30% of Lester's salary, and in the League Secretariat only the Secretary-General himself received more. The high commissioner's salary and expenses were paid for partly by the Danzig Senate and partly by Poland. During a time of economic depression, the cost of the High Commissioner's post was to become a frequent source of contention.

To Lester the appointment probably came as a welcome opportunity for increasing his experience of the League's work at a time when it had appeared more than likely that his activities would be curtailed by Ireland's membership of the Council coming to an end. At the same time, the post as High Commissioner in Danzig was known as a difficult posting, though the source of the difficulties was rapidly escalating—with the result that Lester would soon become internationally known as a prominent public figure. Lester's position as high commissioner was unique since, unlike his predecessors, he was confronted with a series of internal problems to deal with for which both precedents and machinery were lacking.

The Warsaw correspondent of *The Times* reported that the appointment of Lester had been received with satisfaction in political circles: "Mr Lester is well known in Poland because of his work with the League of Nations. The British Council in Danzig reported that both Danzigers and Poles seemed satisfied with Lester's appointment, though outside official circles they showed little interest for the appointment of a new High Commissioner."

Some years later, Major-General A.C. Temperley provided the following sketch of Sean Lester at this moment in time in his book *The Whispering Gallery of Europe*:

> The Irish Free State, like many other small Powers, had a permanent representative at Geneva, and Mr Sean Lester held the post for several years on behalf, first, of the Cosgrave and then of the de Valera Governments. He is a man of great sincerity and moral courage and he did much to shape the course of the Manchuria discussions. He showed to very great advantage as a member of the Council during the Irish tenure of the seat reserved for the Dominions, and this procured for him nomination to the uneasy post of High Commissioner for Danzig. . . The League is the richer for Dominion statesmen, like Lester and Te Water,[21] who have believed that "somehow the right is the right" and have not failed through good and ill to be its champions.

Curiously, de Valera does not seem to have made any statement about Lester's nomination, the first major international appointment for an Irish citizen. De Valera considered Irish membership of the League of Nations to be important and he had worked with Lester in Geneva but, preoccupied with internal unrest and the economic war with the United Kingdom, he may have had more important matters to deal with. It is also just possible that de Valera may have preferred to have a less independent representative in Geneva. Certainly, Lester's successor, Frank Cremins,[22] usually did what he was instructed to do by his government, in comparison with Lester who had followed his inclinations on matters of principle. It was also a time when de Valera reintroduced a few of his supporters into the Department of Foreign Affairs who had left it during the Civil War. Lester, by contrast, had been appointed by the previous Cosgrave administration.

Later, in May 1936 Lester remarked that until then he "had never had one word of appreciation or encouragement from headquarters, personal or official, for my work in the Council or my work in Danzig." His work attracted little attention in Ireland, while even the Irish League of Nations Society in its journal *Concorde* preferred general news rather than covering the activities of Irish representatives in Geneva.

On 6 November 1933 we find Lester equipping himself with a selection of documents on Danzig—treaties, documents, manuals, procedures—and on 18 December he formally resigned his chairmanship of the Council's Leticia Committee.

As High Commissioner in Danzig, a post he was to occupy for almost three years, Lester was clearly no longer a national representative of Ireland since he was on secondment from the League's Department of External Affairs and not subject to Irish governmental policies. He was not yet, however, an international civil servant in the sense of being a member of the Geneva Secretariat; that was to come later with his appointment as Deputy Secretary-General at the beginning of 1937. Rather, he was a special international representative, watching over the League's responsibilities in Danzig, without executive power (here the position differed from that of the League's representative in the Saarland). Yet he was expected to prevent discord reaching the state where a formal report had to be made to the Council. His time in office was destined to be the most troubled time in the twenty-year history of the Free City of Danzig as the nazis tried to destroy the principles on which the League was based. During the next three years, the German-directed Nazi Party of Danzig became increasingly confrontational and Lester, as the League's man on-the-spot, was constantly required to deal with the arrest of innocent people, the suppression of newspapers and violations of the Constitution, all perpetrated by the Danzig Government itself.

During his time in Danzig, Lester would come into contact with a host of politicians, consuls, ambassadors, journalists and civil servants, but three names stand out.

Dr Hermann Rauschning[23] was an agricultural specialist and member of the NSDAP or Nazi Party. He was an educated, cultured and moderate politician belonging to the party that achieved victory in the 1933 elections. When Lester arrived in the city in January 1934, he was president of the Danzig Senate. Rauschning, an excellent public speaker, played his part perfectly as the respectable leader of a right-wing political party that attracted German members of the population fearing communist and Polish ambitions—he was, in fact, being duped by the nazis. At the end of 1934 he realized what was going on, fell out with the Nazi Party and openly denounced nazism, appealing to the public not to vote for them in the 1935 elections. Lester acquired a certain amount of respect for Rauschning who, he said, was the only local politician who had any conception of a world outside Danzig. Rauschning later wrote a best-selling book publishing his conversations with Hitler, which the nazis attempted to suppress since it described only too clearly the *Führer*'s true ambitions. Rauschning was a good leader, but was not a typical nazi and was not anti-Jewish. He was also a bitter rival of the party leader, Albert Forster.[24]

Gauleiter Albert Forster[25] was the head of the Nazi Party in Danzig and controlled the elected politicians. Hitler knew him personally — he had been taught at school by Hitler's sister and was known by the nickname "Bobby"—and had chosen this young colleague as his representative in Danzig, so Forster always had direct access to the *Führer*. He was a Bavarian who had arrived in the city by train dressed in lederhosen and knee socks with his possessions in a cardboard box, but within a year owned a patrician townhouse and a country estate, and travelled everywhere in a Mercedes car dressed in a smart uniform. A fanatical nazi and anti-Semite, he held the prestigiously low Nazi Party number of 158.[26] As soon as he arrived in the city, Forster electrified the local nazis by flooding the town with propaganda and organizing a powerful election campaign with massive public rallies addressed by prominent public figures. The result was that within a couple of years the nazis were ready to take the city over. Lester's opinion was that people like Forster may have been useful during a revolution, but once the revolution had achieved its aims the time had come to remove them. Rauschning's wife, who had no time for her husband's political associates, described Forster as a rabid street fighter. Everyone outside the Nazi Party, including Lester and German diplomats, was curious to know exactly what Forster's role was in the government of the city, since he held no elected post and was not a native of the city, but seemed to hold supreme power. When Hitler paid a visit to Danzig in September 1939, it was Forster who introduced him during a radio broadcast. Throughout Lester's term of office in the city there was persistent friction with Forster and constant talk of removing him, but his position was entirely secure. In a speech to a Dublin audience in 1948, Lester had this to say about Forster:

> More corruptible than easily-acquired wealth was unbridled power and the absence of any control on the growth of a vast vanity. Provided he showed sufficient adulation of the Dictator, he could do as he pleased—a Nietzscheesque lord of the lives of the people. Forster was a great mob orator and a fanatic, very impatient of legal obstacles to the institution of a nazi dictatorship.

The final member of the trio was Forster's rival and Lester's "friend", but also his greatest political foe: Albert Greiser.[27] During the 1920s Greiser had lived comfortably running his own import/export business in oils and fats in Danzig. Finding himself bankrupt in 1929 and with little prospect of finding a new job, Greiser joined the Nazi Party and soon gained a reputation as a good speaker. He rose rapidly through the ranks as a radical German nationalist politician. In November 1934, he replaced Rauschning as President of the Danzig Senate. He was a very complicated person indeed, described by different people as rude, quarrelsome, vain, vicious, opportunistic, imperious, cold-blooded, a treacherous politician, an inveterate schemer; to intimidate people in discussions he was known to display or toy with a loaded revolver. But he was also known as a dutiful son, a devoted parent, an affectionate lover and a faithful family member renowned for his sense of humour—his children adored him. He embodied those opposing qualities that are often portrayed as a stereotype of model nazis: decent and dishonest, cultured and cruel, respectful and ruthless. When dealing with the well-meaning and straightforward Lester, Greiser deployed a whole range of dubious political manoeuvres—lies, deceit, defiance, duplicity, rumours, threats, squabbles and insults followed by charming overtures, reassuring confidences and abject apologies—which meant that he often held the upper hand. There was a violent collision between Lester's desire that the Constitution of Danzig and the Treaty of Versailles should be respected, and Greiser's ambitions that the Free City should become a nazi-dominated stronghold soon to be integrated into the German Reich. Since Greiser could count upon the blatant interference of the German Government in Berlin, while the League of Nations was paralysed with indecision, the outcome was inevitable. Arthur Greiser's life story merits a whole book and such a book actually exists.[28]

Lester made a name for himself in the international press by defending the terms of the Constitution and preserving democratic institutions for nearly two-and-a half years of his mandate. Despite his robust rear-guard action, the member states of the League of Nations were anxious not to provoke Hitler's Germany. They failed to appreciate the gravity of the situation even when, by late-1936, democracy no longer existed in the city. The Berlin-dominated Nazi Party of Danzig was by then in full control.

NOTES

1. Barros, J. *Office without Power: Secretary General Sir Eric Drummond, 1919–1933*, p. 59. Oxford, UK: Clarendon Press, 1979.

2. Barros, p. 85.

3. Sir Richard Cyril Byrne Haking (1862–1945) was a British general, who commanded XI Corps in the First World War and is remembered chiefly for the high casualties during the second Battle of Fromelles in 1916. After the war he had a distinguished career before becoming High Commissioner to Danzig in 1921.

4. League of Nations, Drummond Folder. Geneva, Switzerland: Archives of the League of Nations.

5. Notes on Danzig, Danzig Administrative Commission, 31 October 1919, box 4/1872. Geneva, Switzerland: Archives of the League of Nations.

6. Sir Reginald Thomas Tower (1860–1939) was a British diplomat whose career as ambassador lasted from 1885 to 1920.

7. Edward Lisle Strutt (1874–1948) was a British soldier and mountaineer. After a distinguished military career he became President of the Alpine Club 1935–1938.

8. Mervyn Sorley MacDonnell (1880–1949) worked for the civil service in Sudan and Egypt, where he was acquainted with Lawrence of Arabia. After becoming High Commissioner in Danzig, he worked as a journalist.

9. Gustav Stresemann (1878–1929) was a German politician and statesman who served as Chancellor in 1923 and Foreign Minister 1923–1929, during the Weimar Republic. He was co-laureate of the Nobel Peace Prize in 1926 with Aristide Briand for signing the Locarno Pact.

10. Józef Klemens Piłsudski (1867–1935) was a Polish statesman and marshal. As a young man he had been a socialist and was sent to Siberia for planning the assassination of Tsar Alexander III. He fought for the Austrians against the Russians in the First World War. From 1917 he had a major influence on Polish politics and was responsible for the creation of the Second Polish Republic in 1918.

11. Polish Foreign Minister from 1932 to 1939, Józef Beck (1894–1944) was a diplomat and military officer, but hostile to the League of Nations. A close associate of Piłsudski, he tried to fulfil Piłsudski's dream of making Poland the leader of a regional coalition, but was widely distrusted by other governments. Died of tuberculosis while interned in Romania.

12. Józef Lipski (1894–1958) was a Polish diplomat and ambassador to nazi Germany, 1934 to 1939. Lipski played a key role in foreign policy of the Second Polish Republic.

13. Manfredi Gravina (1883–1932) had been an Italian naval officer, pilot and diplomat, before being appointed High Commissioner for Danzig from 1929 until his death in 1932.

14. Helmer Rostgaard Rosting (1893–1945) was a Danish theologian and diplomat, who became an expert on Danzig in the League's Minorities Section. Head of the Danish Red Cross during the Second World War. Having collaborated with the nazis during the war, he committed suicide in 1945.

15. Sir John Allsebrook Simon (1873–1954) was a successful lawyer and British politician who held senior cabinet posts from the beginning of the First World War to the end of the

Second. He is one of only three people to have served as British Home Secretary, Foreign Secretary and Chancellor of the Exchequer.

16. Edward Hallett "Ted" Carr (1892–1982) was British historian, diplomat, journalist and international relations theorist. Moving increasingly towards the left throughout his career and preoccupied with the study of the USSR, he resigned from the Foreign Office in 1936 to begin an academic career. In the 1930s, Carr was a leading supporter of appeasement.

17. McNamara, P. *Sean Lester, Poland and the Nazi Takeover of Danzig,* p. 50. Dublin: Irish Academic Press, 2009.

18. Konstantin Freiherr von Neurath (1873–1956) was a German diplomat who served as German Foreign Minister between 1932 and 1938. Holding this post in the early years of Hitler's regime, Neurath played a key role in undermining the Treaty of Versailles. In 1946, he was prosecuted at the Nuremburg Trials and spent eight years in prison.

19. William Augustus Forbes Erskine (1871–1952) joined the British Foreign Office in 1894 and served all over the world. Minister and then Ambassador to Poland 1928–1934, he was the first British Ambassador to Poland since the seventeenth century.

20. McNamara, p. 51.

21. Charles Theodore Te Water (1887–1964) was a South African barrister and diplomat. High Commissioner for South Africa in London between 1929 and 1939, he represented South Africa at the League of Nations. President of the Assembly, 1933–1934. He was an ambassador for South Africa, 1948–1949, and Chancellor of the University of Pretoria, 1949–1964.

22. Francis Thomas "Frank" Cremins was the Permanent Representative of the Irish Free State to the League of Nations from 1933 to 1938, when he became the Irish Chargé d'Affaires in Berne, Switzerland.

23. Hermann Rauschning (1887–1982) came from a noble family. Wounded in action as an infantry officer in the First World War. Became a German conservative revolutionary politician who joined the Nazi Party. In 1936, he sold his farm in the Danzig area and fled, eventually settling in Portland, Oregon, United States.

24. Epstein, C. *Model Nazi: Arthur Greiser and the Occupation of Western Poland,* p. 59. Oxford, UK: Oxford University Press, 2010.

25. Albert Maria Forster (1902–1952) was a nazi German politician and friend of Hitler. In the period 1933–1936, he spearheaded the nazi take-over of Danzig. During the Second World War, he organized the extermination of Poles and Jews. In 1948, he was condemned to death by the Polish court for war crimes and hanged in 1952.

26. Epstein, p. 51 – 53.

27. Arthur Karl Greiser (1897–1946) was a German politician, fanatic anti-Christian and member of the Nazi Party. He was the President of the Danzig Senate, 1935–1939. During the Second World War, he was primarily responsible for organizing the Holocaust in the Posen area. Arrested by the Americans in 1945, he was tried, convicted and executed by hanging in Poland in 1946.

28. Epstein, p. 54.

Chapter Ten

Danzig in 1933 and 1934

When Lester arrived in Danzig on 24 January 1934, the arrangements for governing the Free City decided upon by the Great Powers in Versailles in 1919 were clearly in difficulties. Two days after he arrived nazi Germany and Poland signed a non-aggression pact that by-passed the League of Nations. According to this pact, both countries accepted to resolve their problems through bilateral negotiations and not to attack each other for a period of ten years. As a consequence, Germany effectively recognized Poland's borders and undertook to end a customs war which had affected both countries during the previous decade. German policy on Danzig at this time was to limit the clashes with Poland in order to concentrate on the nazi take-over of the city. What this also meant was that Poland had given up on the League of Nations as a guarantor of its security. In a way, the agreement between Germany and Poland was a considerable relief to the League in Geneva since, if the German/Polish border had to be re-negotiated, then perhaps all the frontiers established by the Treaty of Versailles would require revision. Five-and-a-half years later Germany attacked Poland.

The mediaeval city of Danzig had some buildings surviving from the time of the Hanseatic League and was surrounded by seventeenth-century fortifications with elaborate gates at both ends of the city. In the 1930s the city was commercially only a shadow of the port that had once dominated Baltic trade. Lester took up residence with his family in the large German baronial house assigned to the High Commissioner. A formal speech of welcome was given by Hermann Rauschning, president of the Danzig Senate, and replied to by Lester; official visits were made and received. During the following weeks Lester met various other Danzig personalities and soon came to the conclusion that the authorities considered the League and its High Commissioner as an irrelevant nuisance. Apart from his domestic staff, the High

Commissioner had no bodyguard or ceremonial military staff. Because he was more concerned with foreign affairs than the internal management of the city, he had no influence over the police force either. It was the political party that held a majority in the Danzig Senate that ultimately controlled the police. During normal circumstances, this was not significant, but when the nazis came to power the police force became an instrument of political repression. Thus, it could be said that, as High Commissioner, Lester had a multitude of responsibilities, but no authority. He endeavoured to carry out his duties in accordance with the Treaty of Versailles while the governments in both Berlin and Danzig were conducting an aggressive and coordinated campaign to undermine any remaining authority and render the treaty inoperable. Lester had considerable experience as a negotiator in the League's minorities section, but his chances of stopping the nazi juggernaut without any method of coercion, and particularly without the support of the Great Powers, were nil.

Lester had a great deal of contact with the opposition parties who asked for his help. Among the people that Lester would come into almost daily contact was Erich Brost,[1] one of the opposition leaders. Brost passed information to Lester both verbally and in written form about the way the nazis were violating the Constitution in order to impose totalitarian rule in the Free City, and described a number of cases where the difference between the city's administration and the Nazi Party seemed to be blurred.[2] Both Lester and his assistant Enrico Giustiniani[3] had a great deal of confidence in Brost. In November 1934 Brost and two journalist colleagues had been arrested for having connections with German exiles. Brost had been released, but his colleagues had been thrown into a concentration camp in the German Reich. Due to the energetic efforts of Lester, the two journalists were set free. Lester was subsequently accused of working too closely with the opposition. Since the German Government, the Danzig Senate and the Polish Government, while pretending to respect his opinions, would not deal with him in any meaningful way it can hardly have been otherwise.[4]

The Free City of Danzig was governed by a twelve-man Senate elected by the parliament (*Volkstag*) for a maximum period of four years. The parliament itself had seventy-two seats. During the 1920s the political parties in the Free City corresponded to the political parties in Weimar Germany; the most influential parties were the conservative German National People's Party, the Social Democratic Party and the Catholic Centre Party. A Communist Party was founded in 1921 with its origins in the Spartacus League of the First World War and similar to an existing group in East Prussia. Several liberal parties and free voters' associations existed and ran in the elections with varying degrees of success. A Polish Party represented the Polish minority. Up until this time the High Commissioners had consistently supported the decisions of the Danzig Senate, thus tending to damage Polish interests while inadvertently encouraging the return of the city to Germany. Even when it had been a permanent member of the Council of the League of Nations, Germany had no formal say in the administration of the Free City. The official language was German, although the use of Polish was guaranteed by law. There were not many Poles in the city itself, but large numbers of them lived in the surrounding countryside.

In May 1933, several months before Lester's arrival in the city, a bitter election campaign had been fought in which the police showed signs of favouring the Nazi Party. The nazis won just over 50% of votes in the elections. The reason why the population voted for the Nazi Party at this time was that they hoped it would be more successful than its predecessors in dealing with unemployment. This gave the nazis thirty-eight seats and an overall majority in the *Volkstag*, so they took control of the Senate of Danzig with the moderate Hermann Rauschning as president.

Before the 1933 elections, the former High Commissioner Rosting had received Rauschning and Forster, who had promised him that, if successful, they would respect and loyally observe the Constitution — but it was a hollow promise. Rosting had felt that this interview was necessary due to the long series of Danzig/Polish disputes. In fact, Forster had every intention of not respecting the Constitution and of eliminating all opposition in one way or another so that the nazis hold on power was total.

Initially, the National Socialist German Workers' (Nazi) Party had only a small amount of success and was even briefly dissolved. Its influence grew with the onset of difficult economic times following the Wall Street Collapse of 1929 and the increasing popularity of the Nazi Party in Germany proper. Albert Forster was appointed *Gauleiter* or party leader of a regional branch of the Nazi Party in October 1930, by which time the Danzig nazis controlled one-sixth of the *Volkstag* seats and gave their support to a right-wing coalition. When Hitler came to power in Germany at the end of January 1933 he encouraged his Danzig followers to demand a more active share in the government of the city. In March 1933, the Poles were sufficiently alarmed by nazi references to the realignment of frontiers to double the number of troops at their military depot in Westerplatte, located on the eastern bank of the harbour opposite the city, breaking international law in order to test the reaction of the new German Chancellor. The consequence was that the Germans sent police reinforcements into the city. After international protests, the additional troops were withdrawn, both sides climbed down and the situation returned to normal.

Forster was a radical and, once the nazis had a majority, he told Rauschning to suppress opposition newspapers, ban opposition parties and trade unions, and imprison Catholic priests. It should be borne in mind that, apart from being party leader, Forster did not hold any political office in Danzig. He had also made speeches from time to time in which he made the extraordinary declaration that Danzig was a state governed by the Nazi Party. Lester issued a stern warning to Forster that his words were being reported to the Council in Geneva. Anna, Rauschning's wife, believed that the nazis were corrupting young people, even her own children, by enrolling them in youth movements and teaching them that cruelty and immorality were normal behaviour. Girls of 17 were told that it was their duty, in or out of marriage, to become pregnant in order to give the *Führer* young soldiers. She also observed that some sermons from the pulpit in churches were practically indistinguishable from speeches by nazi politicians. Even so, the Catholic Press Agency described nazi ideology as "contrary to the fundamental bases of Christianity".

The Catholic bishop of Danzig, Count Edvard O'Rourke,[5] was also annoyed by two gratuitous measures introduced by the nazi-controlled Senate. Firstly, a decree stated that the collection of money for charitable works would henceforth only take place by post rather than by volunteers passing from door-to-door, leading to a very considerable reduction in church income. Secondly, the parades by the Hitler Youth movement were timed to take place outside churches as the congregation left. The boys formed a line and shouted anti-Catholic slogans and jeered as the people passed. During one of these incidents the police had been called but, despite the fact that the Hitler Youth were wearing easily identifiable uniforms, they had only managed to seize a member of the congregation and charge him with resisting arrest. On both of these matters Lester intervened successfully and was thanked by Count O'Rourke. Lester alerted Geneva that the members of the Hitler Youth movement not only wore military-style uniforms but carried so-called "ceremonial" daggers.

The first moves by the nazis to take possession of the city had already taken place before Lester's arrival with a law of 24 June 1933 giving the Senate power to issue decrees to strengthen public security and order. During 1933 other laws were adopted restricting state recognition to nazi associations (in June and October), providing for "preventive detention" (in June) and a reorganizing and re-equipping of the police (in November). The administration of the Free City did not treat all citizens equally since members of the Nazi Party were clearly favoured. Quite apart from these measures, there were two provocative speeches in October and November by Arthur Greiser, at that time vice-president of the Senate. In the first, he told the police that there would soon be no more political parties and that they must "be faithful to the Nazi Party" if they wished to continue their employment. In the second he seemed to deny the independence of the judiciary. Two newspapers which reported the first of these speeches were prohibited. Their owners and editors petitioned the High Commissioner and three of them were promptly arrested for doing so (the fourth was immune from arrest being a *Volkstag* deputy—at that time the nazis still respected this political nicety). These new developments were clearly illegal and Rosting had taken action in November 1933 by alerting the Council of the League of Nations. The primary function of the High Commissioner was as the guarantor of the Constitution. Article 79 of the Danzig Constitution said: "There shall be no censorship." Rauschning was summoned to Geneva to explain to the Council why the newspaper editors had been arrested without any valid reason. Lester had been present in Geneva when the League had dismissed Rauschning's explanations as totally unacceptable. When Lester later became acquainted with Rauschning he acquired a certain respect for him and came to the conclusion that at this time he was being instructed what to say by Forster.

Before Lester's arrival in the city, High Commissioner Rosting's report to the Council in June 1933 had shown a certain awareness of the way all opposition in Danzig was being eliminated. In the following months, he was deceived by the new government's equivocal replies. Rosting's final report to the Council in January 1934 summarized events since the election, together with the various vague assurances and ambiguous promises he had received from the Senate. He noted that there had been improved relations with Poland, with an exchange of state visits and outstanding disputes being cleared up, but drew attention to the activities of the Nazi Party leader Forster, querying—perhaps for the first but certainly not for the last time—his precise relationship with the government.

One of the steps taken by the Nazi Party to strengthen its position prior to the election involved Rosting. An attempt to nazify the management of some trade unions had succeeded through an astonishing legal pronouncement that these unions were subordinate to parent unions in Germany, which therefore had ultimate control over their property and funds — even though Germany was actually a foreign country and had no say in the affairs of Danzig. The membership of the Danzig unions was largely social democrat and the judge's extraordinary decision provoked a demonstration outside the High Commissioner's residence before being dispersed by the police. Although Rosting refused to intervene "in a political matter which, ostensibly at least, did not infringe the law", he met the union leaders and accepted a petition from them which he forwarded to the Secretary-General of the League in Geneva.

The process of petitioning can be looked on as a mechanism through which only the most severe breaches of the Danzig Constitution were brought to the Council's attention. Petitioning the League of Nations through the High Commissioner was not in fact provided for in the original Constitution of the Free City. In 1925 the Council had ruled that their High Commissioner should accept such petitions, deciding which merited notifying to the Council and, in serious cases, accompanying the petition with a request that the Council should discuss it and take a decision. This ruling was supplemented by another one in 1931 when High Commissioner Gravina (who had requested that his powers be more clearly defined) was told "the High Commissioner can address himself at any moment to the Government of the Free City", which was supposed to provide him with an official explanation that he could then forward to Geneva. A paragraph to this effect was later inserted into the Danzig Constitution. It is clear that providing an "official explanation" is not the same thing as actually attempting to deal with the problem. Lester used these two rulings to submit disputes and petitions to the Senate, but since it was usually the members of the Senate themselves who were responsible for the infringements of the Constitution, the responses were often tardy, evasive and unhelpful. The heart of the problem was that the Council of the League of Nations could only discuss a petition if it had been submitted through the Danzig Senate—an unlikely situation. As Lester explained in his diary: "The criminal must complain of his crime".

It was typical of the nazi style of government that it behaved as if the opposition did not have the right to exist. After coming to power in 1933, it soon became clear that they intended destroying all other political parties, whether based on ideology, religion or ethnicity. Once they had achieved a majority in the *Volkstag*, all opposition was crushed through such measures as banning existing parties and trade unions, seizing their newspapers, arresting editors, politicians and priests, and, if this didn't work, murder. Anybody who protested about these actions was accused in violent language of "provocation" and intimidated into silence by being branded as a "traitor", a "Jew", a "communist" or, worst of all, a "separatist". This last category was reserved for people who did not want Danzig to be reunited with Germany. Whenever their aggressive political methods were likely to be made known to a wider public or revealed to the Council of the League of Nations, the nazis would resort to a number of wearisome delaying tactics: particularly and *ad nauseam* stating that it was their victims who were at fault and not themselves; that they were aware of the problem and it was under review; or that they were undergoing an internal crisis that was in the process of being resolved. This often resulted in the League being lulled into believing that the Nazi Party had come to its senses and the matter was being dealt with in a satisfactory way or that recommendations were about to be implemented or the Constitution respected—when it was simply being cunningly deceived. It was also very characteristic of the nazi leadership that they would make an outrageously provocative speech to their party members and, realizing afterwards that if reported in the press it would lead to a very adverse reaction on the international scene, then arrest any newspaper editor who attempted to print it. They would lie about their immediate political intentions and attempt to justify themselves afterwards with ridiculously implausible excuses. Lester observed that dictators such as Hitler have the conviction that they are "semi-divine" and cannot subsequently go back on their words and actions without "losing face".

The presence of the League of Nations in Danzig, however, still guaranteed a certain level of sanity. Lester could immediately see what the nazi politicians were trying to do and attempted to intervene to defend the rights of the opposition groups. His position as High Commissioner was unique. Unlike his predecessors he was confronted with a series of problems for which there were no precedents and no machinery to overcome them; unlike his successor he was expected to make a serious attempt to defend the Constitution. He had already seen, when dealing with the minority problems in Upper Silesia, the treatment that the Germans reserved for the Jews and he was also aware that the arbitrary arrest of newspaper editors was a classic ploy of nazi policy. Every move by the nazi majority in Danzig was confronted by Lester pointing out that their policies infringed the Constitution. He expected the Senate to carry out free and fair elections, and he was not afraid of raising his voice to make his point. His actions did not go unnoticed in Berlin and a British contemporary at the time half-joked that Lester soon became "the most hated man in the Third Reich". Even the Poles had not expected him to play such an active role in the city's affairs.

There was a rapid, though not complete, spread of nazism during Lester's first year in Danzig. He was soon faced with the most unpleasant aspects of political extremism. While a totalitarian government was trying to eliminate all democratic political parties, Lester was a witness to the suppression of newspapers, members of political parties wearing semi-military uniforms, and innocent people being taken into "protective custody". When Lester pointed out to Rauschning that there was nothing wrong with a newspaper printing an innocuous article, the president of the Senate argued that it was misrepresenting the government and undermining its authority. One newspaper had questioned the sincerity of Rauschning's statements to the League of Nations about the Senate's respect of the Constitution. As a former journalist, Lester explained that, if the reporting was false, it was sufficient to issue a denial or a clarification. Since the newspapers had often printed the plain truth, it was difficult for the nazis to deny it. Therefore, their solution was to suppress the newspaper and arrest the editor on a pretext engineered by their own twisted logic.

There were two sorts of problems during 1935: those concerning breaches of the Constitution by the Senate; and those concerning attacks on opposition political parties, their structure and newspapers by the nazis. Lester quickly learned that anybody who came to his office to complain about the nazi regime was no longer safe. Thus, it was not unusual for family walks in the woods on a Sunday afternoon to be interrupted by someone wanting to have a private conversation with him. Night-time strolls with the dog were interrupted by nazi victims, too scared to be seen at his office, appearing out of the dark to beg him for help.

While the Senate appeared to be respecting the agreements with Poland, the city was in fact responsible for anti-Polish propaganda. What made the situation worse was that the Polish Government had no idea about the monster that it was dealing with and often unwittingly assumed the role of *provocateur*. For instance, the Poles deliberately did not give any support to the opposition parties in Danzig, thus making their destruction considerably easier for the nazis. It had been threats of Polish aggression further stoked by nazi propaganda that had contributed to the local nazis obtaining an absolute majority in the May 1933 elections. It took the Poles a long time to realize that it might be worth supporting Lester in order to defend Polish interests, but Józef Beck, the Polish Foreign Minister, never understood at all. While Kazimierz Papée,[6] the Polish representative in Danzig, seems to have viewed Lester as an honest broker ready to promote Polish interests, Beck in Warsaw wanted the High Commissioner to be politely side-lined so as not to jeopardize Poland's delicate relationship with Germany and Danzig. Polish foreign policy during the 1930s was peculiarly lacking in shrewdness and foresight, while at the same time being the victim of British and French bad faith and vacillation. The behaviour of the previous high commissioners had further undermined Poland's faith in the League of Nations.

Initially, Lester's policy was to settle as many disputes as possible locally. This was carried out either through his own mediation or by encouraging the parties concerned to negotiate. He also suggested that complainants address themselves to their governments or the legal system. He may have accepted Rauschning's argument that sending petitions to the League of Nations too soon weakened the Senate's authority and encouraged discontent. In a discussion with the German Consul General, he remarked that "no one would be happier than I if I were not compelled to report the situation to the Council of the League of Nations". Lester may also have felt there was a better chance of the Council intervening when action was really needed, if it had not previously been pestered with a multitude of minor complaints.

Danzig was discussed at the Council session in September 1934. Before this meeting, Lester took the precaution of having a long talk with Rauschning, backed up by a written summary of their conversation, in which he mentioned various complaints he had received and stressed the need for the Senate to respect the Constitution. He expected that the Danzig Senate would be above reproach when dealing with political opponents. A single party regime was not possible in Danzig, he said, and he hoped that the government "would devote itself to bringing its legislative measures into closer conformity with the existing Constitution". Although the situation in Danzig was almost out of control, the fact that at the beginning of each year Lester was required to submit an annual report to the Council of the League of Nations usually placed pressure on the Danzig Government. The essential honesty contained in these reports brought the delegates in Geneva face-to-face with the uncomfortable truth of what was taking place on the ground. While the inactivity of the League in the face of nazi provocation led to the collapse of its moral authority, Hitler's regime was determined to destroy the very principles on which the League was based.[7]

Although it enjoyed a much higher standard of living than that of the surrounding Poland, Danzig's economy depended on maritime trade, a secret subsidy from Germany and indirectly through the 5,000 or so German pensioners who had retired to the city. As the nazi system succeeded in eliminating all opposition, it was perhaps inevitable that the Danzig Government's finances would run out of control. Germany began to have foreign currency difficulties and Danzig's trade agreements with Poland in August 1934 had involved concessions. The sense of insecurity in Danzig led many people to transfer their money elsewhere, while wasteful and amateurish government spending in Danzig added to the problem. Rauschning was fully aware of the situation and it led to a disagreement with Forster.

In November 1934 local elections were held in two districts of the city. Lester handed to Rauschning (who was still president at this time) a note expressing his confidence that the Senate would ensure that all political parties would be able to exercise their rights according to the Constitution. He was answered with the usual hollow assurances that the government would carry out its responsibilities, etc. One week later the newspaper of the Social Democratic Party was suspended for three days for accusing the police of partiality during the election campaign. However, the truth was beginning to dawn on Rauschning—that he was being deceived by members of his own party, and particularly by Forster.

Already in October the Danzig press had been carrying reports that appeared to describe a rift between Forster and Rauschning. On 23 November, Rauschning finally realized that he was being used as a respectable figurehead to conceal the Nazi Party's true intentions. He resigned from the Senate and renounced his membership of the party. The nazis now began a campaign to isolate and destroy him and his family. His farm was boycotted and notices posted outside the property accused him of being a "traitor". In the Danzig elections held in the following April, Rauschning abandoned the nazis and supported the "constitutionalist" candidates. Furthermore, he wrote articles supporting co-operation with the Poles, which angered the nazis. In 1936 he found himself in personal danger and fled to Poland. Two years later, his wife sold the farm and left with their children for France.

On 28 November Greiser was elected president of the Senate. During this election all forty-one nazi representatives voted for Greiser while all the remaining thirty-one representatives abstained or provided invalid ballots.[8] The replacement of Rauschning by Greiser and the policy changes that this change implied, taken in conjunction with increasing criticism of the

League's function in Danzig and personal harassment, obliged Lester to take his responsibilities more seriously.

NOTES

1. Erich Brost (1903–1995) was a journalist for the *Danziger Volksstimme* from 1924 to 1936. He escaped to Poland in 1936, then Sweden and lived in London from 1942 to 1945 working for the BBC's German section. He returned to Germany in 1945 and founded one of the country's biggest newspaper groups. Created the Erich Brost Foundation in 1994.

2. McNamara, P. *Sean Lester, Poland and the Nazi takeover of Danzig,* p. 71. Dublin/Portland, OR: Irish Academic Press, 2009.

3. Enrico Giustiniani (1898–?) was an Italian diplomat and lawyer. He became *chef de cabinet* of various High Commissioners in Danzig from 1929 to 1938, when Italy withdrew from the League of Nations.

4. McNamara, p. 77.

5. Edvard Aleksander Władysław O'Rourke (1876–1943) was born to a Russian aristocratic family of Irish ancestry. He became a Roman Catholic priest in 1907, bishop of Riga in 1918 and bishop of the Free City of Danzig in 1925. In 1938 he resigned after severe nazi pressure on his position. In 1939 he fled to Rome.

6. Kazimierz Papée (1889–1979) became the Polish High Commissioner of Danzig 1932–1936 and combatted nazi efforts to remove the League of Nations from the city. In 1938, he was relocated to Prague, siding with the Czechs against Germany in the Sudetenland Crisis. Ambassador of the Polish Government-in-Exile to the Holy See from 1939 to 1958. He was related to Józef Beck by marriage.

7. McNamara, p. 4.

8. Epstein, C. *Model Nazi: Arthur Greiser and the Occupation of Western Poland,* p. 76. Oxford, UK: Oxford University Press, 2010.

Chapter Eleven

Danzig 1935

After Rauschning's replacement by Greiser as the President of the Senate, political activity in Danzig speeded up prior to the January 1935 Council meeting in Geneva and the elections for the Senate in the following April. Rauschning had originally benefited from the support of the German Foreign Office and the less extreme political elements in Berlin, while Greiser at times appears to have belonged to the group formed around Hermann Göring.[1] Forster, on the other hand, had direct access to the *Führer* himself and could always count upon his backing. The German Foreign Office was headed at this time by Baron von Neurath, who, according to Lester, had been "little seen at Geneva and heard still less." It was believed that he disliked the League, while his general bearing was that of a superior being of the old school. Germany had left the League in October 1933 and therefore took no further part in the Council's discussions on Danzig. Nevertheless, von Neurath was kept informed of its activities through the German consulate in Geneva, which had a large staff and many contacts within the Secretariat.

In his New Year message to the people of Danzig, President Greiser did not fail to draw attention to the "peaceful disposition of the National Socialist Government". After this extraordinary piece of double-speak, he could not prevent himself from revealing his true feelings by pouring scorn on the remaining opposition parties with the remarkable statement that "they refused to realize that their political role was over." As was usual in speeches by nazi politicians in Danzig, all those who stood in their way were described as "traitors".

On 10 December 1934 Lester had forwarded to Geneva a petition from the Catholic parish priests of Danzig objecting to four Senate decrees that they considered unconstitutional. He had received this petition in August and passed it on to the Senate for its reaction but, predictably, he had been kept waiting two and a half months before realizing that he was never going to receive a reply. Following several interviews with the two parties concerned, he felt that it was not possible to resolve the matter locally. He had therefore submitted it to the Council in Geneva. The second petition forwarded by Lester was from the Catholic Centre Party.

Lester sent a great deal of information on conditions in Danzig to Geneva and London through letters to the Secretary-General and to contacts in the Foreign Office. Thus, when the League of Nations' Council met to discuss Danzig on 18 January 1935 it had before it these two petitions and Lester's report for 1934 in which he contrasted the appreciable improvement in Danzig/Polish relations with profound misgivings over the policies pursued by the Senate. Regrettably and perhaps disastrously, there was also a letter from Lester dated 7 January in which he informed the Council that the Danzig Government now proposed to negotiate with the petitioners. It is a well-worn political trick to pretend to deal with a situation immediately before the likelihood of sanctions seems inevitable. The timing of the Danzig Government's proposal seems to have been designed cunningly to render the Council's discussions meaningless. The Senate must have felt that the Council would seize any opportunity to defer discussion of a sensitive issue and, following Lester's letter of 7 January explaining the Danzig government's proposal to negotiate with the opposition parties, this is exactly what happened. There must have been a sense of satisfaction among the Danzig nazis that the Council took the bait.

The atmosphere in the Council was not improved by the Saar Plebiscite which had just taken place, resulting in an overwhelming vote for reunification with Germany. The Saarland had been placed under a League of Nations mandate to compensate for the French coalmines destroyed by the German Army during the First World War. In 1934 the Saarlanders were allowed to decide about their future. The trouble-free voting in the Saarland (under supervision of international monitors) had been a credit to the League and its much criticized President of the Saar Commission, Sir Geoffrey Knox.[2] Nevertheless, the result was clearly encouraging to the nazis. Refugees were already leaving the region, and it was in this atmosphere that the Council welcomed Lester at its meeting. He was accompanied by Greiser who, upon his first entry into the Council room, immediately made the nazi salute!

Lester's letter had given the Council an excuse to evade action. The British minister and Rapporteur of the Danzig debate, Anthony Eden, proposed not to enter into the substance of the petitions in the hope that a satisfactory solution would be found locally. Eden believed that, even if the Nazi Party represented a majority of the population, it would not carry out policies that were contrary to the Danzig Constitution. He mentioned Lester's report, which had referred to certain unconstitutional tendencies, but thought the Council could expect the Senate's assurances of loyalty to the Constitution to be observed! The nazi-dominated Danzig Senate, on the other hand, was trying to buy time so that the petitions would never be examined—and it had no intention of respecting the Constitution. Greiser shared with the assembled politicians his rather ambiguous views on democracy which included the statement that opposition parties were "unwilling to bow to the principle of the will of the majority", whereas the opposition would soon be harassed and persecuted out of existence. He added the rather contemptuous assertion that Senate would "govern the city within the limits laid down by the Constitution", which meant precisely the opposite.

At the end of the meeting in Geneva, Lester clearly felt that Eden's conclusions were not sufficiently precise, so he summed up the situation himself in much greater detail. He pointed out that every matter discussed by him with the Senate could have easily been dealt with in the way that the Council had suggested . . . had there been any cooperation locally. Lester observed that the nazis believed that the League of Nations "can be confounded by defiance and trickery". He mentioned such details as the doubtful impartiality of the police and the coercion evident in political life, where the majority evidently believed that it could do what it liked.

At this meeting of its Council the League therefore missed the first opportunity to take effective action in Danzig and thwart nazi ambitions. For this Lester may be held to blame in that his letter suggested that a local settlement might be possible, while Eden believed that he was dealing with reasonable people who only needed to be reminded of their responsibilities. In fact, the situation in Danzig was already out of control. What Lester had reported to the Council was only the worst part of the confrontation that had taken place within the city during 1934, while the Council had not understood the relentless nature of nazi persecution. Neither Lester nor any members of the Council had yet realised that reaching an agreement with the nazis was going to be difficult, if not impossible. It was at this time that Lester started keeping a private diary and from it we learn about his preoccupations.

Although Greiser had promised the Council in Geneva that he would observe the Constitution and negotiate with the opposition, upon his return to Danzig he immediately suppressed the Centre Party's *Danziger Volksstimme* newspaper and made a speech insulting the clergy. Lester complained to Otto von Radowicz,[3] the German consul-general in Danzig, that he was affronted by Greiser's perfidy.

Lester had frequent dealings with Greiser's assistant Viktor Böttcher,[4] although Lester did not have a very high opinion of his intelligence, calling him "that timber-headed lout". In later years, Lester declared that if he had ever written a book about his experiences in Danzig, Böttcher with his "solemn stupidity" would definitely be one of the comedy characters. On one occasion, Ludvig Krabbe, a Danish member of the League's Secretariat responsible for the Free City, paid a private visit to Danzig having been urged to do so by both Greiser and Böttcher. Although Krabbe had made the journey entirely on his own initiative and at his own expense, Böttcher complained that he had not been consulted beforehand. Böttcher said to Krabbe that "he supposed he had come up to see the opposition" and proceeded to attack the High Commissioner—which made a very bad impression on Krabbe. The Danzig correspondent for the British newspaper *Daily Telegraph*, Ambrose B. Wareing, summed up Böttcher in three words: "What an ass!"

Böttcher now informed Lester that the Senate had decided to dissolve the *Volkstag* and call for new elections in the spring of 1935, although according to the Constitution there was no need to do so until 1937. Because of their triumph in the Saarland Plebiscite in January 1935, the nazis were obviously hoping that they would benefit from the same success in Danzig. They were still looking for the two-thirds majority in the seventy-two seat *Volkstag*, which would enable them to re-write the Constitution and submit it to the League of Nations as a *fait accompli*. In the following weeks the Nazi Party organized more than a thousand rallies, the local radio station was used exclusively for its propaganda and the display of posters on street pillars was also limited to the Nazi Party. Hermann Göring, Rudolf Hess[5] and Joseph Goebbels[6] came from Berlin to address the rallies, although Danzig was not German territory. The nazis also made liberal use of state funds and public employees to promote their election campaign.[7]

At the same time the opposition parties were subjected to a massive terror operation. Most of them were only able to organize a few public meetings, all of which were disturbed by nazi thugs. The Social Democratic and Catholic newspapers were banned or confiscated at various times. While a communist deputy was giving a speech in the *Volkstag*, he was physically assaulted by a group of nazi deputies "as if on a pre-arranged sign". The journalist Erich Brost, who observed the scene from the press gallery, had his notes confiscated by Greiser and was ordered out of the chamber. Lester's assistant, Giustiniani, had also witnessed the incident and Lester immediately sent a report to Geneva. He also wrote to Greiser telling him that it was the Senate's duty to ensure "liberty of opinion, secrecy of voting, freedom of meeting," and that it had a responsibility to protect all of its citizens "to whatever party they belong". When Greiser actually agreed to Lester's instructions, Papée, the Polish consul-general, declared: "in my opinion, [Lester] has achieved a major political success."[8]

Two weeks later, however, Greiser delivered a speech in which he criticized Lester severely for protecting the opposition and interfering in the city's internal affairs. Both Forster and Greiser were in the habit of making hostile declarations using violent language to their followers about their questionable political intentions for the city, followed by public protestations of innocence and pretended fidelity to the Constitution. Lester summoned Greiser once more for a personal explanation of his speech, during which Greiser was keen to point out to Lester that he was attacking the office and not the man. However, he threatened Lester saying that the High Commissioner risked being the victim of intimidation and non-cooperation, upon which Lester demanded that he should repeat "this astonishing remark". He struck the table with his fist and said that no threats and no force would make him deviate from what he believed to be his duty. Due to Lester's energetic actions, the nazis were held back and the opposition was finally able to conduct the election campaign openly.[9]

Lester then sent a strongly-worded note to the Senate expressing his great surprise that a nazi newspaper had published false information about the League of Nations and the treaties affecting Danzig. News of the difficult relations between Lester and the Senate reached the Polish press, and the Danzig police took immediate action to confiscate all local newspapers to stifle any information on the subject reaching the outside world.

During the election campaign, even the former President of the Senate and former nazi Rauschning protested about the way the opposition parties were being treated. On 25 March Lester heard about four members of the opposition who had been taken into "protective custody". When questioned, Greiser suggested that these people had been guilty of acts which had outraged "the natural sense of justice" and had been arrested by the police "for their own protection". He had not realised that they were also members of the opposition! He agreed to release them while expressing the groundless fears that they were at risk of being "molested by the population".

When new elections took place on 7 April 1935, Lester's defence of minorities, amongst them Poles, Jews, Communists and Roman Catholics, and their right to publish newspapers and to enjoy freedom of speech, were important in preventing the Nazi Party from winning two-thirds of the vote. Although the nazis won forty-three seats, they did not reach the forty-eight that they required for a two-thirds majority. Over 40% of the population did not vote nazi. Albert Forster, who started to announce the results on the radio, cut his speech short, while a planned victory parade was cancelled. Nevertheless, the nazis did possess a majority.

The outcome of the elections clearly frustrated the nazis, who unleashed a tirade of violent words on the opposition. Lester reacted by sending a letter to the Senate saying that he could not accept that members of the opposition were labelled as "traitors" and "separatists". He then came in for a particularly ferocious attack himself for interfering with the nazi take-over of the city rather than acting as a neutral arbitrator. He refused to allow the Senate to discuss the way the High Commissioner carried out his duties. Greiser, on the other hand, felt that the opposition's protests addressed to the League of Nations undermined the Senate's authority—ignoring the fact that the protests had been provoked by the Senate's own actions. In his view, the Senate's persecution of the opposition and the seizure of their newspapers were matters of no importance.

When the new *Volkstag* met on 30 April 1935 President Greiser took the decision that opposition parties could no longer say that they were petitioning the League "in the name of the population of Danzig". Furthermore, although the Constitution expressly forbade censorship, the newly elected government now required all printed publications of a political nature to be shown to the police before being distributed. This decree was subsequently withdrawn in a trade-off with the Council over the election results.

A direct result of the elections was an increase in petitioning by various sections of the opposition and a greater rapidity on the part of the Senate in replying to the High Commissioner's inquiries. The first petitions were handed in to Lester by several Jewish organizations the day after the election. They said that they had decided to approach the High Commissioner reluctantly since they had been hoping that the city's Senate might respect Danzig law. Lester asked for the Senate's opinion and a month later received the stock nazi reply that it was the Jewish associations who were at fault rather than itself. Lester was unimpressed and forwarded the petitions with his observations to Geneva on the same day, asking the Council to consider it at its next meeting. A second petition pointed out that a decree sought to prevent Jews from using one of the local beaches, although Jewish holidaymakers made a major contribution to Danzig's finances.[10] The Jewish community of Danzig complained that Jewish professionals were being discriminated against, Jewish traders were being boycotted and Jewish employees dismissed — all of which must have reminded Lester of Upper Silesia. It was not the general public who were shunning Jewish professionals, but the government of Danzig that was making it impossible for them to carry out their functions. Many Jews began to flee.

Following the election, the opposition parties (except for the Polish Party) immediately filed a lawsuit in the Danzig High Court in protest about the way they had been run. They described numerous examples of illegal manipulation of the voting by the nazis, including direct threats of dismissal to people who did not support them. The secrecy of the ballot had not been guaranteed, while people who were not citizens of Danzig had been brought into the city by bus and train to vote. However, some months later on 14 November 1935 the Supreme Court of Danzig decided that, despite "irregularities . . . widespread fraud and violence", the elections had been valid "overall"! The Supreme Court did, however, reduce the proportion of the Nazi Party vote from 59 to 57%, which set off a furious reaction in the Senate.[11]

Even though it had not achieved a two-thirds majority in the election, the Nazi Party behaved as if it had been given a clear mandate to impose its policies on the city. Decisions by the Danzig government systematically favouring the Nazi Party seemed to assume that it represented the entire population—which was far from true. For instance, Lester wrote that "the Senate's idea of what constituted reasonable criticism by the press seems to have been based upon National Socialist principles rather than upon those laid down in the Constitution." The distinction between the government of Danzig and the Nazi Party became increasingly blurred. Meanwhile, the differences of opinion between, on the one hand, Forster, Greiser and Böttcher and, on the other, Lester and the League became more manifest.

Both Lester and Papée, the Polish consul-general, expressed doubts about the validity of the elections. At its May meeting, the League's Council looked again at the actions of the Danzig Senate and reminded it that the High Commissioner was the guarantor of the Constitution. The Council condemned Greiser's excuses and upheld the High Commissioner's position, but decided to delay a decision about re-running the elections until a Committee of Jurists consisting of legal experts from the Netherlands, Sweden and Switzerland appointed by the League had examined the legality of the elections. Two months later, the jurists concluded that the conduct of the April elections was unconstitutional and the banning of newspapers was incompatible with the freedom of the press. Even though it was now clear that the elections had been a reversal for the nazis and their economic policy was in ruins, astonishingly the Council took no action, such as ordering a re-run. Forster and Greiser both knew that the Council would avoid confrontation and, given that the High Commissioner was backed by no military force and had no influence over the police, he was ultimately powerless against bold defiance. The League expressed its full confidence in Lester and confirmed his authority, but both he and the opposition parties were about to be sacrificed in the interest of power politics. Although Lester was deeply concerned about the situation in Danzig, the Governments of France and the United Kingdom were at this time both fully preoccupied with the Italian invasion of Ethiopia and the question of introducing an oil embargo against Italy. Lester was aware that neglecting Danzig could be the spark that would ignite international chaos, but the British and French failed to appreciate its importance at this time.

Between May and September events in Danzig were dominated by an economic crisis involving a dispute with Poland. Even though Forster had managed to keep the matter quiet during the election campaign, in the spring of 1935 the day of reckoning for Danzig's economy could no longer be postponed. Competition with the port of Gdynia had damaged Danzig's livelihood, the constant quarrelling and turmoil in Danzig continued to have a negative effect on the economy, while the reckless spending by the nazi government had brought the city's finances into a deficit. Hitler's rearmament programme had resulted in surreptitious financial support from Germany being withdrawn. In March 1935 Hitler had announced the existence of a German Air Force and an Army of 550,000 men. The gold reserves of the Bank of Danzig declined and the foreign asset reserve fell to a dangerous level, leading to a devaluation of more than 40% in the Danziger *gulden*. Lester was aware that the nazis had placed the city's finances "in a terrible financial and economic muddle". The British magazine *New Statesman* wrote: "Within two years the National Socialists have succeeded in ruining Danzig." It was clear that Forster's meddling with the economy was at the origin of the problems, and once again there was talk of him being transferred elsewhere within Germany. However, this did not happen since Forster was extremely skilful in transferring the blame on to other people. In this case, who else but the Jews could be responsible for the devaluation? For good measure, seven members of the opposition were arrested and thrown into prison for not supporting the government. Lester threatened to call an emergency meeting of the Council and Greiser quickly released six of the seven victims.

By 21 May there were fears of a further devaluation and there was no money to pay state salaries. On 4 June, the Senate panicked and closed the banks in order to check the flight of *gulden*. Speaking to Howard Kennard,[12] the British ambassador in Warsaw who was on an official visit, Lester said that the Free City was living way beyond its means. Kennard visited both Danzig and Gdynia. In Danzig, he was horrified by the swastika flags, the constant military processions and political rallies on every street corner. In contrast, he was delighted to visit the busy port of Gdynia, which was now a thriving town where there had previously been "a fishing village and a peat bog".[13] Given the constant turmoil in Danzig, many foreign importers now preferred Gdynia.

Due to the financial crisis, Lester had heard that Poland was expecting to seize control of the city. To prevent the Poles from taking advantage of the crisis at the expense of the Bank of Danzig, it was quickly decided in Berlin that foreign exchange control should be introduced. The High Commissioner was to be given a factual explanation of the position and asked to apply to the League's financial committee for support in the form of a short-term credit for Danzig from the Bank of International Settlements. This ruse was designed less to achieve financial stability than to foil a Polish take-over. In fact, the idea that Poland might seize control was enough to persuade the German population of Danzig to support the Senate. On the subject of the League's financial help, Secretary-General Avenol wrote that he could not approach the Bank of International Settlements without knowing more about the problem. He suggested sending René Charron[14] from the League's Financial Section to Danzig. Lester took up this idea with the Senate but found that they preferred to send someone of their own to Geneva.

In mid-July Lester left for a holiday, but it had to be interrupted. On 1 August Greiser declared a state of emergency and ordered the opening of the Danzig-German frontier for customs-free imports of coal and foodstuffs. This provoked a sharp reaction from Poland which insisted that imports into the country came through Gdynia, bringing trade in Danzig to a halt. There were renewed negotiations and a settlement was reached on 8 August just before Lester arrived back. Under pressure from Berlin, Danzig and Warsaw both made some concessions and the confrontation stopped.

During this period of financial chaos the popularity of the Nazi Party fell, but the strategy to turn the city into a "Brown Dictatorship" continued relentlessly. As the nazis gained in confidence, Forster boasted that the opposition would be thrown into concentration camps and the days of the League of Nations were numbered. Forster claimed to exercise his authority in Danzig as a representative of Hitler, but Lester was quick to draw his attention to the fact that Hitler was the leader of a foreign country. Forster held no political office in Danzig's affairs and Lester said that he would be obliged to inform the League of Nations in Geneva of this anomaly. Lester describes Forster, as "a young man, very self-opinionated . . . a pure revolutionist". As a personal friend of Hitler, he was unable to accept any criticism of himself or the nazi regime. Lester concluded that while Forster's political skills might in normal circumstances be useful to Germany, in the international context of Danzig he was "a danger to everybody".

Despite all the political confrontations, social life in Danzig carried on almost as normal. In his capacity as High Commissioner, Lester held regular dinners for the local diplomatic corps, politicians, and visiting personalities and dignitaries. At the end of August, Lester held a banquet for the officers of the visiting German pocket battleship *Admiral Scheer*, followed by a reception for 150 guests. When Senate President Greiser saw that his predecessor Rauschning was present at the reception, he left abruptly and required all the other Nazi Party members present to do the same, but the ship's commander and his officers remained. There was perhaps a gulf between British/Irish protocol and German etiquette, since in London or Dublin it would have been perfectly normal practice to invite members of the opposition to an official reception. Greiser, however, saw it differently. The next day Lester requested Greiser's presence and told him that his lack of courtesy to the naval officers could not be excused on the grounds of the sensibilities of one political party. Lester pointed out that during the Senate's dinner held the day before the High Commissioner's reception, he had been affronted because the captain of the *Admiral Scheer* had been given precedence—but he had said nothing. Although Greiser's attitude was mild and apologetic, Lester was very annoyed, suggesting to Secretary-General Avenol that the moment had come to appoint a commission of inquiry to expose the misconduct of the Danzig administration. But nothing was done. Over the course of the next year, the local nazi newspapers tried to turn this affair into a major diplomatic incident saying that Lester had deliberately attempted to insult the Nazi Party by inviting its opponents to the reception. Since, by this time, the nazis controlled all the media in Danzig, they made sure that their interpretation of the Admiral Scheer Incident was the only one possible. It is obvious that the nazi politicians were ready to criticize any and all of the High Commissioner's actions.

When the League's Council came to discuss Danzig again on 23 September 1935, it had before it the report of the Committee of Jurists published in July which had found the April elections to be fraudulent. The report also stated that a number of Senate decrees had been unconstitutional, either legally or in the way they were applied. The Council had also received a new petition from the Jews of Danzig, and one from two municipal workmen who had been dismissed for left-wing views and had lost their case at Danzig's supreme labour court. Finally, there were three opposition party petitions complaining about the recent amendments to the penal code whose "nebulous principles . . . open the door wide to arbitrary proceedings". The Danzig Senate had amended the Criminal Code to bring it into alignment with German (i.e. nazi) law. One of the new measures stated that a person could be convicted "in accordance with healthy [i.e. nazi] public opinion even if his offences were against no law". Justice was now being dictated by the subjective opinions of the Nazi Party.

Lester describes a case where the ineptitude of nazi politics approached the comic. Lester had asked the Danzig government to withdraw the amendment to the law because it was unconstitutional, but the Senate had refused saying that the decree was "perfectly correct". Faced with this refusal, Lester said he would refer the matter to the League's Council in Geneva. The representative of the Senate then said that, if this was the case, he would place the matter before the Permanent Court of International Justice in The Hague. Lester pointed out that either of these actions would draw the illegal actions of the Danzig government to the attention of the whole world, at the same time as putting on trial the actions of the German Government in Berlin. Two months later this observation filtered through to "what passes as a political mind in Danzig", and the nazi newspaper *Danziger Vorposten* expressed its regret that a matter of this kind should have ever have gone to the Permanent Court rather than being settled by goodwill!

With the Danzig government's illegal actions evident for all to see, one would have thought that the League would insist that the Senate should obey the law, and yet in his September rapporteur's report Anthony Eden merely proposed in the most genteel diplomatic terms that the Senate should be asked "to take the necessary steps to bring their legislation and its application into conformity with the Constitution and should report progress on this through the High Commissioner". He expressed the hope that the Senate would cooperate in the future with Lester. It is evident that Eden, like many of the politicians who followed him, had no idea how far the nazis were prepared to go in carrying out their ambitions. Yet another opportunity to halt the Senate's ambitions was lost.[15]

The Danzig opposition had asked the Council of the League of Nations to declare the April elections invalid. However, on 27 November Greiser informed Lester and Robinson, the British consul-general in Danzig, that whatever the Council decided the Senate had no intention of implementing its recommendations. He gave two reasons for this: one was that the British and French Governments were far too busy dealing with the Italy/Ethiopia crisis to pay any attention to what was happening in Danzig; and secondly, with German rearmament the power base in Europe had fundamentally changed in Germany's favour. Furthermore, Greiser now blamed Lester for the devaluation of the *gulden* due to the high cost of maintaining the High Commissioner's post. Since neither the United Kingdom nor Poland were prepared to insist on Forster's dismissal, it was now being suggested that Lester was the one who should lose his job. Lester felt that Greiser's words had not originated in Danzig and was determined to conceal nothing from the League. He also shared with Papée, the Polish consul-general, his forewarning that in the next few years he would not be surprised if Germany did not start to consider moving its border eastwards. Papée agreed that Greiser had carried out "a quite tasteless attack on the League of Nations and her representative in Danzig". Lester declared that in his next report he would conceal nothing of Greiser's "disloyalty, unscrupulousness and arrogance" and he would call for drastic measures to discipline the Senate. Against a background of Polish anxiety, continuing petty disorder took place in Danzig provoked by its own government.[16]

In the autumn came renewed pressure on the Danzig opposition, including another truculent speech by Greiser. The Polish Government was sufficiently alarmed to invite Lester to Warsaw for an official visit. He told the Polish authorities that radical action was required to discipline the Danzig Senate and he went so far as to mention the possibility of Polish troops being called in. He also asked Kennard, the British Ambassador in Warsaw, to communicate his concerns to the German Ambassador, von Moltke.[17]

This period as a whole was much more stressful than the preceding one, marked by the increasing importance of Council meetings and of outside events. Lester seems to have decided that if the Council were to be involved in dealing with Danzig's problems at all, it might as well have a comprehensive picture of the situation and he made less effort to negotiate with the city's politicians. In November Lester warned Greiser again about the dangers of pursuing nazi policies but, by the end of the year, he noted that all attempts to restrain the nazi leaders in Danzig "have become utterly useless. They answer with bland prevarication."

At the beginning of December Lester and Robinson, the British consul-general in Danzig, were invited for lunch with Greiser and Böttcher at the latter's house. After a gratuitous insult of Anthony Eden, Greiser announced that the Senate had decided not to implement the Council's decisions. This incident was followed by a defiant speech offensive to the League and to Lester himself. Lester was subsequently informed by the German Foreign Minister, von Neurath, that he was astonished by the threats and insults of which the High Commissioner had been a victim and that they were in no way inspired by the German Government in Berlin. Nevertheless, Lester could not believe that Greiser could have made his declarations with such brazen confidence without being inspired by "someone" in Berlin. After his official visit to Warsaw, Lester was not surprised to receive an invitation to visit Berlin on his way to Geneva for the Council's annual meeting on Danzig. After some hesitation about the diplomatic significance of dealing directly with a government that, in theory, had nothing to say about Danzig and its internal affairs, Lester agreed to visit von Neurath to discuss the behaviour of Forster in Danzig. During the meeting, Von Neurath suggested once again that Forster should be removed from the Free City—although, since Forster was a favourite of Hitler, it was von Neurath's position that was the more insecure. In a moment of candour, von Neurath said to Lester: "You know our policy on Danzig. It is to keep turning the knife in the wound." Lester subsequently received a series of half-explanations and half-protestations from von Neurath, Forster and Greiser about their attitude towards him, after which he drew the only useful conclusion—that there was a difference of opinion between the latter two. Lester was not the only person interested in seeing the departure of Forster. Greiser would have been extremely pleased to see him go since, he later confessed, "Forster was ruining and killing him."

In November Lester wrote: "A trench is being dug in the garden this morning – ostensibly to repair drains. It is symptomatic of conditions here that I take note of any operations of this kind. The telephones are of course tapped. My butler is a spy." One of Lester's daughters had inadvertently witnessed devices being installed in order to tap the telephones at the High Commission.[18] He had previously been informed by Rauschning that the Senate had considered digging a tunnel under the High Commissioner's residence in order to install listening devices. During his absences from Danzig, Lester gave strict instructions that no workmen should be allowed to approach his office "under any pretext". Visitors to his office were blatantly photographed on the steps of the building by plain-clothes detectives, while on one occasion Lester himself was accosted while getting out of his car and surrounded by four young men, who examined his papers and then withdrew. He had no idea whether they were plain-clothes police or nazi heavies—and it was difficult to tell the difference. Lester had already been informed by an indignant official working in the Danzig main post office that his mail was being intercepted and read by Nazi Party members. In view of the assurances that he had previously received from the city's government, he threatened to make a public scandal of this affair. Lester was outraged and dismissed his mail clerk. Henceforth, all correspondence was sent through the British consul-general's diplomatic bag.[19] When Lester went to Geneva to attend the Council meeting in December, the nazis tried to prevent his return on the grounds that he had "injured Danzig's interests" during his statements to the Council.

Lester had described the Danzig opposition parties as fickle and untrustworthy. He was astonished that he had to tell them to stop making hostile remarks about Poland and should rather approach Warsaw in order to seek protection. At this point, the opposition parties decided to stop fighting each other and form themselves into a cohesive unit ready to take on the nazis. They considered sending a delegation to Geneva but were not sure that the Council of the League of Nations would receive them. It was then decided to send two delegates to London in December 1935 to see the British Foreign Secretary. Lester was informed, but did not express any opinion. Unfortunately, it was a very bad time to visit London. It was the Christmas holidays, the Foreign Minister Samuel Hoare had just resigned, being replaced by Anthony Eden, King George V was dying and the British Government was deeply concerned by the Italian invasion of Ethiopia. Nevertheless, the two delegates spoke to the press and were received by officials at 10 Downing Street and at the Foreign Office. They begged the British Government to re-run the *Volkstag* elections that had taken place in April since a nazi defeat could now be assured. Regrettably, it came to light during the discussions that the League of Nations had no legal way of calling for a new election and no physical way of enforcing its guarantee of the Danzig Constitution. Finally, the British Government was indifferent and decided that it and the League had enough problems to deal with so that no action could be expected from either of them. To add to the confusion, news of the Hoare-Laval Pact had broken in early December where it was learned that the French and British Governments intended to hand Ethiopia over to a belligerent Italy. Joseph Goebbels, the Reich Minister of Propaganda, gloated over the League of Nation's tarnished image as "the conscience of the world".

But what if a new election had been called in Danzig? Given what had happened prior to 7 April, one could be sure that the nazis would resort to all their usual tricks of arresting opposition politicians, banning their newspapers and sabotaging their meetings, while using public funds and staff to organize a massive campaign of public rallies for themselves. It would also be certain that their propaganda machine would turn the High Commissioner of the League of Nations into the interfering villain who had required the elections to be re-run. It was therefore essential that a neutral body should be in charge of organizing the new elections. But, of course, this never happened.

Lester and the leaders of the opposition had offered the League the opportunity to deliver a severe blow to the nazis by re-running the elections at a time when the Nazi Party's popularity had dropped to less than 30%. The powers behind the League, including the British, French and Polish Governments, decided not to provoke Hitler by allowing an election that would have been the first democratic rejection of nazism. When Hitler heard about the suggestion of re-running the election, he became so incensed that he demanded Lester's removal. While in his official reports Lester highlighted nazi electoral violations in unequivocal language and questioned the legal basis for calling the April elections in the first place, the Council of the League of Nations was not prepared to exercise its authority. Had it done so, Danzig would almost certainly have become the first place where ethnic Germans threw the Nazi Party out of power. As well as this, the rejection of a nazi administration in Danzig would have removed from Hitler his main justification for attacking Poland in September 1939—to "rescue" Germans outside the Reich's borders. On 31 December 1935 Lester was informed by the Bishop O'Rourke, that fifteen men of Hitler's bodyguard had arrived in the city in order "to assault, if not kill, the leaders of the opposition".

NOTES

1. Hermann Wilhelm Göring (1893–1946) was a German politician, military leader and leading member of the Nazi Party. An ace fighter pilot in the First World War, he was awarded the coveted "Blue Max". When Hitler took power in 1933, he became second-in-command. He founded the Gestapo and was appointed commander-in-chief of the Luftwaffe. In 1946, Göring was convicted of war crimes at Nuremberg and sentenced to death by hanging, but committed suicide beforehand.

2. Sir Geoffrey George Knox (1884–1958) was an Australian/British diplomat. President of the Saar Commission and later British Ambassador to Hungary and Brazil.

3. Otto von Radowitz (1880–1941) entered the German diplomatic service in 1910. German consul-general in Danzig, 1933–1936. Supported Rauschning in his conflict with Forster, and tried to weaken the Nazi Party in the city.

4. Hans Viktor Böttcher (1880–1946) was a German administrative lawyer and Nazi Party politican. In Danzig he was a close friend of Greiser and from 1935 became responsible for the city's foreign affairs. He remained close to Greiser during the Second World War and was employed in eliminating the Polish language and culture.

5. Rudolf Walter Richard Hess (1894–1987) was a prominent politician in nazi Germany. Appointed Deputy *Führer* to Hitler in 1933, he served in this position until 1941, when he flew solo to Scotland in an attempt to negotiate peace with the United Kingdom. He was taken prisoner, tried and convicted, serving a life sentence.

6. Paul Joseph Goebbels (1897–1945) was a German politician and Minister of Propaganda in Nazi Germany from 1933 to 1945. As one of Hitler's closest associates, he was known for his zealous anti-Semitism, which led him to support the extermination of the Jews. On 1 May 1945 Goebbels with his wife Magda killed their six young children, and then committed suicide.

7. McNamara, P. *Sean Lester, Poland and the Nazi takeover of Danzig*, pp. 90–91. Dublin/Portland, OR: Irish Academic Press, 2009.

8. Ibid., pp. 86–7.
9. Ibid., pp. 88–9.
10. Ibid., p. 112.
11. Ibid., p. 118.
12. Sir Howard William Kennard (1878–1955) was a British diplomat, Chargé d'Affaires, and British Ambassador to Poland at the outbreak of the Second World War and to the Polish government-in-exile until 1941. He had previously been ambassador to Switzerland and to Yugoslavia
13. McNamara, p. 108.
14. In 1926 René Charron (1894–?) was a French diplomat of Jewish origins. Sent by the League of Nations in the 1920s to work with Bulgarian refugees. Participated in the French Resistance during the Second World War. Later, he became the French delegate to the United Nations in New York.
15. McNamara, p. 116.
16. Ibid., p. 119–23.
17. Hans-Adolf Helmuth Ludwig Erdmann Waldemar von Moltke (1884–1943) was a Silesian landowner who joined the German Foreign Service in 1913. From 1924 to 1928, he served at the German Embassy in Constantinople and from 1931 to 1934 he was ambassador in Warsaw. He died in Madrid in 1943.
18. McNamara, p. 117.
19. Ibid., p. 144–5.

Chapter Twelve

Danzig, 1936 and Beyond

At the beginning of January 1936, Lester received a visit from Böttcher, Greiser's hapless assistant, who came to express New Year's greetings and to assure him, in case there was any doubt, of the Danzig Senate's appreciation of him. A few days later, Lester invited the principal officials of Danzig to a dinner at his residence where food and drink were provided in generous quantities and good feelings abounded. Lester concluded that Greiser was "really not a bad chap—apart from his politics". Private contacts between Lester and Greiser remained amazingly cordial; Greiser and his wife would frequently have lunch with Lester and his family at the High Commissioner's residence; they went horse-riding together and hunting in the local forests. In Geneva during the Council meetings Greiser and Lester would often dine together, even though they disagreed strongly about policy in Danzig. Nevertheless, 1936 was to be the year that Greiser would drive Lester out of the Free City.

After Lester had been removed from Danzig, Greiser spoke about him in a very friendly manner and claimed that "he had always attacked the office and not the man"—although, being Greiser, he was also reported to have said exactly the opposite. Another of Greiser's very flattering remarks about Lester was that he "never said or wrote a word that was untrue". Lester also claimed that his successor as High Commissioner, Carl Burckhardt,[1] had "developed a sneaking sympathy with poor Greiser". On the other hand, Lester described *Gauleiter* Forster as an "impertinent and irresponsible" young man. Outward rivalry between Forster and Greiser continued until the beginning of the Second World War, although Greiser would not forget to write an annual dissembling newspaper article for publication on the occasion of Forster's birthday. On one occasion in the following years, Burckhardt said that Greiser broke down in tears when describing his situation in

Danzig. The relationship between Forster and Greiser is intriguing. Although Greiser often gave the impression to Lester, Burckhardt and the Polish diplomats in Danzig that Forster was a thorn in his flesh, their activities frequently complemented each other in a remarkable way to achieve a common goal. However, during 1935 the relationship soured and, in 1936, deteriorated beyond repair. The regime in Berlin would, nevertheless, maintain the power-sharing between them until the outbreak of the Second World War. Neither could get rid of the other.

A few days later Greiser was the host for a grand dinner in the *Rathaus*, at which he made a speech praising the High Commissioner and drew attention to their cordial collaboration. Lester noted in his diary that: "Anyone listening to this complimentary speech would have thought that there was not a cloud on the horizon." However, it was evident from Greiser's empty words that this euphoria could not last. The Council of the League of Nations met every year in January to review the situation in Danzig and Lester had already noticed that in the prelude to this meeting, where he had to submit an annual report, there was a marked improvement in the behaviour of the nazi leaders in the city and open defiance ceased in order to create a good impression. It was obvious that Lester was going to use the presentation of his annual report as an opportunity to force the League of Nations to take action over the way the city of Danzig was run.

At the League's Council meeting on 17 January he presented a detailed description of just a few of the incidents that had marked daily life in Danzig during 1935:

- Despite several warnings from the Council, the Senate had obstinately pursued its policy of turning Danzig into a nazi bastion.
- The elections in April had been designated by the Council itself as unconstitutional.
- Freedom of the press had been curtailed by an impressive number of suppressions of newspapers and the arrest of their editors.
- The *Volkstag* had been restricted to a sham parliament with questions first vetted by a nazi-dominated committee whose sole purpose seemed to be to deny the opposition an opportunity to speak.
- Although the deputies were supposed to benefit from parliamentary immunity, several of the opposition leaders had been arrested many times.
- Although Forster held no political office and was not a citizen of Danzig, he interfered directly in the city's government, civil service and police force.
- Forster made speeches that praised Hitler, denigrated the League of Nations and predicted the destruction of the opposition.
- The Danzig police were not protecting people on the streets, unless they were nazis.

- Danzig's Supreme Court had ruled that the display of swastika flags and portraits and busts of Hitler was unconstitutional, but the Senate continued to do so blatantly.
- The Danzig Senate announced that it had no intention of carrying out the Council's recommendations and accompanied this refusal with speeches containing brazen falsehoods about the League of Nations.

Lester attempted to be just and fair, but his report to the Council that January outlined in the clearest terms that Danzig's Nazi Party and government were attempting to take total control of the city by illegal means. Evidently, the objective was to present the League with a *fait accompli*. During the local election campaign in April 1935 he had seen that the nazis resorted to violence, intimidation and fraud, and it was therefore not difficult to imagine what life in a totalitarian state would be like. He reported that Greiser had made direct threats about eliminating the role of the League of Nations, suggesting that only Germany and Poland would decide on the future of the Free City of Danzig. Lester added that, despite the Council's recommendations and the Senate's promises to implement them, the situation in Danzig had continued to deteriorate steadily. He concluded his report by saying that 43% of the population (approaching half) was opposed to the Nazi Party and deserved the protection of the League of Nations. Perhaps the nazis no longer represented the majority of the population. Even Forster himself had declared that membership of the Nazi Party represented only 10% of the Free City's population.[2]

Avenol, the Secretary-General, received Lester's annual report with the statement "This is literature", but Lester was keener to know if it was also good politics. His report was described by an expert on international affairs as "a dignified and tactful document, which throws the clearest light on nazi methods". But, with an atmosphere of appeasement reigning in Geneva and with the League powerless to implement its will, nobody had any clear idea of what to do about it, except Lester himself. While he wanted the League to curtail the nazi politicians of Danzig, appeasement was an attractive policy for France and the United Kingdom since it was other countries that were likely to pay the price. During 1935, the Council had already let pass three occasions to intervene decisively in Danzig.

At first, "appeasement" did not have pejorative associations. The original idea was to create a situation of patience and tolerance during which negotiations in favour of stability could take place in a calm and constructive atmosphere. It was easy to understand that Germans might feel bitter following the First World War. Politicians who opposed appeasement, such as Winston Churchill and Sir Robert Vansittart, were at first seen as cranks and warmongers. While we now know that appeasement of Hitler's policies was clearly the wrong way to go, the politicians of the 1930s felt that they had a very limited choice. A robust confrontation by the British and French Governments over Hitler's and Mussolini's ambitions could have alerted public opinion to their true ambitions. From many sides there were demands for action to halt the nazis, but it was the attitude of the British Government that was the key to any action the League might pursue in Danzig. However, it was not a good moment for the British, with Sir Samuel Hoare being replaced as Foreign Secretary by Anthony Eden, and the illness and death of King George V. Lester pointed out that the activities of the nazi-dominated Senate in Danzig were illegal, and his views were supported by the British consul-general in Danzig, L.M. Robinson. Did the British Foreign Office appreciate the irony of protecting an Irish international official when there was an on-going confrontation between the United Kingdom and Ireland?

The Danzig delegation to Geneva at the January Council meeting was led initially by Böttcher, who was not at all happy with Lester's report and remarked that the only source of trouble in Danzig was the High Commissioner himself! This pretext, a typical explanation of events by nazi politicians, had already been used over and over again in one way or another as a reason to avoid the truth. It was evident that the Free City was once again going to be the focus of international tension. Lester described the nazi regime in Danzig as consisting of "wilful, blind, unintelligent partisans". The delegates at the Council meeting expressed their complete confidence in him, but were annoyed with Greiser who had not yet arrived in Geneva and did not appear to be in a hurry to do so. Eden was astonished by Greiser's cavalier attitude and summoned him to attend the Council meeting at once. He soon arrived in Göring's private aeroplane. However, when he addressed the delegates, he dismissed lightly the failure of the Senate to carry out the Council's recommendations. One of the journalists present remarked: "Such an impudent speech I never heard."

The day that the Council was to discuss the situation in Danzig was overshadowed by two major events: the British King George V died and the French cabinet of Pierre Laval collapsed. The adoption of the Council's report on the Free City gave rise to outrageous manoeuvring on the part of the Danzig authorities to avoid accepting any responsibility for the situation they had created and to play down all criticisms of their actions, particularly those of Forster whose behaviour was, according to Lester, damaging the image of Germany and nazism. There followed a session of horse-trading over the wording of Eden's final report of the meeting. Would the Senate's actions be condemned? Would the elections be re-run? Would Forster be forced to leave? Would the League wash its hands of Danzig? Would a committee of investigation be set up? Would the entire machinery of the League's Assembly be brought to bear on a wayward Baltic provincial town? Finally, none of these options were mentioned in the report and all references to Forster were removed in return for Greiser's "promise" that the Senate would respect certain guarantees in the future. The final sentence of the Council's report did, however, contain the phrase that Poland should lend "any aid that may be required by the High Commissioner".

Although Lester's annual report had described exactly what was going to happen in Danzig, the Council chose to ignore it. The League was already attempting to appease Hitler's regime in Berlin by not publishing the frank truth about the Free City. On the other hand, Lester's opinion was that making concessions in the belief that they would lead to moderation was misguided. Greiser had been given numerous opportunities to redeem himself and had simply pursued totalitarian policies with increased vigour. Some German diplomats, including the Foreign Minister von Neurath, spoke as if Forster's removal from Danzig was imminent. But when it was proposed that the situation would improve if Forster was dismissed, Hitler claimed that he would never desert an "old comrade". Both Eden, who was the Rapporteur for Danzig, and Lester left Geneva with profound misgivings about the future since the administration of the city seemed likely to pursue nazi policies that were unconstitutional. At this stage no one realized to what lengths Hitler was prepared to go.

Among the decisions that the Council did *not* take in its January 1936 meeting was to appoint a committee of investigation to examine the functioning of the administration in Danzig and to order the holding of new elections. Lester's suggestion to appoint this body was understood as a cry for help, but the Council decided to postpone the matter to a later date — which would turn out to be never. The League therefore missed an opportunity to attack the Danzig nazis at their most vulnerable point following the financial crisis during the summer of 1935 — added to which it was believed that they no longer represented the majority of citizens. Upon learning of the League's decision not to guarantee the Free City's constitution, the opposition parties in the city were further demoralized. Although the window of opportunity for re-running elections in Danzig went on into 1936, the Council continued to dither, particularly through inertia on the part of the British and Polish Governments, which had most influence on this question. Danzig, in the opinion of London and Warsaw, was a sideshow when put in the context of maintaining good relations with Berlin. From this viewpoint, although Lester's attempts to maintain democratic institutions in the Free City and to protect the civil rights of its citizens were admirable, they should not be allowed to interfere with international power politics. The slow-burning fuse smouldering in the city, known as "the powder keg of Europe", had not been extinguished and would soon reach the point of no return—if it had not already done so.

The high tension and duplicity of the January 1936 Council meeting could be regarded as a defeat for Lester and placed a great strain on his nerves. A patient man by nature, he had become disillusioned with the empty promises of the Danzig Senate to stop violating the Constitution and persecuting its democratic opposition in a barbarous and mediaeval manner. He admitted that he was under constant stress, never had an opportunity to relax and began to suffer from sleeplessness. Nevertheless, in January 1936 his post in Danzig was renewed for another year by the Council. Secretary-General Avenol understood that if Lester had to give up his post, it would be a humiliating blow for the League of Nations, and he therefore urged Lester to stay and even to accept a further prolongation of his appointment during 1937. The new Deputy Secretary-General Walters mentioned that the entire Council would be "on its knees" with gratitude if he accepted to remain in Danzig. It is possible that Lester was tempted by the prospect since his colleagues in Dublin had informed him that there was no suitable position waiting for him in the Irish Government.[3]

One British politician visiting Danzig in 1936 wrote that: "Mr. Sean Leste [sic]—a high-minded person of sterling qualities and plenty of courage — were it not otherwise it is doubtful if active members of the minorities would be able to secure even a bare livelihood there just now." Although the Polish representative in Danzig, Kazimierz Papée, had frequently reported that the city had become a testing-ground for an aggressive German foreign policy that directly threatened Polish interests, the foreign minister of Poland, Józef Beck, continued to ignore these warnings on the pretext that they might cause difficulties with Berlin. Beck suggested that the problems with Danzig could be resolved if the next High Commissioner were Polish. Despite Beck's expressions of satisfaction about Poland's excellent relationship with Germany, Lester knew otherwise. In the meantime, the Polish Government started to invest heavily in armaments.

Nevertheless, Lester's report to the League's Council in January 1936 did have some impact and a chastened Danzig Senate attempted to live peacefully with the High Commissioner during the following months. Greiser realised that matters might have been much worse for the Senate and adopted a cordial, respectful, almost apologetic approach to the High Commissioner, while Forster kept a very low profile even though violence towards opposition groups continued during the winter and spring of 1936. Amazingly, Greiser and Lester's relationship also included a number of joint breakfasts, lunches and dinners. Lester appreciated the relative calm and even wondered if the full revelation of nazi methods employed in Danzig had caused a change of tactics. Had the firmness of the Council's attitude in January restored the League's prestige with the Danzig Senate? He continued to state that he expected the administration of the city to be based on the agreed Constitution but wondered if the Senate was actually listening to him. The next Council meeting would take place in May and the Senate seemed to be determined that Danzig should not appear on its agenda. All it required was for the Council to continue with a firm and unequivocal position regarding the respect of the Danzig Constitution. What happened after the Council meeting was another matter.

In February the Danzig Senate adopted the new press laws, which allowed full scope for the nazi-dominated government to ban any periodical that offended its sensibilities. The prohibition did not come into force until May, but when it did the newspapers of the Social Democratic Party, the Catholic Centre Party, the Jewish Party and the Communist Party were all suspended. Greiser justified these moves on the preposterous grounds that opposition newspapers "abuse the Government unreasonably". It was obvious that the Senate would make it impossible for newspapers that held views different from its own to survive economically, but to do so they seized upon any flimsy pretext enabling them to ban almost anything, such as "a danger to public security", "the incitement to strike" or "contempt of officers of state".[4]

On 7 March 1936 the German Army reoccupied the demilitarized zone of the Rhineland and Hitler denounced the Locarno Pact. Lester felt that, while one might sympathize with Germany recovering part of its territory, Hitler's audacity was likely to spread alarm throughout Western Europe because the Germans had broken the Treaty of Versailles as well as the Locarno Pact, which they had themselves proposed. The Locarno Pact had been agreed between Aristide Briand of France and Gustav Stresemann of Germany in 1926. At this moment the French Government was divided and undecided, while the British Government felt that no aggressive act had been committed. The Italians were already being sanctioned for their attack on Ethiopia, so it was unlikely that they would be motivated to put pressure on Germany to evacuate part of its own territory. Since the leading European nations did not react to this violation of treaties, the League of Nations remained silent. However, it clearly encouraged Hitler to see how far he could go. Already the most farsighted people feared that war was coming and Lester began to consider how to place his family out of harm's way. Greiser explained to Lester that the Rhineland coup could not be repeated in Danzig since it was essential to keep on good terms with Poland.

The ninety-third session of the Council of the League of Nations took place between 9 and 13 May 1936—a very short session. The Italian occupation of Ethiopia was now considered as a *fait accompli* so did not figure largely on the agenda. Lester reported that remarkably, since January, the Danzig Senate seemed to be making an effort to respect the Constitution. So, this matter too did not involve the Council in long and arduous negotiations. As usual, Greiser had lunch with Lester, who wrote in his diary "I might say that Greiser's attitude to me in Geneva was of the most friendly." It was Greiser's submissive attitude during this May meeting that further encouraged Secretary-General Avenol to extend Lester's term of office into 1937.

Nevertheless, there were worrying signs of seismic activity. Upon returning to Danzig, Greiser made a speech to his followers in a café during which he declared that the Polish/Danzig Pact would not last and soon the Nazi Party would triumph. The Polish consul Papée protested and received a complete denial from Greiser. Lester asked Greiser for an explanation and was told to his face: "Do you think I would be so stupid as to make such a speech?" In his diary Lester makes no comment about Greiser's assertion but it is not difficult to read his thoughts. For good measure, the *Volkstimme* newspaper that had printed his speech was suppressed for two months for "false" reporting. Forster then made an inflammatory speech using a loudspeaker saying that his hooligans were ready to seize control of the streets of Danzig in place of the police force. This time his words could be heard some distance away. Someone wrote them down and passed the text to Lester. When Lester told Greiser that he possessed Forster's speech, Greiser pretended to be ignorant of it and asked to have a copy.

Nonetheless, a sort of honeymoon period seemed to endure and on 3 June Greiser wrote a grovelling letter asking if there was anything he could do to encourage Lester to accept a second term as High Commissioner. This was to be his last act of deception before the storm broke.

Lester had been away from the city, but when he returned on 13 June he faced an excited crowd of people outside his house who claimed that nazi ruffians had stormed the meeting of another political party injuring fifty people, many of them elderly. The leaders of the opposition angrily showed Lester the weapons that had been seized from the attackers. Another group had asked the police for protection at their meeting, but Forster's men had cleared the police away before attacking. It seemed that the police were in some way acquiescent. Forster had the nerve to protest that fifteen of his men had been injured in the attack, one of whom subsequently died, becoming a martyr for the nazi cause. It subsequently transpired that the death of the man who died could be attributed to the consequences of syphilis.[5] More riots followed with the police looking on, so an atmosphere of fear settled on the city. Polish people were also being attacked. Lester told Greiser that if the situation appeared to him to be out of control, he had been authorized in January to request the intervention of the Polish Army and would also ask the Council to put the matter once more on its agenda. For this reason, he intended seeing Papée at the Polish consulate and would draw the attention of the Council to the matter in its special session to be held at the end of June. Greiser reacted immediately, saying he would regret these moves very much and gave his explanation for the disturbances: it was, of course, the opposition that was to blame! He declared that there was (once again) a rift between himself and Forster— but it was not the first time Lester had heard this one. Lester then visited the German consul-general in Danzig, Otto von Radowicz, drawing attention to Forster's activities who had, in the meantime, been made an honorary citizen of Danzig. Von Radowicz said that Forster did not represent the *Führer*—but in this respect he was wrong. Lester also observed that most of what was written in the nazi press was blatant lies, while newspapers that published the truth were banned. Greiser, Forster and von Radowicz all gave different accounts of the troubles and were summoned to Berlin for "talks". While Greiser and von Radowicz met with Göring, only Forster had access to Hitler and this would explain what happened next.

Because of Lester's resistance to the nazis, he was now seen as an exasperating nuisance. He had prevented Forster and his men from taking over the streets of Danzig; he had defended the opposition parties during the election process; he had even stated that Hitler's friend Forster should be removed from the city; finally, he had insisted that the Senate should respect the Constitution. The complete nazi victory in the 1935 elections had been thwarted by Lester and he had subsequently dared to suggest that the elections ought to be re-run due to widespread fraud. If they were re-run, it was now clear that the nazis would be heavily defeated. Lester's actions were so troublesome that the nazis wanted him gone, but Forster and Hitler were frustrated to learn that his appointment had been prolonged for yet another year by the Secretary-General of the League. Berlin had been looking for a reason to precipitate Lester's demise as High Commissioner, which they considered essential if the Free City was ever to become a part of Germany again. Thus, to achieve the desired result, a contemptuous and carefully planned diplomatic snub was engineered. The opportunity occurred when the German cruiser, *Leipzig*, visited Danzig on 26 June 1938.

In his position as High Commissioner for Danzig, Lester hosted a continuous series of dinners, luncheons and receptions for the large number of visitors to the city. All governments had been informed some years earlier that the officers of naval vessels visiting the port were required to pay a series of courtesy visits, including one to the High Commissioner. Lester's staff and that of the Senate and the Polish and German consulates had agreed all the details of the programme of visits some days previously. A reception had been arranged at the High Commission, food and drink had been ordered and guests invited. However, while waiting for the officers to arrive, Greiser sent one of his subordinates to inform Lester that they had completed their programme of official visits and would not attend the High Commissioner's reception. No explanation was given for this act of disrespect but apparently the officers were following instructions from the naval high command in Berlin. Lester immediately wrote a short report describing the event for the benefit of the Council.

The authorities in Berlin and Danzig threw the blame on each other. The German Foreign Ministry declared that it had no hand in "The Leipzig Incident", while the local nazis suggested it was a matter that concerned Berlin. It was therefore a remarkable coincidence that the Danzig nazis—party, Senate and press—unleashed a tirade of abuse against Lester at exactly this same moment, accusing him of being a financial burden, a mouthpiece for the democratic opposition, as well as "meddling in Danzig's internal affairs". *Time* magazine wrote: "young Albert Forster, supple-muscled leader of the Danzig Nazi Party, declared next day in his Nazi news-organ that the adjective which best describes both the League of Nations and its High Commissioner is 'superfluous'!"[6] Forster organized daily protest marches of up to a thousand uniformed nazis on the streets outside Lester's office. It was clear that the Greiser and Forster had pulled off a major diplomatic coup, and had severely weakened the High Commissioner's position without making any concessions or running the risk of reprisals. Eventually, the Polish Government expressed its concern to the Senate about the turmoil going on in the city and law and order returned.

Eden asked Lester to attend a short formal discussion of this serious international incident at the Council meeting to be held in Geneva on 30 June. Greiser was also summoned by Eden. On his way, he passed through Berlin and had a briefing with Hitler, Göring and Forster, who told him to make "a bombshell" of a speech—and thus he was to make his mark on history. What he said when he arrived on 4 July was described by various journalists as "unprecedented in the history of the League" or "more suited to a bar-room than to a meeting of the League Council". During the morning session a Czech spectator had committed suicide in the League's Assembly. Exactly one hour after the Assembly had voted to lift sanctions against Italy and refused to succour Ethiopia, Greiser marched into the Council session and with calculated insolence addressed British Foreign Secretary Anthony Eden in German. Among his more absurd allegations was that the Danzig opposition, which numbered nearly half of the population, consisted of dishonest criminals and cowards, while the majority of honest citizens (i.e. those who supported the nazis) were terrorized by the minority—and it was all Lester's fault! In unprintably coarse language, Greiser attacked Lester on personal grounds and demanded a free hand for the nazis to administer Danzig. The way for the League to secure peace was to remove Lester and give the responsibility to the President of the Senate (i.e. himself). He claimed to speak on behalf of the whole German nation: "The German people expect from the League of Nations in the coming months actions that will permit me . . . to appear no more at Geneva!" As he stormed out of the meeting room amid uproar making the Hitler salute, there were shouts of abuse and a burst of derisory laughter from the press gallery. Greiser stuck out his tongue and "cocked a snook" with his fingers to his nose. He declared that the next time he came to Geneva would be with a fleet of bombers! Greiser, whom Lester declared to be "full of schnapps", had brought international diplomacy down to the level of a schoolboy jape. One British newspaper deplored the fact that "a single ill-mannered clown" had overshadowed the tragedy that was taking place between Italy and Ethiopia at the very same moment. The next morning a Berlin newspaper announced that Greiser had been "insulted at Geneva" and threatened by the press box at which he had thumbed his nose because—it will surely come as no surprise—"Jews were conspicuous". Two weeks later Danzig was further eclipsed from the agenda when the League became totally preoccupied with the Spanish Civil War.

This Leipzig Incident put both the League of Nations and Poland in a quandary about demanding an explanation from Berlin since Germany was no longer a member of the League. Beck, who had learned beforehand about what was going to happen in Danzig on 26 June, did not pass this information to either Lester or Papée. Furthermore, Lester found that Beck's reaction to Greiser's speech was decidedly offhand. Did Beck actually support the League of Nations in Danzig? Lester told Beck's second-in-command, Michał Łubieński,[7] that the High Commissioner's mission had ended and that the situation was beyond the possibility of action for an official provided with such limited powers. However, it was unacceptable to pass the Leipzig Incident over in silence, so some way had to be found to approach the German Government for an apology. Rather than supporting the authority of the High Commissioner, the United Kingdom, as the League member in charge of Danzig questions, squeezed out of its responsibilities by requesting Poland to obtain a German apology. The legal situation was that, as the arrangements for the visit of the *Leipzig* had been previously agreed with Poland, Germany had interfered directly in the affairs of a foreign territory and Poland had been offended. It could be concluded that Germany felt free to conduct any policy it liked in Danzig. Poland was put in the position of apology-seeker while weakening the authority of the High Commissioner, whose office was a vital political buffer between Poland and Danzig and, ultimately, Germany. While in Geneva, Lester had a conversation with Beck during which the Polish Foreign Minister stated that his troops had been moved up to the Danzig frontier and warships in Gdynia were ready to intervene at short notice. Lester told him: "Make sure the Germans know it."

After the June meeting of the Council, Lester's colleagues in Geneva begged him to stay at his post and return to Danzig as soon as possible, even though there were fears for his safety. While still in Geneva, he was informed by a bunch of excited journalists that his house was in flames and his family in flight. Lester telephoned his wife and discovered this alarming news to be entirely fabricated.

After the Council meeting, Greiser was welcomed home to Danzig like a hero amid tumultuous scenes of celebration. He gave interviews to the foreign press stating that the League of Nations no longer had any say in Danzig's internal affairs, while it was Lester's support of the opposition parties that represented a danger for Polish/German relations. It was obvious that, following the Manchurian and Ethiopian fiascos, Hitler's government was ready to call the League's bluff. There was, however, one potentially disastrous consequence for the Danzig nazis. When he observed the terrific impact of Greiser's speech, Forster went to Hitler and claimed to have written the speech together with Greiser. Göring implored Greiser not to turn this untrue statement into the source a nasty quarrel, but now that the League of Nations had been eclipsed Greiser and Forster had lost a common enemy. This incident cemented their rivalry.

When Lester returned to Danzig, he did not know what to expect. He was met by his wife, dog and driver at the station, while Danzig nazis stood and stared at him. In an act of considerable courage, he sent the driver away and walked home arm in arm with his wife. The Polish delegation had given assurances that its armed forces were ready to intervene in an emergency; all Lester had to do was inform the Polish consul-general. However, when questioned, Papée became very evasive about what his government had actually promised to the High Commissioner, saying that it needed to be confirmed at the ministerial level. Papée's reports to Beck from Danzig that summer clearly described how Poland's lack of support for Lester meant that the High Commissioner could no longer defend Polish interests, neither locally nor internationally. Although Beck seemed to be indifferent to the fate of the Danzig opposition, Papée did not share this attitude. The Danzig opposition felt it had been rebuked by the League and that Lester was also no longer able to protect its members, who began to look upon the Polish authorities as their saviour. It was Papée who now found himself besieged by the opposition and was required to remind Greiser that there was a gulf between what the Senate was expected to do and what it actually did. He also had to listen to Greiser's litany of lame excuses. For instance, Greiser explained that Lester was so hated by the entire population of Danzig that his house had been placed under police protection. Papée knew otherwise; the police had placed Lester under surveillance so that no members of the opposition could approach him.

The Jewish newspaper *Danziger Echo* was suspended for ten months. The only other opposition periodical still appearing, the Catholic *Volkszeitung*, was cancelled after printing a letter from Bishop O'Rourke in which he wrote: "The Senate has made war on all the Free City's Christians. I appeal to all Catholics to rally around the clergy." Lester reported to Geneva that the Senate refused to answer his questions about the constitutional basis for these arbitrary nazi decrees.

The nazi victory was now complete. From this moment on Lester was boycotted and played no further part in the affairs of the Free City. Danzig became a totalitarian state and the High Commissioner was rendered powerless since the Senate refused to cooperate with him. Any attempt by the opposition to contact him now became a criminal offence.[8] Visitors were interrogated by the political police; even diplomatic personnel had to prove their identity. A British journalist, Elizabeth Wiskemann,[9] paid Lester a visit upon his return from Geneva—the next day she was arrested by the Gestapo in Berlin and, after six hours of interrogation, expelled from the country. Lester abandoned his diary at this time, fearing his office would soon be subjected to a police raid and his papers seized. The most outrageous lies were also circulated in the city by the nazi propaganda machine about Lester's imaginary attendance at fictitious meetings, and his hypothetical speeches and declarations—which he treated with a certain amount of humour. Particularly, Forster blamed Lester for the deaths of nazi agitators on 12 June, a day upon which he had been absent from the city. Lester noted in his diary that he had even received thanks for these non-events. He took his wife and dog fishing in Ireland, making Poland's responsibilities perfectly clear.

The Danzig nazis had won the battle for control of the city following the Leipzig Incident. Lester was forced out of Danzig because he insisted on carrying out his instructions in accordance with the Treaty of Versailles. The drive to get rid of him obviously originated from Hitler himself, who complained about the tactics employed by Lester to frustrate the nazis and his "interference" into the smallest details of the Danzig administration. If only the High Commissioner would stop defending democratic values, protecting the minorities in Danzig and insisting on respect for the Treaty of Versailles, the nazi takeover would have been so much easier! During a visit by Jan Szembek,[10] Beck's deputy, to the 1936 Summer Olympics, Hitler protested bitterly about the Irishman, stating that "the presence of Lester in Danzig is, from the point of view of the doctrine of the regime governing Germany, unacceptable". It was important that "there was a change of personnel in the post of High Commissioner and it would be appropriate to bring up the matter with the British once again". Later the same day, Hermann Göring said much the same thing, while Foreign Minister Joachim von Ribbentrop[11] saw the Irishman's difficult situation as "a result, to a large extent, of a lack of tact in his behaviour"—it was certainly not the nazi's fault! It was particularly a victory for Forster and also Greiser—Lester's erstwhile friend. Even Beck, the Polish Foreign Minister, considered Lester as a problem. He observed that "if only the High Commissioner fulfilled his mission with more discernment a *modus vivendi* could be established."

Lester spent most of the late summer and early autumn of 1936 hoping that Poland would soon secure a morally satisfactory apology from Berlin for the Leipzig Incident. It took a long time for an official German response to be issued, but when it did eventually arrive it was no surprise that it took the form a worthless scrap of paper. It stated entirely deceitfully that the Leipzig Incident had been a personal attack on Lester and had not been directed against Danzig, the League of Nations or Poland. Nevertheless, it was clear that Berlin's real aim was to eliminate the League from Danzig. There was no apology. However, as the German text had been kind enough to include a further guarantee of Polish rights in the Free City, Józef Beck left it at that, satisfied that Poland had shown the League that its word still counted with Berlin; he was not too perturbed about the fate of Lester or the democratic opposition. Despite frequent reports from consul-general Papée praising Lester's activities in favour of Poland, Beck failed to appreciate the gravity of the Leipzig Incident so that Polish foreign policy remained detrimental to its own interests. If Poland, as an armed sovereign state, had stood by Lester, his defence of the press and the opposition parties, the ability of the Senate to pursue nazi policies might have been severely restricted. Elizabeth Wiskemann, the British journalist, later wrote that Beck had "prepared for the destruction of Poland" and was "essentially worthless". Diana, the wife of the British politician Alfred Duff Cooper, described Beck's "drunken boasting rather a bore" and went with him to a night club where there was "much pinching of thighs".[12]

Thanks to Beck, Poland remained blissfully unaware of the great peril that it was now facing, but there would be a heavy price to pay. It slowly began to dawn on the Polish Government in Warsaw that the Polish population of Danzig might be at risk. In November 1936 some Polish officials, realising that the nazi regime in Berlin thrived on bullying its victims, warned that Poland was the most likely future candidate. What the Poles had not yet realized was that Hitler was determined to recover land in Germany's former eastern territories which lay in Poland. Józef Lipski, the Polish ambassador in Berlin, attempted fruitlessly to meet with Göring to discuss the increase in anti-Polish words and actions in Danzig. The British public, at least, no longer had any illusions about German ambitions.

Greiser's return from Geneva in July 1936 was the beginning of the end for the League of Nations and the signal for the complete nazification of the free city. The fact that its decrees were illegal did not stop the Senate issuing them. Within a few months the opposition had been drowned by what Lester calls "the brown tide". Once Lester was no longer in a position to protect them, the opposition politicians were overcome within a few weeks. Lester himself told journalist Erich Brost to flee the city. On 6 October seventy-four members of the Social Democratic Party were arrested and publicly marched through the streets. A week later the party was banned on the pretext that weapons had been found in the offices of its newspaper. The next day 200 socialists were arrested, causing those who had not already been murdered or imprisoned to flee either to Poland or to Scandinavia.

Neither the League nor Polish Foreign Minister Beck saw that their face-saving exercise had not eased Lester's impossible position. He was, more or less, on his own. The Council had adopted a policy of cynically deliberate indecision, while paying lip-service to the League's ideals. The High Commissioner's authority did not come from the League but from whichever country or power was standing behind him. Everyone was aware of the great peril in which Lester and his family lived so the Poles did intervene to ensure that Lester was not in danger of being physically assaulted.[13]

In 1936 the League moved into its magnificent new Palais des Nations overlooking the Lake of Geneva and the Alps. At its meeting on 28 September in Geneva, the League's "Committee of Three" (originally France, Portugal and the United Kingdom, but Sweden soon replaced Portugal) proposed that the mandate for the Free City of Danzig should be given to Poland, thus rendering the High Commissioner's post useless. The Council was faced with Lester's report summarizing events since troubles began in 1934. In this he mentioned the slowness of the League's machinery for enforcing respect of the Constitution, the more hopeful signs in the first half of 1936 and the abrupt change of policy in mid-June leading to the eclipse of the High Commissioner's functions. There was now a total lack of contact between himself and the opposition leaders, the administration in Danzig and even with his daughters' school friends. At this point, Secretary-General Avenol said that he had an interesting proposal to share with the Council. Avenol suggested that the recent resignation of Azcárate, the Spanish Deputy Secretary-General, who was quitting his post in order to become Spanish Ambassador in London, offered an unexpected opportunity for removing Lester from Danzig under cover of a promotion. Avenol pointed out that Azcárate's position had to be filled by a small power national and he wrote that "in searching among those whose services to the League were marked by great competence and devotion, the Secretary-General's attention was at once fixed on Mr Lester." If the Council had no objection to Lester leaving his present difficult position, Avenol proposed to nominate him to this new post. Beck, who had not been informed and wanted the next High Commissioner to be Polish, was furious that Poland was likely to be presented with yet another *fait accompli*. However, with a few modest qualifications, the Council approved, asking that the new appointment should not come into effect until a successor had been appointed in Danzig. Thus, the Council managed to find a dignified way out for the Irishman through a prestigious promotion as Deputy Secretary-General. Due to this appointment, Lester would become the second highest official in the League of Nations and would be in charge whenever Avenol, the Secretary-General, was absent. Anthony Eden pointed out to Lester that he would almost certainly be the next Secretary-General. "If I thought so," Lester replied, "you wouldn't see my heels for the dust."

In drawing a line under Lester's period in Danzig, the international press concluded that he had made several ineffective attempts to force the League to intervene in the free city, but paid tribute to his "courage, dignity, self-sacrifice and political sense". Nevertheless, news of Lester's "resignation" or "recall" caused wild jubilation lasting for many weeks among nazis both in Danzig and in Germany. Both Poles and Germans openly welcomed Lester's withdrawal, and there was justifiable panic and consternation among the free city's opponents to the nazi regime. Still out of touch with reality, Beck suggested that the Senate was a more reliable source of information than the High Commissioner, thus granting the Senate the victory that it could hardly have expected from the Polish Government.

High Commissioner Lester finally left Danzig on 22 December 1936. He did not write a final report for the Council's January session, believing that his report for the previous September had already provided a complete description of the situation. For much of the last two months of his mandate he was absent from Danzig, but it did not make a great deal of difference since, on orders from Berlin, nobody made contact with him. Thus, he was no longer subject to police harassment as before, being reduced to the status of an observer. Both Erich Brost and Hermann Rauschning had taken refuge in Warsaw. The Catholic Bishop of Danzig, Edvard O'Rourke, was also overwhelmed by the increasingly bitter politics that operated in his diocese. At one stage Greiser had assured him that the Roman Catholics could carry out their religious activities unhindered. In view of the past record of nazi assurances, O'Rourke should have been prepared for the series of attacks on Catholic youth organizations and property that followed. O'Rourke was criticized both by the Senate for defending the independence of the Christian elements of the population too energetically and by the Catholics for not defending them with sufficient vigour. In June 1938 O'Rourke was forced to resign after he had tried to appoint four additional Polish nationals as parish priests. Lester was very fond of Bishop O'Rourke remarking that he played "a quite impossible game of bridge":

> I think it was his great—(or [simply]) grandfather who left Ireland and eventually took service with the Czar, winning wealth and high place as a soldier. His descendants were mostly in the Army and Navy, and the family estate in what is now Lithuania. Speaks, Polish, Russian, Italian, German and French very well; English not so good and the rumour which (I confess) rather alarmed me before I arrived, that he also spoke Irish was unfounded. Probably more Polish in feeling than anything else, the Bishop maintains a certain sentimental regard for Ireland, and is proud of his Irish descent. . . . We like the bishop very much, and are glad he so often comes to see us . . . A gentle Christian is how I most often think of him.

At the Council meeting in January 1937 Lester told Avenol that the most decent way out of the Danzig crisis would be for the League to admit its "powerlessness". Avenol's reply was that this could not happen as it would represent a revision of the Treaty of Versailles. The Council itself was not in a hurry to appoint another High Commissioner, but decided to do so under pressure from the Poles—who had done so much to undermine the High Commissioner's authority. Furthermore, in a conversation which left Eden, the British Foreign Secretary, speechless, Greiser pressed for a new High Commissioner to be appointed without delay. Lester and Eden were intrigued by this attitude and came to the conclusion that both Poland and Germany were anxious not to be confronted with a situation where they had to deal with each other face to face.

After a number of candidates had been rejected or had refused to accept the appointment, the German-speaking Swiss diplomat Carl Burckhardt became the new largely meaningless High Commissioner in February 1937. Following his departure from Danzig, Lester took a great interest in events in the Free City and was kept informed by reading Burckhardt's reports—"amazingly well-written"—and through numerous conversations with the new High Commissioner whenever he visited Geneva. Lester said of Burckhardt: "His sense of humour and drama makes him an excellent 'raconteur'." Burckhardt treated Forster, the *Gauleiter*, in a brusque manner with a mixture of flattery and playful teasing. When Burckhardt found his butler had the habit of standing close enough to overhear his conversation, he gave the man his cigarette to hold for two minutes—after which he kept his distance. Still gloriously ignorant of the true situation, Józef Beck warned Burckhardt not to count on the support of the Polish State in the case of difficulties with the Senate or the Nazi Party. During Burckhardt's period in office the uselessness of the High Commissioner's position was demonstrated by the complete nazification of Danzig and the annihilation of the last opposition, particularly the Jewish members of the population. Burckhardt tried to shift the blame for his failure to defend the opposition parties by saying that they showed "a lack of character and courage"! The last component of the nazi paraphernalia was the building of a concentration camp at Stutthof, a few miles from the city, in September 1939.

Burckhardt promoted the appeasement process since his approach to the position of High Commissioner was to establish personal contact with the political elite in Danzig and Berlin. Greiser found in him an important ally since Burckhardt refused to deal with Forster. He was also brought into contact with Hermann Göring, Reinhardt Heydrich,[14] Heinrich Himmler, Joachim von Ribbentrop and even with Hitler himself. This situation obviously pleased von Ribbentrop, who described Burckhardt as "an admirable exception compared to many of his predecessors". Lester had been very careful about having contacts with the German Government and was alarmed by Burckhardt's actions in case they upset the Poles. Beck, on the contrary, seems to have appreciated Burckhardt as a channel to pass messages to the German hierarchy and to sound out their attitude. The new High Commissioner met Hitler for the first time in October 1937, but was hardly able to utter a word since the German Chancellor spoke "alone, copiously and, at moments, passionately". Burckhardt also believed that he might be able to exert a restraining influence on Hitler, but no-one shared this assumption.

Carl Hambro summed up Burckhardt's ambitions with brutal irony: "We didn't realise what a master-statesman we had amongst us."

The death of Poland's charismatic leader Piłsudski in May 1935 had left Beck almost entirely responsible for Polish foreign policy, so the following years read like a sad litany of ham-fisted errors contrary to national interests. Despite Papée and his colleagues in the Polish consulate in Danzig drawing attention to Lester's efforts as a conscientious and honest broker on behalf of Poland, Beck pursued the unrealistic and ultimately fruitless ambition of replacing him with a Pole. For all his qualities, High Commissioner Burckhardt, encouraged by Beck, would be a disaster for Polish interests. Following the First World War Czechoslovakia had seized a disputed area in southern Poland known as Teschen. When Germany occupied the Sudetenland as a result of the Munich Agreement of September 1938, Polish troops took advantage of Czechoslovak disarray to re-occupy Teschen. While this may have satisfied a Polish grievance, it was very clearly in Polish interests to have threatened Hitler and to have stood firm with Czechoslovakia rather than take advantage of her weakness in an ignoble manner.

German policy on Danzig came into the open immediately after the Munich Conference in October 1938, when Minister of Foreign Affairs von Ribbentrop demanded the incorporation of the Free City into the Reich. As in Germany, the Danzig nazis introduced the racialist Nuremberg laws a month later. By this time Lester felt that the responsibility of the League of Nations was at an end. In April 1939, High Commissioner Burckhardt was told by the Poles that any attempt to alter the city's status would be answered with armed resistance on the part of Poland. Extraordinarily, on 11 August 1939 Hitler had sent his private aeroplane to bring Burckhardt and Forster to Berchtesgaden for a personal meeting during which the German Chancellor appeared at times almost normal, making inconsequential small talk at teatime and, after sending Forster away, threw in the casual remark that he had no ambitions about the Free City! Hitler did explain that Germany needed more land to grow food for its expanding population. Two subjects that came up in the conversation, however, resulted in Hitler exploding with a maniacal fury: the attitude of Poland and the French press. Burckhardt said that he felt pity for Hitler's outbursts, since he seemed to be like "an unbalanced woman". When they parted, Hitler said ominously that he would like to meet Burckhardt again, "whatever happens . . ." Because he had not been in the room during Hitler's emotional outbursts, Forster remarked to Burckhardt as they drove away: "You seem to have a tranquillizing effect on him."

Three weeks later on 1 September 1939 the Second World War began with the shelling of the Westerplatte and the Polish post office by the battleship *Schleswig-Holstein*. Burckhardt had met the captain of the ship a few days previously and had been intrigued by his remark that: "Sometimes an officer was compelled to do a thing that he would never dream of doing as an honest private individual." On the evening of 31 August, *Gauleiter* Forster had assured Burckhardt that Hitler's conversation with him represented the true German attitude towards Danzig, to which Burckhardt had replied he was tired of his "jokes". That night the Gestapo burst into his residence and cut the telephone lines. Burckhardt was awoken at 4.30 a.m. when the first explosions blew in the windows. At 8 o'clock in the morning Forster arrived at the High Commissioner's residence armed to the teeth and ordered Burckhardt to leave the city within two hours. Then, in a rather melodramatic manner, Forster added: "I hope this will not interfere with our private relations." To which Burckhardt replied: "Sir, I never had any private relations with you and never wish to have." With a Gestapo man in each room he packed his bags and at 10 o'clock was ready with his Swiss secretary, typist, valet and two small dogs. Burckhardt then found himself on the street amid a considerable crowd. Greiser did not participate in these events having just lost his job as Danzig President to Forster.

Burckhardt's wife and children had returned to Switzerland some days earlier. He had been solemnly promised by Ernst von Weizsäcker[15] of the German Foreign Ministry that if ever he had to leave Danzig he would be properly treated and offered every facility in reaching Switzerland. Von Weizsäcker had particularly advised Burckhardt, who had intended leaving his private car in Berlin, to bring it with him to Danzig since "it might be very useful!" Nevertheless, Burckhardt's journey with his own car and official car back to Geneva followed a circuitous route through East Prussia to Kaunus in Lithuania, then Riga in Latvia, then by boat to Stockholm in Sweden. Three weeks later, he travelled across Germany to Switzerland. Once there, Burckhardt reported to his colleagues in Geneva that the attack on Poland was supposed to have taken place on 26 August but had been postponed for a week because Hitler was unsure how the British and French would react. The German Chancellor was under the illusion that, once he had conquered Poland, London and Paris would sue for peace and was taken by surprise when they declared war.

Polish civilian post-office employees had received military training and were in possession of a cache of weapons—mostly pistols, three light machine guns and some hand grenades—and were thus able to defend the Polish post office for fifteen hours. Upon their surrender, they were tried and executed. (The sentence was officially revoked by a German court as illegal in 1998.) The Polish military forces in the vicinity of the city held out until 7 September. Up to 4,500 members of the Polish minority were arrested with many of them being executed. The Free City was then formally incorporated into the newly formed *Reichsgau* of Danzig-West Prussia.

During the Second World War, both Forster and Greiser became regional governors in occupied Poland. Given their record of behaviour in Danzig, one might have been led to believe that Forster was the more extreme nazi and Greiser the more moderate, but their subsequent actions were rather the opposite. As governor of the Warthegau province, Greiser implemented ethnic-cleansing policies in a ruthless manner, ordering the mass expulsion of Poles, summary executions and the extermination of the Jews. On the other hand, in his district Forster interpreted the racial laws in a more flexible and judicious manner. Nevertheless, both were executed by the Poles following the war.

Five and a half years after the bombardment of Westerplatte, the city was re-taken by the Red Army on 30 March 1945, but Danzig had been reduced to ruins. It is estimated that almost the entire population of its pre-war inhabitants were either dead or had fled. A number of inhabitants of the city perished when the cruise ship *Wilhelm Gustloff* used for evacuation was sunk by a Russian submarine on 30 January 1945. It had over 10,500 refugees on board at the time, of whom by one estimate 9,400 drowned, including about 1,000 seriously wounded soldiers and sailors. There are many different estimates of how many people died, but all of them agree that it was the largest loss of life through the sinking of a single ship in maritime history.

At the Yalta Conference in February 1945, the Allies agreed that the city would become part of Poland and would be known by its Polish name, Gdańsk. The frontier between Poland and Germany was established on the line of the Rivers Oder and Neisse. This meant that the whole Polish state moved bodily some 300 kilometres to the west with the result that today the city of Gdańsk lies well within Poland.

Lester's work and bravery in defending the constitutional rights of the Danzig population were largely forgotten, both in Gdańsk and in Ireland. However, in 2010, the Irish Ambassador to Poland, Declan O'Donovan, along with members of Lester's family, raised the topic with Gdańsk city council leaders that there should be some kind of symbol of remembrance for the role he played in the city's history and his courage in delaying the inevitable take-over by the nazis. The city offered to rename one of the rooms in the City Hall, itself the former residence of the League of Nations High Commissioner, in honour of Sean Lester and this was officially opened in August 2010 at a ceremony attended by the President of Gdańsk, the Irish Ambassador to Poland, city council members and also Lester's daughter Ann Gorski. She recalled that her father's actions had resulted in the family being shunned by friends, their telephones tapped, their staff forming part of the nazi surveillance team and how nazi rallies were very deliberately routed to pass by the house on Saturdays and Sundays.

After Lester had left Danzig, Hitler reassured Burckhardt that, since the departure of Lester and the advent of a new High Commissioner, the city no longer represented a flash point threatening European peace. The irony did not escape Lester: "I would feel somewhat unhappy . . . if I had earned praise from Hitler."

NOTES

1. Carl Jacob Burckhardt (1891–1974) was a Swiss diplomat and historian. His career alternated between periods of academia and diplomatic postings. High Commissioner for the Free City of Danzig (1937–1939) and President of the International Committee of the Red Cross (1945–1948).
2. McNamara, P. *Sean Lester, Poland and the Nazi takeover of Danzig,* pp. 131–5; 200. Dublin/Portland, OR: Irish Academic Press, 2009.
3. McNamara, p. 148.
4. Gageby, D. *The Last Secretary-General: Sean Lester and the League of Nations,* p. 113. Dublin: Town House, 1999.
5. Epstein, C. *Model Nazi: Arthur Greiser and the Occupation of Western Poland,* p. 96. Oxford, UK: Oxford University Press, 2010.
6. *Time,* 20 July 1936.
7. Michał Tomasz Łubieński (1896–1967) was a Polish diplomat and Chief of Cabinet to Foreign Minister Józef Beck.
8. McNamara, p. 187.
9. Elizabeth Wiskemann (1899–1971) was an English journalist of Anglo-German ancestry and an outspoken critic of nazism. During the Second World War, she managed to halt temporary Jewish deportations from Hungary by deliberately sending an unencrypted telegram to the Foreign Office in London suggesting that the offices of the Hungarian Government should be targeted by bombers.
10. When Poland regained its independence in 1918, Jan Szembek (1881–1945) joined the Polish Foreign Service. He was one of the most influential figures in the later years of the Second Polish Republic, a close associate of Józef Beck. On 17 September 1939, he left Poland, together with other members of the government. He died suddenly in July 1945 at Estoril near Lisbon.
11. Ulrich Friedrich Wilhelm Joachim von Ribbentrop (1893–1946) was Foreign Minister of nazi Germany from 1938 until 1945. A businessman, he was appointed German Ambassador to the United Kingdom in 1936. Arrested in June 1945, he was tried at the Nuremberg Trials, convicted of war crimes and hanged.
12. McNamara, p. 216–7.
13. McNamara, p. 201.
14. Reinhard Tristan Eugen Heydrich (1904–1942) was a high-ranking German nazi official and one of the main architects of the Holocaust. Heydrich was attacked in Prague on 27 May 1942 by a British-trained team of Czech and Slovak soldiers. He died from his injuries a week later.
15. Ernst Freiherr von Weizsäcker (1882–1951) was a German diplomat and politician, who served as State Secretary at the Foreign Office of nazi Germany from 1938 to 1943, and as Ambassador to the Holy See from 1943 to 1945. He was arrested in 1947 and was put on trial for the deportation of French Jews to Auschwitz. He was found guilty and sentenced to seven years in prison, but soon freed.

Sir Eric Drummond, the first Secretary-General of the League of Nations.

Joseph Avenol, the second Secretary-General of the League of Nations.

Carl Hambro, a Norwegian politician and Lester's long-term ally. He eventually became President of the annual Assembly and the powerful Supervisory Commission.

Arthur Greiser, President of the Senate of the Free City of Danzig, 1934–1939.

Albert Forster, Gauleiter of the Nazi Party in Danzig during the 1930s.

Residence of the League's High Commissioner in the Free City of Danzig, now containing the Sean Lester Room.

Józef Beck, the Polish Foreign Minister who failed to realise that supporting High Commissioner Lester was in Poland's best interests.

Carl Burckhardt, the High Commissioner in Danzig following Lester, who was, in his turn, driven out of the Free City on 1 September 1939.

Anthony Eden, a British politician and diplomat, who was variously Rapporteur for Danzig, Secretary of State for Foreign Affairs, Secretary of State for Dominion Affairs and Secretary of State for War.

Alexander Loveday, Director of the League's Economic and Financial Organisation, was one of Lester's close colleagues.

Arthur Sweetser, an American journalist, was at one stage the League's Director of Information and one of Lester's most prolific correspondents.

Éamon de Valera, an Irish independence fighter and politician. He was President of Council of the League of Nations from September 1932 to January 1933, and President of the Assembly of the League of Nations, 1938.

Adolfo Costa du Rels, a Bolivian diplomat and writer, who played a key role as Acting President of the Council in the League's final years.

Seymour Jacklin, the League's Treasurer, who became Lester's principal ally in the summer of 1940.

Ludwik Rajchman, a Polish doctor and one of the most outstanding staff members of the League before the Second World War.

Francis Walters, Lester's neighbour, who was the League's second Deputy Secretary-General.

Thanassis Aghnides, who briefly became right-hand man to Joseph Avenol in the summer of 1940 but remained loyal to Lester.

Edward Phelan, Lester's first acquaintance in Geneva, who eventually became Director-General of the International Labour Organization.

Chapter Thirteen

Ethiopia/Abyssinia

Although Lester had very little to do with the Italo-Ethiopian Crisis since he was fully occupied with the situation in Danzig, it is necessary to describe what happened because it was one of the League of Nations' greatest political disasters.

On 5 December 1934, at the remote Wal-Wal oasis in a disputed area between Italian Somaliland and the Ethiopian province of Ogaden, a clash occurred between Ethiopian troops and local troops under the command of Italian officers. This was a prelude to a full-scale war between a modern European industrial power and an undeveloped African nation. There seemed little doubt that Italy, from the outset, intended to take possession of Ethiopia by force.[1]

In the 1930s, Italian Prime Minister Mussolini was looking for a military conquest to bolster his image and to give renewed vigour to his fascist regime. The most obvious candidate for invasion was the independent African country of Ethiopia, also known as Abyssinia, which lay between the two existing Italian colonies of Eritrea and Somalia. The term Abyssinia strictly applies to the north-western part of Ethiopia, although it has been used throughout history as another name for Ethiopia. This country was, with Liberia, the only African country that had not been colonized during the nineteenth century. Ethiopia had been admitted as a member of the League of Nations in 1923.

Following the Wal-Wal Incident and faced with the Italian rejection of arbitration, on 14 December the Ethiopians turned for help to the League of Nations. However, at this time the French and British Governments were very keen to obtain the support of Italy against the alarming rearmament of nazi Germany and wanted Mussolini on their side. Both the United Kingdom and France wanted Italy to join them in opposing Hitler's ambitions. The

French Foreign Minister Pierre Laval[2] had already met with Mussolini in Rome and signed the Franco-Italian Agreement of 4 January 1935. This agreement proposed that Italy should have a free hand in Abyssinia in return for supporting France against any German aggression. Laval had been pursuing anti-German alliances with Mussolini's Italy and with Stalin's USSR. Subsequently, on 14 April 1935, the Stresa Front was an agreement signed in a town on the banks of Lake Maggiore in Italy, between Laval, British Prime Minister Ramsay MacDonald and Mussolini. This agreement discreetly encouraged Mussolini's African ambitions by giving unambiguous signals that neither France nor the United Kingdom would intervene if Italy attacked Ethiopia. During the subsequent Italian invasion in October 1935, these two countries condemned the attack in order to conceal their true role in this affair. Moreover, Mussolini wanted to end the Ethiopian war quickly due to the poor performance of his general, Marshall Emilio De Bono,[3] and the unexpectedly firm Ethiopian resistance. The British ambition was to reach a further agreement with the Italians before the Germans did. Thus, an agreement was negotiated by Dino Grandi,[4] Italian ambassador in London, and Sir Robert Vansittart,[5] Permanent Under-Secretary at the Foreign Office. Vansittart was concerned about the weaknesses of British defence, particularly in the Mediterranean, Egypt and the Middle East.

The Secretary-General of the League of Nations, Joseph Avenol, did not look sympathetically upon the Ethiopian protests about the Italian invasion. On the contrary, he seemed to go to extraordinary lengths to make excuses for the Italian aggression. This pro-Italian stance was observed by Baron Pompeo Aloisi,[6] the Italian delegate to the League of Nations, who believed Avenol to be strongly in favour of closer Franco-Italian relations. For instance, Avenol sought to have the Ethiopian question disposed of quickly. During the initial phase of negotiations he attempted to keep the matter outside the League and preferred a solution to be found through bilateral discussions between Italy and Ethiopia. The Italians' refusal to negotiate during these early days and Ethiopia's clear references to the terms of the League's Covenant did not make Avenol's task any easier. The Ethiopians maintained that the Wal-Wal Incident had been caused by the Italians (it lay well within Ethiopia) and they therefore believed that it should be settled according to Article 5 of the Italian-Ethiopian Treaty of Amity, Conciliation and Arbitration of 1928. Deviously, the Italians claimed that it was the Ethiopians who were the aggressors and demanded apologies and reparations. It was because of this situation that the Ethiopians had approached the League in the first place.

Throughout the first nine months of 1935 a long series of accusations and counter-accusations took place between Italy and Ethiopia both within and outside the context of the League of Nations in which Italy distinguished itself by its perverse attitude. The initial attack by Italy was a preliminary to a series of military manoeuvres throughout 1935 culminating in a full-scale invasion in October. It seems that the Italians had already established their invasion plan in 1933 and had merely been waiting for the end of the rainy season before bringing it into operation. In October, Lester observed that: "Yesterday [Mussolini's] airplanes dropped 1,000 bombs on an Abyssinian town. If the Abyssinians can hold them for six months, international law may gain a success which should mean several new orientations in Europe."

On 7 October 1935, the League of Nations declared Italy to be the aggressor and started the laborious process of imposing sanctions on Italy. Lester wrote in his diary on 2 November 1935: "May well be described as an historic day in international affairs. Fifty States have agreed to apply sanctions to a great power found guilty of making war in violation of the League Covenant, and to apply these as from 18 November. Will they be effective?" Finally, the embargo was never seriously applied since the United States—not a League member—continued to supply Italy with oil throughout this period, a vital resource in the mechanical war being carried out in Ethiopia. As previously arranged, the United Kingdom and France did not undertake any serious action against Italy (such as blocking Italian access to the Suez Canal). Even Italy's use of chemical weapons on innocent populations did not stimulate the League to action. Lester observed that countries were "each hoping to keep out of trouble and looking the other way when trouble occurs". The big powers regarded Italy as a vital element in the preservation of the international balance of power. It had also become clear that, as soon as the League attempted to discuss matters that a member state considered vital to its national interest, action was taken to settle the matter through bilateral negotiations.

While the Italian invasion of Ethiopia was pursuing its course, British Foreign Secretary Samuel Hoare[7] and the by-then French Prime Minister Pierre Laval were plotting to appease Italy. They concluded the Hoare-Laval Pact which foresaw the war ending inevitably with the partition of Ethiopia. According to this pact, Mussolini's goal of making the independent nation of Ethiopia into an Italian colony would be recognized. Italy would gain the best parts of the Ogaden and Tigray provinces, as well as economic influence over all the southern part of Ethiopia. Nevertheless, the unoccupied part of Ethiopia would have access to the sea ("a corridor for camels") via the port of Assab. Mussolini was ready to agree to this, but he deliberated for some days before making his decision known. This delay was to prove fatal. The international press learned about the pact and the affair erupted into a tremendous scandal.

The news spread quickly and provoked public outrage in the United Kingdom, France and elsewhere throughout Europe. The moral indignation against this apparent sell-out of the Ethiopians led to Hoare's resignation as Foreign Secretary at the end of the year. His successor was Anthony Eden.

When the details of the pact were released in France, Laval too was forced to resign in January 1936 and driven completely out of ministerial office until he joined the Vichy Regime during the Second World War.

Historians have differed over the significance of the pact, but it has been suggested that it was "the blow that killed the League of Nations". It showed clearly that France and the United Kingdom were not prepared to respect the principles of the League. People throughout the world lost confidence in it.

On 5 May 1936 Addis Ababa was occupied by the Italian forces and Mussolini announced that Ethiopian campaign was over. The King of Italy, Victor Emanuel III, signed a decree making himself successor to the Emperor of Ethiopia. Thus, a member state of the League of Nations, a modern financial, industrial and technical power able to produce weapons on an industrial scale, had attacked another member state, a minor pastoral nation possessing neither armaments nor resources. Rather than introducing the measures stipulated in the Covenant of the League, the whole matter was passed off hastily on the international scene with the pretence of regret. The League of Nations, under pressure from the French and British had done practically nothing to come to the aid of Ethiopia. As Lester wrote: "The League appeared to have been defeated"—one may add, by itself.

On this occasion, Kerstin Hesselgren,[8] a representative of the Swedish delegation at the League of Nations, spoke her heart as a woman. Hesselgren was sceptical about the way in which international diplomacy operated—she was not alone. Her speech was published in American and French newspapers. Part of what she said is as follows:

> Fifty nations let a small power, one of its members, fall to the ground. However can we, after this, hope that any *small country* can have any hope for the future? When last autumn [1935] fifty nations rose to help one of its small members of the League against deadly aggression, we took hope. The League was after all a real protector. It had not shown itself so before, but now had come the time when it would show its strength—when we would learn that our homes and our children could be safe under its wings. And the result! . . . The small nation that the League went to help is wiped out and the belief in the League of Nations is shaken to its foundation.

But this was not the end of the affair. The Emperor of Ethiopia had fled the country with his entourage. Who would now represent Ethiopia at the League of Nations? If the King of Italy had declared himself to be the head of state and from now on pretended to represent the Government of Ethiopia, what was the position of the Ethiopian delegation in Geneva? Aloisi, the Italian delegate, expected the Council to make a choice—"either him or me"—and he would not accept "the so-called Ethiopian representative being present at the Council table". Even the Swiss Government refused to grant Haile Selassie[9] the title of Head of State when he visited Geneva. When he arrived the

Italian delegation walked out and left the country. If Italy were ever to enter the League again, it would be necessary to re-write or suppress Articles 10 to 16 of the Covenant. From his outpost in Danzig, Lester asked his colleagues in Geneva to make sure he was informed of the next untoward event, otherwise he would find himself the sole representative of law in Europe!

It seems that, above all, Avenol viewed the League of Nations as a club for the so-called Great Powers, and particularly the European ones. Germany had withdrawn (as well as Japan) and now Italy was on the point of doing the same thing. He was determined to "leave the door open" at any cost so that these countries might one day return to their rightful places. His manoeuvring over the coming months and years was designed always to show Germany and Italy that they could come back at any time and all would be forgiven. In the face of the Covenant, in the face of justice and in the face of moral principles, from now on Avenol pardoned every act of aggression—even, unbelievably, the invasion of his homeland, France. But, in 1936, the question was what country would be the next victim?

There was a gulf between what the small number of Great Powers considered as politically expedient through secret dealings and what public opinion in both large and small countries believed to be justice and respect of the rules. To put it another way, the Great Powers looked upon the League as a private club for executing their policies, while the lesser powers considered it as a democratic forum for protecting the rights of small countries and for conducting mediation and conciliation. On 28 May 1936, the Argentine Foreign Minister, Carlos Saavedra Lamas,[10] requested an emergency meeting of the Assembly of the League of Nations in order to pronounce on the non-recognition of the Italian conquest and its annexation of Ethiopia. In fact, the small states wanted Italy to be expelled from the organization or, the Argentinians feared, smaller countries would soon start leaving the League through disgust. Before calling such a meeting, Avenol wanted there to be wide consultations and he secretly hoped that the meeting might reach a decision in the opposite sense: the Italian occupation of Ethiopia would be recognized and sanctions dropped, thus encouraging Italy to stay in the League. Avenol's lack of respect for the Covenant and the opinions of small states would continue to undermine the image of the League for some years to come.

At the extraordinary Assembly meeting in June 1936, Haile Selassie rose to speak amidst a storm of abuse from the Italian journalists present. He described what Ethiopia had endured and went on to warn "the Governments assembled in Geneva . . . of the deadly peril which threatens them." He pointed out that the Italian forces had used poison gas and had attacked peaceful civil populations in remote regions with aircraft in order to terrorize and exterminate them. He had first-hand experience that this was the way that wars were going to be conducted in the future. Nobody listened. The only concrete outcome of the meeting was that sanctions against Italy were lifted!

There remained the question of recognizing Italian sovereignty over Ethiopia. The French Foreign Ministry pointed out that there was no Ethiopian Government on the national territory and if the Assembly took decisions affecting that country the delegates present could not implement them. On the other hand, the participation of Italy was essential for peace in Europe and the admission of a powerless Ethiopian delegation would only ensure that Italy left the League. At this point Avenol made an error he would later regret. He paid an unofficial visit to Rome to gauge the Italian Government's attitude. He told them that, for the regular session of the Assembly in the autumn of 1936, there was the possibility that the Ethiopian delegation's credentials might not be recognized and, therefore, the Italian delegation should hold itself ready to attend. He does not seem to have seriously considered the opposite scenario: that the Assembly would recognize the Ethiopians' credentials and the Italians would be humiliated. When the member states of the League heard about Avenol's visit to Rome, it provoked the sharp reaction that he had been "dealing with the enemy".

When the credentials committee met on 23 September 1936 for the annual session of the Assembly of the League of Nations, they assessed the situation of the Ethiopian delegation and came to the conclusion that there was no reason why its credentials should be refused. The plenary of the Assembly then overwhelmingly voted to accept the Ethiopian delegation. It was obvious that Avenol's flying visit to Rome had persuaded a number of wavering countries to support the Ethiopians. The Italian Government, particularly the Foreign Minister Gian Galeazzo Ciano,[11] was so bitter about this outcome that it immediately established close relations with Berlin—an arrangement that came to be known as the Axis.

The next session of the Assembly was scheduled to take place in May 1937, which was a special meeting convened to admit Egypt to the organization. Avenol looked upon this as another opportunity to throw out the Ethiopian delegation and expected Belgium, Poland and Switzerland to carry out the necessary actions on his behalf. This did not happen and the "unreality" of the Ethiopian delegation went on. Meanwhile, although Italy had made no move to leave the League, its association with Germany intensified and the two states together became involved in the Spanish Civil War on the side of the Nationalists. After abstaining from the League's meetings since June 1936, the Italians finally left in December 1937.

NOTES

1. Fox, J.; Fosse, M. *The League of Nations: From Collective Security to Global Rearmament,* p. 83–8. New York: United Nations, 2012.

2. During the time of the French Third Republic, Pierre Laval (1883–1945) served as Foreign Minister and Prime Minister. Following France's surrender in 1940, he also served the Vichy Regime as head of government from 1942 to 1944, signing orders permitting the deportation of foreign Jews to the nazi death camps. After the Liberation in 1944, Laval was arrested, found guilty of high treason and executed by firing squad.

3. Emilio De Bono (1866–1944) was an Italian general, marshal and member of the fascist Grand Council. De Bono fought in the Italo-Turkish War, the First World War and the Second Italo-Abyssinian War.

4. Dino Grandi (1895–1988) was an Italian fascist politician, Minister of Justice, Minister of Foreign Affairs and President of the Parliament. He eventually revolted against Mussolini in July 1943 and fled the country.

5. Sir Robert Gilbert Vansittart (1881–1957) was a senior British diplomat in the period before and during the Second World War. He was Principal Private Secretary to the Prime Minister from 1928 to 1930 and Permanent Under-Secretary at the Foreign Office from 1930 to 1938. He adopted a hardline stance towards Germany during and after the Second World War. He was also a poet, novelist and playwright.

6. Pompeo Aloisi (1875–1949) was an Italian admiral, secret agent and diplomat. Following the First World War he had been ambassador in Copenhagen, Bucharest, Tokyo and Ankara. In 1932 he became Minister of Foreign Affairs in Mussolini's cabinet until 1936.

7. Samuel John Gurney Hoare (1880–1959), more commonly known as Sir Samuel Hoare, was a senior British Conservative politician who served in various Cabinet posts in the Conservative and National governments of the 1920s and 1930s.

8. Kerstin Hesselgren (1872–1962) was a Swedish politician, the first woman elected to the Swedish parliament in 1921. She was active on gender and social issues; access of women to all political positions; equal salaries for both sexes; the legalization of sex education and birth control; and lowering the punishment for abortion.

9. Haile Selassie I (1892–1975), an Ethiopian Orthodox Christian throughout his life, was Ethiopia's regent from 1916 to 1930 and Emperor from 1930 to 1974. He departed from Addis Ababa with his family on 2 May 1936 and re-entered the city five years later on 5 May 1941.

10. Carlos Saavedra Lamas (1878–1959) was an Argentine academic and politician. His work in ending the Chaco War between Paraguay and Bolivia led to him becoming the first Latin American Nobel Peace Prize recipient. He was noted for his sartorial elegance and was elected President of the Assembly of the League of Nations in 1936.

11. Gian Galeazzo Ciano (1903–1944), Benito Mussolini's son-in-law, was Foreign Minister of Italy from 1936 until 1943. On 11 January 1944 Ciano was shot by firing squad at the behest of his father-in-law, Mussolini, under pressure from nazi Germany. Ciano left a massive diary.

Chapter Fourteen

Deputy Secretary-General, 1937–1940

On 30 September 1936, the Council of the League of Nations had decided to appoint Lester as Deputy Secretary-General to replace Pablo de Azcárate, although his appointment as High Commissioner in Danzig had previously been prolonged for another year. In the following months, Lester did not return to Danzig for any length of time, before taking up his new responsibilities in Geneva in February 1937. His departure from Danzig caused consternation among the opposition and satisfaction among the nazis, who regarded Lester as an obstacle to the establishment of their total domination of the city. Alongside the other Deputy Secretary-General Massimo Pilotti, Lester became the second highest official in Geneva and would be in charge whenever Avenol, the Secretary-General, was absent.

On 18 February 1937, Sean Lester wrote in his diary:

> Take up new duties as Deputy Secretary-General of the League. Elsie [his wife] recalled to my mind yesterday that it is less than eight years since I left Ireland—about the middle of April 1929. I had never before been in either Paris or Geneva! In four and a half years I had attended scores of conferences, been a member of the Council for three years, and over several of its committees—notably the Peru-Columbia [sic] and the Chaco affair—and been asked to go to Danzig as [High Commissioner]—I sometimes wonder what on earth I'm doing here, being a man without ambition.

The position to which Lester had been appointed had evolved over the years. A single deputy secretary-generalship—the second-in-command at the League of Nations—had been established in 1922 and was first held by Jean Monnet. Its second occupant was Joseph Avenol who remained in the post until his promotion in 1933 to become Secretary-General. By then, with each of the Great Powers seeking posts among the higher direction of the Secretariat and small powers pressing to have a place in the hierarchy, it had been agreed that there should be two deputy secretaries-general, one of whom should represent the small powers. Thus in 1932, Pilotti of Italy and Azcárate of Spain had been appointed, but the small powers—for whom Lester was the spokesman—remained dissatisfied. Since Spain was a permanent member of the Council and therefore potentially a Great Power, did it really represent the small powers' interests? When Azcárate left in 1936 to become Spain's Ambassador to London, the opportunity arose to satisfy the small powers' desire to choose a deputy secretary-general and at the same time to resolve the Danzig impasse.

On many occasions the member states of the League had betrayed the Covenant and broken their solemn undertakings in dealing with an aggressor. In this context, on 25 May 1937 Lester made a declaration to discharge his functions and to regulate his conduct with the interests of the League alone in view. In the years that followed, only Lester, among the high direction of the Secretariat could honestly claim to have kept this promise to the letter. The four under secretaries-general were political appointments representing the Great Powers and were by their very nature a point of liaison with their home governments rather than effective administrators—and they often had little do. The two deputy secretaries-general were more a true part of the Secretariat. Avenol had been a staff member since the early years of the League. Azcárate had been an efficient Director of the Minorities Section. With the withdrawal of Italy, Pilotti soon retired and was replaced by the British official Francis Walters, who had also worked his way up in the hierarchy. Lester had been working with the Secretariat officials in various capacities since 1929.

When Lester actually took up his position, not only was it the first time a citizen of a genuinely small state joined the highest officials of the League but it was soon made clear that he was the senior Deputy Secretary-General. At a meeting of the Supervisory Commission in May 1937, Lester's friend, the Norwegian delegate Hambro, drew his attention to the fact that Pilotti's name appeared first on the budget list, remarking "but you are Avenol's second". Thus, during Avenol's absence, Lester would be in charge. While Avenol was bound by the Assembly's decisions, he confessed to having great difficulty dealing with Italy. This potential source of friction was, however, short lived because Italy withdrew from the League and Pilotti's place was taken by Walters, a close personal friend and neighbour of Lester's—he was also, like Lester, an angler. The hierarchical relationship between Avenol's and Lester's functions would take on its true importance in the summer of 1940.

Lester was to spend over three years as Deputy Secretary-General. Much of his work was trivial and insignificant due to the deteriorating world situation and the decline in the League's prestige itself, factors over which Lester had no control. Hambro joked that the members of the League wanted to hang on to all their privileges, but were ready to give up their principles.

Lester's post gave him responsibility for the League's general internal organization. This meant that when the League's machinery was functioning normally his work was unnecessary and when the machinery was functioning badly his work was unpleasant. His activities in 1937–1938 involved him in what were probably to him too many trivial duties. In April 1937, he took part in making the official League film, delivering the English version of Avenol's speech. In June he gave a party to which 750 guests had been invited. His life became a round of official receptions and dinners, acting as president of clubs, being a guest of honour, receiving important visitors, making speeches and unveiling statues. This obviously conflicted with his Protestant upbringing, since Lester observed: "This past two or three weeks we have averaged about four parties a day. Appalling."

Lester was also made head of liaison with member states, which gave some added significance to the position since for the first time a national from a small power was able to engage in political work from the vantage point of one of the principal officials, but by 1937 the extent of the League's political action had declined drastically and Lester's work remained primarily administrative.

Of the entire top seven officials in the Secretariat, Lester was the only one free from government pressures. Avenol was only too ready to adapt to British, French, German and Italian influence, and Walters, although a good international civil servant, was part of the system whereby the League was never supposed to discuss questions which would embarrass the United Kingdom or France. In fact, there were political advantages in this system: through these officials, Avenol could communicate rapidly with governments and they, in their turn, could make their governments' views known to him. If a country did not possess "its own" official in the hierarchy, it could be difficult for its views to be taken into consideration. Except on the matter of birth control, it was unlikely that Dublin would apply pressure on the League.

Although his position as second in the League hierarchy left him a free agent, Lester was often to find the work frustrating. Under Drummond the position had carried more dignity than actual responsibility. Azcárate had been put in charge of all internal administration while Pilotti had taken responsibility for the political side. This situation would have suited Lester well but for two circumstances. Firstly Azcárate had become ill during his term of office and two Secretariat officials had taken over most of his work. Lester on his arrival found little to do. Secondly, and more importantly, a growing friction between Avenol and Lester resulted in the latter being pushed aside or ignored in matters of importance, in particular on political issues, where Lester had considerable experience.

With the departure of Germany and Italy, the affairs of the League of Nations depended largely on the whims of the British and French Governments. The French Governments of the Third Republic were renowned for short periods in office and sudden collapses, while the British Governments suffered from unremitting indecision as they steered a tortuous course in pursuit of their "vital national interests", which were often short-sighted and not always moral. As a result, the small states asked themselves what purpose the League of Nations served when the Great Powers seemed determined to betray the Covenant and weaken the League. Chile and Venezuela announced their intention of quitting the League to save money. When the British Prime Minister Neville Chamberlain[1] insisted on treating Mussolini as a reliable ally, Lester's friend Anthony Eden, the British Foreign Secretary, resigned on 25 February 1938 and was replaced by Lord Halifax. Lester had a very high opinion of Anthony Eden. On the contrary, he had a very low opinion of Lord Halifax and this view would be reinforced in January 1939 when Halifax attended the League's Council meeting for just one day. Eden's resignation could be interpreted as yet another victory for the Axis powers as they extended their hegemony over Europe. The United Kingdom and France recognized Italian control of Ethiopia in April 1938 and people asked themselves: would the League's position be any different?

Lester named Chamberlain as "a short-sighted blunderer hastening to disaster" for his policy of appeasement. The first few months of 1937 had been devoid of Hitler's "surprises" as everyone waited for his next move. Nevertheless, Lester's suspicions were aroused when the Austrian Chancellor Schuschnigg[2] paid a visit to Mussolini in Venice and was told to "admit more nazis into his patriotic front government", which suggested that German interest lay in this direction. Germany was only willing to give a guarantee to the territorial integrity of Belgium and the Netherlands provided they ignored Article 16 of the League's Covenant—which mentioned "the free passage of troops"—so perhaps Hitler's ambitions lay in this direction too! Lester hoped that the Western powers would resist threats and blackmail by Germany and Italy and yield no further, but at this stage he was to be disappointed. On 8 November 1937 Japan joined Germany and Italy to form a tripartite Axis, another step towards war.

Up until this time, the senior officers of the German Army had represented a restraining influence on the Nazi Party, but with the resignation of eighteen generals in February 1938 this control evaporated. The nazi extremists now took over complete control of the German Government and its policies. The Foreign Minister von Neurath resigned and was replaced with von Ribbentrop, a dedicated nazi disciple described as "pompous, conceited and not too intelligent" and "aping Herr Hitler at his worst". At this point Hitler summoned the Austrian Chancellor and, treating him like a wayward domestic servant, ordered Schussnigg to admit nazis into his government.

This was obviously a prelude to the disappearance of Austria, which took place predictably on 12 March 1938—another member state gone. When the British and French Ambassadors to Berlin requested further information about this event, they were told that it was none of their business. Even the Italians, the so-called allies of Germany, realised with apprehension that the German frontier now lay in northern Italy. At last, the Poles began to feel anxious about German ambitions in Danzig—and not only Danzig. To people like Lester, it was obvious that Czechoslovakia was also on Hitler's list of annexations. When Germany starting amassing troops on the Czech border in May, the British began to make arrangements to evacuate their embassy in Berlin—and calm returned momentarily.

Nevertheless, the Czechoslovak crisis came back with a vengeance in September 1938. Hitler had created a huge army of 1.5 million men and placed troops on the German/Czech border near the Sudeten area where there was a majority of German-speakers. Since the spring of 1938, Sudeten nazis led by Konrad Heinlein[3] had been agitating for autonomy, while an economic situation resulting in high unemployment had made nazism very popular in this region. British Prime Minister Neville Chamberlain met with Hitler in Berchtesgaden on 15 September and agreed to cede those areas of the Sudetenland with more than 50% of German speakers; three days later, French Prime Minister Édouard Daladier agreed to do the same thing. No Czechoslovak representative participated in these discussions. Lester knew that, at the Versailles Conference in 1919, the Czech leader Beneš had tried to persuade the Great Powers not to include the Sudetenland within the borders of Czechoslovakia due to the high number of German speakers. They had decided to do so with the intention of weakening Germany rather than aggrandizing the newly created country. A week after the first meeting with Hitler, the British Prime Minister flew back to Germany and it was no surprise to anyone familiar with nazi methods that the price had gone up. Hitler now demanded not only the annexation of the Sudetenland but the immediate military occupation of these territories. Since the Czechoslovak Army had prepared defences along the border with Germany, they had to abandon them without a fight and adapt to the new frontier. To achieve a solution, Italian dictator Mussolini suggested a conference of the major powers in Munich. On 29 September, Hitler, Daladier and Chamberlain met and, agreeing to Mussolini's proposal (actually prepared by Göring), signed the Munich Agreement allowing the immediate occupation of the Sudetenland by Germany. On 30 September, the Czechoslovak Government, which had not been involved in the talks, submitted and promised to abide by the agreement. It should further be noted that, rather than protesting or rushing to Czechoslovakia's aid, the Polish Government observed these events with misguided serenity. While Avenol was congratulating Chamberlain and Daladier in "vibrant terms" for what they had achieved in Munich, Lester wrote: "There is something indecent about this." It was evident that each successive concession to Hitler had not satisfied his appetite for conquest and undermined the position of the League of Nations. Lester also noted that his own daughter had begun to pronounce Chamberlain's name as "J'aime Berlin" [I like Berlin]. The Spanish delegate in Geneva observed that the League of Nations had been made "the laughing stock of the whole world." Six months later the Germans invaded the remainder of Czechoslovakia.

Europe now entered into a period when all that mattered was brute military force. As Winston Churchill pointed out: "We had the choice between war and dishonour. We chose dishonour but, even so, we will have the war." Hitler then made his infamous announcement that he had no more territorial ambitions in Europe—it seems extraordinary nowadays, but the Poles do not seem to have realised yet that they were next on his list. It was not until two months later that the Polish Government recognized its desperate situation and began to look upon the USSR as an ally. Lester wrote:

> What Chamberlain has done is a logical sequence of the policy pursued by Britain and France during the past two years; they paralysed the League of Nations; they gave no help to the weak attacked by the strong; they ran away every time a threat was uttered; now they have given Germany, for nothing but temporary peace, the fruits of a great campaign. . . . The Nazi and Fascist systems have made so great a victory that one wonders how long it may be before France, and even England, are forced to adopt something of their system and methods.

The nineteenth Assembly of the League of Nations—the central world agency for peaceful international co-operation based on law and justice—took place from 12 to 30 September 1938 in an anguished atmosphere of impending catastrophe. Neither the French nor the British Foreign Ministers attended. On the day it opened Hitler made a closing speech at the nazi rally in Nüremberg in which he described, in his own irrational way and not for the first time, his uncompromising attitude towards the Jewish race:

> When the question is still put to us why National Socialism fights with such fanaticism against the Jewish element in Germany, why it pressed and still presses for its removal, then the answer can only be: Because National Socialism desires to establish a true community of the people . . . Because we are National Socialists we can never suffer an alien race which has nothing to do with us to claim the leadership of our working people. Because we are socialists we cannot tolerate an alien race dominating us . . . We are fighting the Jews so fanatically because National-Socialism wants to create a true unity of the nations.

The Assembly ended on the day after the Munich Agreement. As the delegates tried to hold their discussions and the journalists attempted to write their reports, an air of panic ran through the corridors of the Palais des Nations—war was coming! Instead of achieving important international agreements on the advance of civilization, the delegates rushed out of the committee rooms with anxious faces desperate to learn the latest news. All attempts at peaceful negotiation were swept aside by the triumph of violence over law, which had crippled any constructive work that the League could do. By November 1938 the nazi machine was running amok with the destruction of synagogues, the seizing of Jewish assets and the sacking of church property. The concentration of power into the hands of a few fanatics had overcome the apathy of those who believed in the humanizing and civilizing activities of the League.

Avenol had taken office four months after Japan had announced its withdrawal from the League, which was followed by Germany five months later and then Italy four years later. Avenol's biographer, James Barros, stressed his continual hope for the return of these states, which meant that he often cut short any discussion of their aggressive behaviour. For instance, in 1933 Avenol preferred to avoid League political action in Manchuria, which Japan had invaded in 1931. When Italy invaded Ethiopia in 1935, he attempted to maintain Italian membership by recognizing some of Mussolini's claims and opposing Ethiopia's right to attend meetings as a member state. Behind the scenes, he worked against the sanctions the League had imposed on Italy. However, Avenol had been frustrated because eventually Italy renounced its membership. With regard to Jewish refugees fleeing nazi Germany, Avenol resisted efforts to make the League responsible for intergovernmental action on their behalf. When Germany annexed Austria in 1938 Avenol simply removed Austria's name from the list of member states. Germany's invasion of Poland and the commandeering of the home of the League's High Commissioner Burckhardt in Danzig in 1939 did not lead to any expression of outrage from Geneva. Avenol's actions thus diminished the role of the Secretary-General and weakened the organization as a bulwark of collective security. Avenol's disguised sympathy for the totalitarian regimes remained unknown to the public at large at the time. To be fair, it should be said that, in pursuing these policies, Avenol was not alone in the League of Nations. Many other leading political figures—Stanley Bruce of Australia,[4] for example—realised that the League had absolutely no power of coercion and it was necessary to steer a course between the desirable and the feasible.

The League's salvation was believed to lie in technical activities. Thus, at the nineteenth Assembly, since the League's role in the political domain seemed to be at an end, the delegates turned their attention to its technical activities in the field of justice, economics, finance, public health, nutrition and housing. There was plenty to do. The League's staff consisted of a number of acknowledged experts in the economic domain who were well placed to gather data, co-ordinate inter-governmental co-operation and develop new socio-economic policies. In the financial domain it was necessary to reach international agreements on agricultural and industrial credits, the fluctuation in the balance of payments and the principles of fiscal regulation. The delegates accepted the League's role in carrying out studies on demographic problems, deforestation and soil erosion, and the standard of living. There were social questions associated with poverty demanding attention such as child welfare, the traffic in women, refugees, as well as penal and penitentiary problems, intellectual co-operation and the encouragement of cultural relations between countries. Furthermore, since its beginnings, the League had been involved in efforts to limit the opium trade. Finally, as the Second World War loomed on the horizon, the League represented a centre of international collaboration where morality and cooperation were still valued. In defence of the League's ideals, one of Lester's colleagues wrote:

> One who goes through this long record cannot but burn with indignation at the double fact, first, that [the League] is not more actively and courageously supported by those people who believe that this type of thing is the ideal for which civilization should be built, and second, that it is so completely thrown off balance by others who feel they seek to achieve their ends by violence. . . . the question in many minds is not whether the League method is right; it is rather as to how long it will be before the better, more positive, more constructive elements in human society wake up from their lethargy and demand that the rich opportunities which life has to offer be given full freedom of expression unhindered by relics of barbarism.

The Spanish Civil War was by this time causing considerable loss of life, with neither side gaining the upper hand. While the Republican Government was recognized by most member states as the legitimate regime and was being reinforced by the USSR, Germany and Italy were supporting Franco's Nationalists. Other European powers were trying to remain strictly neutral. The British Government, for instance, was pursuing policies associated with its immediate interests, while attempting to persuade Italy, Germany and the USSR to steer clear of Spanish affairs. Guided by the British and French Governments, Avenol's policy was to keep the League of Nations out of the Spanish conflict, while avoiding any resolution that would label Germany and Italy as aggressors. The outcome was a further decline in the League's prestige. France and the United Kingdom accepted Franco's victory and recognized his government in February 1939. The diplomatic community, including Lester, waited to see whether Franco would now be attracted by British and American money or by Italian and German fascism. Rather like Ireland and Switzerland, Spain succeeded in avoiding any involvement in the coming conflict.

Meanwhile, in the Far East a ferocious but undeclared war was taking place between China (a member State) and Japan (a non-member State), with

China handicapped by a lack of mechanical weapons. The military action undertaken by Japan could not be justified by law or self-defence, but in June 1938 Avenol refused to allow a Chinese Government film to be shown at the Palais des Nations—in case it offended Japanese sensibilities.

Soon after Lester's return to Geneva from Danzig in 1937 he was made Chairman of the Council's Committee on Technical Collaboration between the League and China. By this time some of the early impetus had slackened. Work had begun in 1929, mainly as a result of an earlier report by Dr Ludwik Rajchman on China's problems and future. It involved successful activities at a time when the League's prestige began to decline. The problem that concerned the League's technical departments directly was the spread of epidemics in China as a result of the war. Supervising the League's activities in China renewed Lester's contacts within the Health Department, with whom he had worked earlier as Council rapporteur, and with Rajchman, perhaps the most dynamic and inspiring member of the Secretariat, but a man whose left-wing political views were not appreciated by the hierarchy.

The policy of concentrating on non-political activity with the hope of winning back former members and increasing the United States' participation had begun to emerge in 1933. This process was accelerated by the political failures of 1935–1936 and received formal statement in the Bruce Report of 1939. This, though obviously of little importance at the time due to the outbreak of war, prepared the way for the complete administrative separation of technical and political activity—which is today a characteristic of the United Nations.

An unexpectedly positive note mentioned by Lester was that Éamon de Valera continued to put in an annual appearance in Geneva for the League's Assembly. In earlier years Lester had complained that, as President of the Executive Council of the Irish Free State, de Valera had often arrived in Geneva ignorant of foreign affairs. However, according to the new Irish Constitution of 29 December 1937, de Valera's position had automatically become that of *Taoiseach* [Prime Minister] with considerably more power, including the personal authority to dismiss ministers and to request a dissolution of the *Dáil* [Parliament]. Lester reported that he had been a very good President of the League's Assembly in 1938 and was highly regarded by the international community.

Lester's diary also makes clear that he maintained an awareness of Irish affairs and on Ireland's position in international life. After his return from Danzig, he was better able to keep in contact with Irish affairs, both through home visits and meeting Irish delegates in Geneva. Cremins, the Irish permanent delegate, had less scope than Lester since Ireland was no longer a member of the Council. He was, in any case, Lester thought, exceptionally cautious—"Cremins . . . is not really courageous". On 25 April 1938 the United Kingdom and Ireland signed an Anglo-Irish Agreement that brought an end to a trade war between the two countries. Among other concessions of material and political benefit to Ireland was the understanding that Irish ports would not be used for military purposes without the permission of the Irish Government. During the Second World War this permission was not granted to either side.

In June 1937, at the age of 48, Lester learned to drive a car. This meant that he was able to spend his weekends driving to different parts of the Swiss and French Alps, and walking with his family in the mountains. In August he spent a whole month with his family in Ireland. Nearly the entire time was consumed by fishing on the loughs in the west of the country and in the Atlantic Ocean. He learned that his name was being circulated in Dublin as a possible President of Ireland, but realised that as a Protestant this was never likely to happen. However, news of this rumour filtered through to the Senate in Danzig, who then realized with alarm that the man they had treated so badly when he was High Commissioner might soon become Head of the Irish State. Burckhardt, the new High Commissioner, told Lester not to disillusion the Danzigers!

In June 1938 the Lesters bought Ardagh Lodge near Clifden in County Galway on the west coast of Ireland; they would also purchase another house in Dublin. Since in Geneva there were visible signs of preparing for war—the mining of bridges and digging of tank traps—Lester began to consider what to do with his family if hostilities broke out. Ireland was obviously attractive as a refuge. It was decided that, in the event of war, attempting to drive by car from Geneva to Ireland was not a good idea since, even if they had been able to buy fuel, the car could easily be seized by the military and would probably have to be abandoned upon reaching the French coast. Therefore, it was better to make the journey by train. Unless Geneva itself was invaded, Lester would have to stay at his post, so it would be his wife and children who made the journey. The children's old governess would accompany them. They assembled clothing and food for the journey, withdrew a large sum of money in French and British currencies . . . and waited. Elsie, Lester's wife, said that upon reaching Ireland safely she would return to Geneva—although Lester himself had few illusions on the subject. One of Lester's colleagues, the Scotsman Alexander Loveday, who later became the Director of the Economic and Financial Organisation, announced theatrically that he would commit suicide rather than fall into German or Italian hands. Lester's plan was less dramatic—he would attempt to escape on foot—at which point Loveday said he might join him! Although there were signs of panic and confusion at their children's school, Lester and his wife decided not to share their concern about the international situation with their three daughters. However, the children saw Lester packing the family's valuables into boxes and immediately understood exactly what was going on.

Lester summed up 1939 as "a terrible year" and concluded "Munich now clearly a ghastly mistake". The Secretariat, though by now greatly reduced, was still able to carry on much of the routine work of the sections since communications with the outside world remained open. The League at this time may be compared to a ship battened down for a storm. What remained to be decided was the ship's destination and, as things turned out, who should be its captain. Could the League survive and, if so, where, and in what form? These were the issues in the early months of 1940, before the German attack on and rapid collapse of France, which was accompanied by a crisis concerning the leadership of the League that was not resolved until September.

NOTES

1. Arthur Neville Chamberlain (1869–1940) was a British Conservative politician; Prime Minister of the United Kingdom from May 1937 to May 1940. He is best known for signing of the Munich Agreement in 1938, which avoided war but did irreparable damage to his reputation.

2. Kurt Alois Josef Johann Schuschnigg (1897–1977). Chancellor of the First Austrian Republic, following the assassination of Dollfuss in July 1934, until the *Anschluss* in March 1938. He was arrested by the Germans and imprisoned in various concentration camps. Liberated by the Americans in 1945, he spent most of the rest of his life in academia in the United States.

3. Konrad Ernst Eduard Henlein (1898–1945) was a leading Sudeten German politician in Czechoslovakia. Upon the German occupation, he joined the Nazi Party and was appointed *Reichsstatthalter* of the Sudetenland in 1939. On 10 May 1945, while in American captivity in the barracks of Plzeň, he committed suicide by cutting his veins with his broken glasses.

4. Stanley Melbourne Bruce (1883–1967) was an Australian/British businessman, lawyer, prime minister of Australia (1923–1929) and statesman. He was wounded in the First World War at Gallipoli, winning the Military Cross and the Croix de Guerre avec Palme. President of the League of Nations Council in 1936. He was infamous for wearing spats.

Chapter Fifteen

War Begins, 1939

As early as 1937, the Foreign Office in London considered the League of Nations to be "defeatist and Avenol inadequate to the situation." It had already been mentioned in a report dating from April 1938 that Avenol might resign as Secretary-General and accept a diplomatic post from the French Government. Nevertheless, he had a ten-year contract with the League of Nations that was not due to expire until July 1943, so there he stayed.

However, changes were taking place in the League. The once non-political Secretariat was increasingly becoming divided into right- and left-wing factions. The right-wing elements consisted of those inclined to support the fascist states and who thought the Munich Agreement was an important diplomatic milestone. These were often staff members who were in close contact with and respected the instructions of their home governments. In contrast, the left-wingers, who included many of the longest serving and ablest members of the Secretariat, found themselves opposed to the right-wingers not because they were necessarily socialists but because the enemies of the League were so clearly on the right. As a group they were much less likely to be intimidated by outside pressure from Germany and Italy, who had reduced the League to virtual helplessness. The left-wing faction was led by Dr Ludwik Rajchman, the director of the League's Health Section. He was described as a man "with a revolutionary past, a sympathy for left-wing movements of all kinds, unwearying energy and extraordinary intelligence". He was particularly in charge of the technical assistance to the Kuomintang Government of China. At the same time, Japan—a non-member State—was putting pressure on Avenol to remove Rajchman on the pretext that he was going beyond his mandate of providing assistance to the Chinese and that his actions were harming Japan's interests. Growing awareness of Avenol's shortcomings and respect for Rajchman and others as efficient Secretariat officials inclined Lester towards the left-wingers—the group under pressure.

Secretary-General Avenol looked sympathetically on the Munich Agreement of September 1938 and regretted the departure of Germany and Italy from the League. Before he became Secretary-General, Avenol had supported Japan against China in the Manchurian Crisis, even though Japan was clearly attacking another helpless member state. Then, in the League's decisive test—when Italy invaded Ethiopia in 1935—his main concern was not to stop Mussolini's forces from attacking a harmless African member state but, rather, to maintain Italy's membership of the League at all costs as an ally of France against Germany. The British Foreign Secretary Anthony Eden recalled having to listen to Avenol going to great lengths in his speeches to excuse Mussolini's behaviour. Well before this, supposedly left-wing members of the Secretariat had been attacked by some sections of the French press and the British Foreign Office had made discrete inquiries about their political sympathies. For instance, for a year Avenol's chef de cabinet Marcel Hoden[1] had been a victim of attacks in the pro-fascist French press saying that he was "a Jew" and "a communist", which were the tedious ways of describing anyone who criticized fascism. They adopted this attitude because Hoden had dared to suggest that the moment had come to prepare for war as the only way to halt fascism. It was also stated that his conduct had given offence to the British and French Governments because he appeared to condemn the Munich Agreement as a terrible mistake. The time for a purge had come.

Following the nineteenth session of the Assembly of the League of Nations in September 1938, the first in a long series of clearly disturbing signs occurred in Avenol's conduct. In October he wrote a memorandum to his chef de cabinet. It described a number of incidents that had aroused Avenol's dissatisfaction during the Assembly and was, in fact, a letter of dismissal, but the message was so muddled that Hoden completely failed to grasp the point. Hoden, in reply, agreed that there had been misunderstandings and that the two men should meet to discuss their future relations. Avenol then sent a response making it quite clear that their collaboration was at an end and Hoden dismissed, but the chef de cabinet rose to defend himself. Hoden listed a number of situations when he had served the Secretary-General steadfastly and had often been thanked personally by Avenol for his devotion, vigilance and tact, but that recently he had not been kept up to date with the Secretary-General's intentions and decisions. Hoden emphasized that he remained faithful to the principles of the League's Covenant and had always given Avenol his sincere opinion in the defence of these ideals; it could be inferred that Avenol had not been as faithful to these ideals as Hoden. Furthermore, Hoden stated that many of the reproaches raised by Avenol were simply untrue. Here we have the first concrete evidence that Avenol was prepared to lie to justify his actions. It was as if there was external pressure on Avenol to dismiss Hoden coming from the French Government, particularly two politicians who had been involved in negotiating the Munich Agreement—Prime Minster Daladier and Foreign Minister Bonnet.[2] To counter this, Hoden now sent copies of his correspondence with Avenol to some of France's most eminent politicians: Léon Blum,[3] Édouard Herriot, Georges Mandel[4] and Paul Reynaud.[5] Hoden was, inevitably, dismissed. He was the first in a long line of officials who were sacked because their loyalty to the League came before obeying the instructions of their governments or, indeed, those of the Secretary-General.

Over the next few days the American consulate in Geneva reported that another fifty or sixty officials were dismissed. The reason given was the need for economy and reorganization of the Secretariat, although Avenol told the Americans that London and Paris were putting pressure on him to "purge" the Secretariat of those staff members who had leftist leanings and had protested about British and French submissiveness towards the dictatorships. It was even stated in the American consulate report that Berlin and Rome had provided a list of League officials whom they wished to see removed from their functions. The report ends with the extraordinary statement that the League was doing this in order "to pave the way for the return of Germany and Italy". There is no evidence that any of Avenol's justifications were true, but that in removing staff members not to his liking he was merely attempting for his own motives to satisfy the British, French, German and Italian Governments. Untruthfulness was to become a tiresomely familiar trait in the coming years.

The 1938 Assembly had called for economies, since membership was decreasing and contributions slow to come in. There was no doubt that the decline in membership had resulted in less revenue, which could have been overcome by increased contributions—but there was sure to be resistance to such a measure on the part of member states. It was clear then that there must a reduction in the League's expenditure and that could only be achieved by letting staff go. Throughout 1939 the staff was drastically reduced so that by the end of the year the work was done. Lester noted that he was "much overworked in November and December 1939 with the Axe Committee cutting down staff, mobilized men problems, etc. We have reduced comparing 1 January 1939 with 1 January 1940 by 50% on staff. Over 300 have gone—a dreadful business." Lester's responsibility for cutting down staff had involved him in an almost impossible situation. His simplicity, humanity and fairness did something to alleviate the situation—a point borne out by several letters from departing officials. There was at the same time also a series of farewells to departing permanent delegates.

The task of dismissing Rajchman fell to Lester. The reduction in staff members was designed to diminish expenditure, and the fact that these people belonged to a particular faction could easily be camouflaged. On the particular case of Rajchman, Lord Halifax, the British Foreign Secretary, explained that, despite his remarkable contribution to the League's technical activities, he had contributed to Poland's negative attitude towards the League. In view of the Polish Government's enthusiastic efforts to circumvent the High Commissioner during the Danzig crisis and to undermine the League's authority, it is difficult to imagine how Rajchman could have possibly made the situation worse. Since taking up his functions in Geneva, Lester had spent some time trying to establish good relations between Avenol and Rajchman, but had come to the conclusion that "the same house cannot hold both". Avenol felt strongly that Rajchman and his closest colleagues had to go and was pleased to count upon the support of the British Government in this manoeuvre.

Given Rajchman's subsequent career, he had no reason to be disappointed by his dismissal. His services had been deeply appreciated by the Chinese Government, who now appointed him as advisor to the Bank of China and special representative of China to the United States. When the United Nations Relief and Rehabilitation Administration (UNRRA) was established in 1943 to bring assistance to war-ravaged countries, Rajchman advised it on health matters. After the Second World War it was decided to liquidate UNRRA, but several million children remained without aid. With the support of Herbert Hoover, Rajchman helped to found the United Nations International Children's Emergency Fund (UNICEF) on 11 December 1946. He was appointed its first chairman and established the fund's primary activities: the distribution of antibiotics (especially against syphilis); DDT (against typhus); the production and distribution of powdered milk; and a BCG immunization campaign (against tuberculosis). As the Cold War intensified in the 1950s, Rajchman was suspected at the same time of being a pro-American agent by the Eastern-bloc communists and of being a communist spy by the McCarthyists in the United States! In 1957, he left the United States hastily and settled permanently in France. During the period 1950–1965 he co-founded the International Children's Center (ICC) in Paris with Robert Debré,[6] being appointed by France a *Commandeur de la Légion d'Honneur*. When he died in 1965 at Chenu (Sarthe, France), Jean Monnet and Robert Debré were the speakers at his funeral.

After the departure of Italy, the Englishman Francis Walters had replaced Massimo Pilotti as the second Deputy Secretary-General. Walters had returned to Geneva from London in January 1939 and told Lester that the British Government was expecting "a fresh and this time probably fatal crisis" within a few weeks provoked by either Hitler or Mussolini that would be the trigger for the next war. Avenol, on the contrary, felt that public opinion in Germany and Italy might restrain Hitler and Mussolini from undertaking any further desperate gambles. In this respect he was soon to be proved wrong when German troops occupied the remainder of Czechoslovakia on 16 March. Since Hitler had sworn to respect the territorial integrity of Czechoslovakia, it was obvious that he was unlikely to feel any further restraint in attacking neighbouring countries. A British politician called him "A traitor thrice perjured"; he was, unfortunately, also dictator of the German state. Germany now issued threats and ultimatums in the direction of Romania where there were oil wells. A few days later Romania signed a trade treaty granting Germany a monopoly on its petrol production. Not only Romania, but Hungary as well, had become a vassal state of Germany.

As tensions in Europe continued to grow, it was expected that Germany would make a move against Lithuania. Thus, on 20 March, German Foreign Minister von Ribbentrop delivered an ultimatum to the Lithuanian Foreign Minister demanding the surrender of the town of Memel (Klaipėda in Lithuanian). Memel had the finest harbour on the Baltic and had been detached from Germany by the Treaty of Versailles. Lithuania, unable to secure international support for its cause, submitted to the ultimatum and, in exchange for the right to use the new harbour facilities as a free port, ceded the disputed region to Germany two days later. Lester described Memel as "dirty and insignificant as an Irish provincial town." Hitler personally visited the harbour and delivered a speech to the city's residents. This was Hitler's last territorial acquisition prior to the Second World War. The significance of Memel was that it controlled the mouth of Poland's second river, the Niemen, in the same way that Danzig controlled the Vistula. It was at this point that Lester made the ominous remark: "The pincers close on Poland." Given Hitler's successes, Mussolini was desperate to share in the fruits of victory. A month later Mussolini invaded Albania and Lester noted gloomily in his dairy: "Another League member has gone."

One of Lester's early acquaintances in Danzig, Herman Rauschning, had written a book entitled *Hitler Speaks* which became a best seller. The book was a record of conversations that the author had had with Adolf Hitler in the early 1930s, when the dictator had been very candid with his acquaintances about his true ambitions. Rauschning had broken with the Danzig nazis in November 1934. He wrote that Hitler's objective was total world domination to achieve which he would "shrink from no crime" including "mass exterminations" and "bacteriological warfare".[7] Lester described the book as "Shocking. If I didn't know [Rauschning] for a solid, reliable man I'd suspect exaggeration and propaganda." Switzerland banned the book, while German delegations throughout Europe rushed to purchase all the copies they could before the public could buy them—but Lester believed that "nearly everyone has already read it".[8]

The British Government had launched a vast scheme to manufacture armaments and increase the strength of its armed forces, which was likely to result in British politicians adopting a firmer tone with Hitler and Mussolini.

It brought a certain measure of relief that the British Prime Minister, Neville Chamberlain, stated categorically that Britain and France would stand together, while any attempt to dominate the world by force would be resisted by the United Kingdom "to the utmost of her power". Despite Avenol's opinion that it was a diplomatic masterstroke, the Munich Agreement was now considered null and void. It had completely destroyed Chamberlain's reputation, but now he began to criticize the League of Nations, which Lester said, given British policy over the previous decade, was "unfair and unfriendly" and he hoped that Chamberlain would have an opportunity "to eat some of his hard words". In March Hitler announced his "generous offer" to guarantee Poland's frontiers in return for Danzig and a route to East Prussia. Given the location of the Polish port of Gdynia to the north of Danzig, this would obviously create more problems than it solved. On 31 March 1939 Chamberlain announced that the French and British Governments would guarantee the independence of Poland, Greece and Romania. European politicians now turned towards Stalin's USSR as a possible ally that might halt Hitler's ambitions, but on 23 August there was a bolt from the blue in the signing of the Ribbentrop-Molotov Non-Aggression Pact between Germany and the USSR, thus weakening Poland's position—the last piece was now in place for the beginning of the Second World War. During August 1939, the French and British Governments repeatedly stated that they would stand by the defence of Poland, while the Polish Government declared that it was not prepared to enter into negotiations with Germany while being menaced.

The period from April to August 1939 was a time of psychological turmoil for Lester during which he abandoned his diary. Beyond the criminal folly of Hitler's march towards a European war, he disagreed with Avenol about how the League of Nations should be prepared for a period of conflict. Relations between the two men broke down and for two-and-a-half months they had no contact. In August, Lester's wife and children had gone on holiday to the South of France while he went fishing with some friends in Connemara ("the worst season for many years"). He was later joined by his family in western Ireland. When he learned of the signing of the Ribbentrop-Molotov Pact, Lester rushed back to Geneva and he and Avenol started speaking to each other again. By September, Lester reported that, despite petrol rationing, he was cruising on Lake Geneva seated comfortably in the stern of Avenol's luxury motorboat.

With great foresight, Lester had purchased Fairfield House in Dublin and had moved the majority of his possessions there where his family now resided. He lived alone in Geneva on the rue des Contamines with his dog "Bully", having laid in provisions for a long war and purchased "a good pair of boots".

Brushing aside any principles of human morality or pretence at negotiation, Hitler's forces invaded Poland without declaring war on 1 September

1939. The Second World War began two days later when the United Kingdom and France declared war on Germany as a result of its invasion of Poland. When the United Kingdom and France sent in notifications of their declarations of war, they pointedly did not invoke the Covenant of the League of Nations—Part I of the Treaty of Versailles. Instead, they cited the Kellogg-Briand Pact, a 1928 treaty renouncing war that had been signed or ratified by every world power and almost all independent nations. According to their recent guarantees to Poland, the two allies had announced quite clearly that they would carry out their pledges if that country were attacked. Lester observed that Hitler's motives "appeared to have no relevance to any considerations that move civilized governments when they handle matters on which the lives of millions hang." The paradox was that the solid and sober German people had fallen into the hands of a "clique of febrile and hysterical rhetoricians".

Although he expressed sympathy and admiration for the Polish people, Lester believed that the Polish Government had been very short-sighted in trying to play the role of a Great Power during the 1930s. Above all, Poland had stood aside cynically while Czechoslovakia was dismembered. Poland—and particularly the "too clever Beck"—had played a major role in its own destruction by crudely supporting Germany's efforts to bring down the League of Nations, and behaving in a manner likely to lose the support of friendly nations. It had seemed obvious to everyone except the Poles that their turn would come. One of Lester's correspondents later remarked: "Your friends the Poles certainly made a mess of their affairs. If only they and the Czechs could have worked together." On 17 September the USSR invaded Poland from the east. On the same day, Lester noted that the Netherlands would be next. "The nazis must be beaten if there is to be any decency in such life and civilisation as may survive."

His opinion about his own country was that, in contrast to 1914 when Ireland considered itself to be occupied by the British, it was now an independent country and that its national interest lay in the victory of the United Kingdom and its allies. Nevertheless, Ireland would remain strictly neutral throughout the war. Due to its neutrality, the Irish economy would suffer terrible shortages during wartime—wheat (and therefore bread), steel, coal, petrol and paraffin—resulting in unemployment. A very peculiar situation could have arisen with the appointment of the Irish ambassador to Berlin since the official letters of credence were still issued by King George VI of the United Kingdom, who would be obliged to address Adolf Hitler as "his beloved cousin". During the war the Irish Government attempted to appoint an ambassador to the Holy See in Rome without the signature of the British king, but the Pope rejected his credentials. His opinion was that, since both Ireland and the Holy See were neutral, there was no reason why they should not respect the proper protocols, i.e. bearing the signature of George VI.

Throughout the 1930s, the Great Powers had failed to use the League of Nations in the way it had been intended and had failed to appreciate the ambitions of the nazi abomination. In any event, Secretary-General Avenol thought that Article 16 of the Covenant of the League of Nations—"Should any Member of the League resort to war in disregard of its covenants . . . it shall ipso facto be deemed to have committed an act of war against all other Members of the League"—must either be abolished or made more binding. He thought that the League was "politically dead" and any action it took in this sphere potentially disastrous. In the event of war, he had even contemplated closing down the Secretariat. Both Avenol and the Assembly had reached the conclusion that the League should concentrate on its technical activities. In January 1939 Avenol had already disclosed plans for the reduction of the League's nine directorships to three in order to focus on these activities. However, Carlos Pardo,[9] an Argentine member of the League's Supervisory Commission, pointed out that the United States was playing an increasingly active role in technical activities and, while its financial contribution to the League was practically nil, it would tend to dominate these activities.

At the same time, signs of indecision on the part of Avenol became more frequent. Avenol agreed that the League's Treasurer, the South African Seymour Jacklin, would send duplicates of the League's accounts to what was considered a safe haven in France. Lester's opinion was that Avenol had only agreed to do this because he had observed the International Labour Organisation doing the same thing under the guidance of Irishman Edward Phelan, its deputy director. Avenol and Phelan were neighbours with residences and boats on the Lake of Geneva. Avenol stated that, in the event of war he would evacuate the League from Swiss soil, believing that the Axis powers might use its presence there as a pretext for invading Switzerland. The idea was to make a preliminary move to a safe town somewhere in central France before seeking a permanent home for the League in a neutral country. Fatefully, Avenol's choice of refuge for the initial move was the spa town of Vichy.

The most important unit in any move was the Economic and Financial Organisation (EFO), which would not be able to continue its activities in an unsafe environment with poor communications. Now that war had been declared, should the League stay in Geneva? What was the purpose of an organization devoted to peace during a time of war? In the spring of 1939, Avenol had already suggested that the staff of the EFO might be transferred to the United States, which is an extraordinary statement when compared with his own actions in the summer of 1940.

Once the plans for evacuation existed, Avenol turned his attention to a thorough reorganization of the Secretariat, particularly its technical activities. In May 1939 a committee was formed to "suggest any new solutions or procedures" under the chairmanship of the Australian representative to the League, Stanley Bruce. In fact, there were two Bruce reports, but the one that concerns us here is *The Development of International Co-operation in Economic and Social Affairs* published on 22 August 1939. After a review of past economic and social activities largely prepared by Loveday, the Bruce Committee recommended the establishment of a Central Committee for Economic and Social Questions, a non-political organization entirely separate from the League's Council. Given the League's political inertia, the Bruce Report argued that its survival depended upon the humanitarian dimension of its activities and making economic and social work its primary mission. The League should abandon attempts to resolve political problems such as peace and disarmament, although the report did not propose to abolish the Council and the Assembly. If the valuable technical units could be salvaged and separated from the League's political role, more countries might feel tempted to join and, more importantly, participate financially. In 1938, President Roosevelt had even hinted that, if the League disbanded the Council and concentrated on non-political questions, the United States might join an independent Economic and Financial Organisation. Such an arrangement would parallel that of its membership of the ILO.[10]

The procedure for adopting the Bruce Report caused great apprehension because it would require a unanimous vote at the League's annual Assembly meeting towards the end of 1939. Avenol was particularly nervous about the way the USSR would vote. Unknown to the Secretary-General and, no doubt, to Bruce himself, the recommendations of the Bruce Report were to have far-reaching consequences and would be fundamental in the founding of the United Nations after the Second World War. Lester noted that the international community and the International Court of Justice needed a "policeman" to enforce their judgements and declarations.

If Avenol could be accused of adroitness, it was in avoiding issues. When he was informed that Italy had invaded Albania in April 1939, rather than bringing the matter to the attention of the Council, he waited one day and was informed that Albania had withdrawn from the League. When Germany took possession of Austria and the rump of Czechoslovakia, neither France nor the United Kingdom reacted, so neither did Avenol. However, when Hungary occupied the Czechoslovak region of Ruthenia—which bordered on the USSR—the Russians provided their support to the Czechs, so the Council was obliged to discuss the matter at its meeting in September 1939, where the USSR held the chair. While occupying this important post, the USSR invaded Finland and at last there were expressions of indignation within the Secretariat leading to an examination of Russia's membership by an extraordinary session of the Assembly on 14 December 1939. The question of unanimity on the Bruce Report was quickly solved by expelling the USSR. Politicians present at this Assembly were intrigued by the fact that the move to expel the USSR was being expedited with extraordinary vigour and wondered where the pressure was coming from. Was it Whitehall or the Quai d'Orsay? It eventually became clear that it was Avenol himself who was determined to eject the USSR ignominiously from the League. Given the energy, skill and swiftness with which Avenol acted on this occasion, one can only wonder at the way he had dragged his feet over Danzig, Manchuria, Ethiopia, the Rhineland, Czechoslovakia, Memel and Albania. Was the crime of the USSR greater than those of Germany, Italy or Japan? Or was it simply a way of helping Finland? The Assembly had adopted a number of recommendations requesting member states to come to the assistance of Finland by providing aid. During January and February 1940, Avenol persistently obstructed the efforts of staff members Aghnides, Walters and Vigier to apply these resolutions in favour of Finland. Unable to understand Avenol's attitude, Lester concluded: "Finland mattered nothing to him. Did the League?" The Assembly would not meet again until 1946.

The British Foreign Office described Avenol as incompetent and incapable of taking a decision. If he did take a decision, it was the wrong one and further diminished the League. For example, the action of expelling the USSR would ultimately prove to have been hasty and ruinous—the last nail in the League's coffin. Negotiations were already taking place between Finland and the USSR over the possibility of exchanging territory which was acceptable to both parties. And by the summer of 1941 the USSR had become an ally of the United Kingdom and the United States.

At the end of 1939, it was Lester's job to dismiss the last remaining Soviet staff member—Under Secretary-General Vladimir Sokoline.[11] Rather than returning to the USSR—where an uncertain fate awaited him—Sokoline wanted to stay in Geneva and participate in the League's activities in one capacity or another. Lester described him as "clever, intellectual, cultivated and agreeable"—but he had to go.

For Christmas 1939, Lester, suffering from tonsillitis, travelled the long cold journey home across France and England to Ireland by train and ferry with an Irish colleague from the League, William Hill. It was wartime and all towns imposed the blackout, particularly London which Lester describes as "a nightmare cavern . . . exceedingly depressing". The family decided to spend Christmas at their house on the Atlantic coast, but Ireland was covered in freezing fog and the cross-country journey from Dublin by car turned into an ordeal. On his return journey to Geneva, Lester stopped in London for an impromptu meeting with Anthony Eden at the Dominions Office. At the beginning of 1940 he arrived at a Palais des Nations where, as elsewhere in Europe, people waited uneasily for the Phoney War to become real. He did not recover from his illness until some ten days after his return to Geneva. He would not see Ireland again until the end of 1944.

NOTES

1. Marcel Désiré Hoden (1888–1963) was a member of the Secretariat of the League of Nations from 1921 until 1938, ending as Chef de Cabinet to the Secretary-General. Subsequently authored numerous books about international affairs.

2. Georges-Étienne Bonnet (1889–1973) was a French politician and leading figure in the Radical Party. Bonnet was appointed Foreign Minister in 1938 and firmly opposed taking military action against German expansion, preferring to follow a course of appeasement.

3. André Léon Blum (1872–1950) was a French politician of Jewish origin who was three times briefly Prime Minister. When the Germans occupied France in 1940, he escaped but was arrested by the French authorities and put on trial for treason. His trial was such an embarrassment to the Vichy regime that the Germans stopped it. He was imprisoned in Germany until 1945.

4. Georges Mandel (1885–1944) was a French journalist, politician and French Resistance leader of Jewish origins. He was arrested in 1941 in Morocco on the orders of Pierre Laval and sentenced to life imprisonment. Churchill tried unsuccessfully to rescue him. He was then transferred to a German prison and later shot by French Milice loyal to Vichy. Laval was ultimately executed for his murder.

5. Paul Reynaud (1878–1966) was a French politician and lawyer prominent in the interwar period, noted for his stances on economic liberalism and militant opposition to Germany. He was the penultimate Prime Minister of the Third French Republic.

6. Robert Debré (1882–1978) was a French doctor who gave his name to the most important paediatric hospital in Paris. He is the father and grandfather of French Government ministers. In 1946, he wrote with Paul Rohmer *Traité de Pathologie Infantile,* a reference manual for paediatricians.

7. McNamara, P. *Sean Lester, Poland and the Nazi takeover of Danzig,* p. 110. Dublin/Portland, OR: Irish Academic Press, 2009.

8. In 1983, the authenticity of the discussions Rauschning claims to have had with Hitler was challenged by Swiss researcher Wolfgang Hänel. While the book cannot be regarded as a verbatim account, it is nowadays considered as an accurate guide to Hitler's ambitions from someone who conversed with him.

9. Carlos Alberto Pardo (1898–1976), Secretary-General of the Argentine Permanent Delegation to the League of Nations. Subsequently ambassador to Belgium and Luxembourg.

10. Clavin, P. *Securing the World Economy,* pp. 231–58. Oxford, UK: Oxford University Press, 2013.

11. Vladimir Sokoline (1896–1984) was born in Geneva of Russian Jewish parents, both doctors. He fought in the First World War in the Russian Army and was wounded. After taking part in the Russian Revolution, he gravitated towards diplomacy. After various postings, he was appointed Under Secretary-General to the League until 1939. Lived in Geneva as a Russian teacher.

Chapter Sixteen

The Summer of 1940

The German invasion of Western Europe began on Friday, 10 May 1940 with the attack on the Netherlands, Belgium and Luxembourg. The Germans rapidly penetrated the Allied lines by a surprise attack through the Ardennes and by 17 June the French were asking for an armistice. The rapid collapse of France seemed incredible since it was, with the United Kingdom, one of the Great Powers that dominated the League of Nations. These events initiated a series of crises in the Palais des Nations in Geneva which affected the leadership, personnel and future structure of the organization. The outbreak of the Second World War itself in September 1939 had already led to further staff reductions to the point that people, like Lord Robert Cecil, who had played a key role in founding the League, feared that its activities were being crippled.

There had been a 20% reduction of staff in 1938 supervised by Lester, but on 1 January 1939 there were still nearly 700 people of all categories employed by the League, the International Labour Organization (ILO) and the Permanent Court of International Justice in The Hague. Upon the declaration of the Second World War in September 1939 120 people of different nationalities had resigned, but some of them were replaced. The Assembly meeting on 14 December 1939 decided on measures to deal with a number of urgent problems, among which was the need for further staff reductions. The delegates proposed two alternatives: staff could either resign or be suspended. Those who resigned would receive one year's salary payable in four annual instalments. This last measure allowed the League to spread compensation over a four-year period, thus avoiding a major financial melt-down in 1940. These exceptional measures obviously did not correspond to the terms of people's contracts and thirteen staff members appealed to the Administrative Tribunal for non-respect of the staff rules. Due to the wartime situation, these appeals were never dealt with.

Through these measures the number of staff of the League and the ILO was reduced from 511 on 1 January 1940 to 320 by April. This was far from the end, since between May and December another 212 people left the organization bringing the total down to 108, about 15% of what it had been at the beginning of 1939. By the end of 1942 the figure of 99 would be reached, but this was the nadir since it was observed that some units could no longer function and some former staff members had to be re-recruited. Annual expenditure on salaries dropped from nearly 8 million Swiss francs in 1939 to 1.3 million in 1942. From 1943 staff numbers increased modestly reaching 128 by September 1945.

Sometime in the middle of April 1940, Lester had tried to persuade Secretary-General Avenol to create contingency plans for a possible evacuation of the Palais des Nations. With the combined Secretariats of the League of Nations and the ILO, there were still several hundred officials living and working in Geneva at that moment. Avenol dismissed the proposal nonchalantly, saying that Lester was suffering from an attack of "funk" and that everything was ready for an emergency. Lester replied that nothing was ready, to which Avenol's answer was: "We will share the same fate as the Swiss people." Lester decided that, having attempted vainly to raise the matter, his responsibility was at an end.

When the German Army invaded in May, Western Europe was seized with panic. In Switzerland, troops were mobilized, the stock exchange closed, people withdrew their money from the banks and the population of the city of Basle began to flee. With Germany's forces on its northern frontier, it was expected that Switzerland would be invaded on the night of 15–16 May either by parachutists or by a mysterious "Fifth Column". The Geneva authorities anticipated seaplanes landing on the lake and taxi-ing up to the city laden with heavily armed soldiers.

The Secretary-General then made plans to transfer a limited number of officials to a place of safety to act as a nucleus around which the League's responsibilities could be rebuilt. On 14 May, to Lester's surprise, there was a change of strategy. The Swiss Government invited the League of Nations to leave the country, so Avenol ordered procedures to be drawn up for immediate evacuation. Avenol added callously that he would not accept any responsibility for the safety of people's families. This statement set off a wave of alarm in all those staff members with families who immediately abandoned their posts so as to make arrangements to send their wives/husbands and children to safety. Avenol was angry about their absence and made the insensitive remark that families should be ignored! It was exactly these circumstances that led Neville Shute to write his best-selling novel *The Pied Piper*, first published in 1942.

From now on a rupture appears between what the Secretary-General wanted to do and what his colleagues considered prudent. Furthermore, he continually changed his instructions. Writing to a colleague, Lester observed: "I am unable to forecast policy here and in some respects I may confide it has changed with extreme rapidity." All secret documents and some of Avenol's personal effects, together with the luggage of some staff members, were temporarily sent to the French spa town of Vichy, but it was soon concluded that as a place of refuge it would be impossible for this town to accommodate the League's officials. Without telling any other members of staff, on 20 June Avenol sent the League's vehicles to fetch his personal affairs back. Later (22 June) some documents were brought back and—most unfortunately for future historians—a great many of them were burnt, particularly those concerning private conversations that the former Secretary-General Sir Eric Drummond had held with various individuals during his years in office. The reason behind the destruction of these documents was the expected invasion of Switzerland, a fate shared with Belgium, Denmark, France, Luxembourg, the Netherlands and Norway. If the Secretariat's files had been seized and examined by the nazis and their agents in Geneva, it was only too likely that the content of Sir Eric Drummond's conversations and other private correspondence would lead to a spate of arrests, deportations and assassinations. This is what happened following the nazi occupation of other neutral countries. An observation on page 440 of Lester's diary seems to indicate that he was involved in the destruction of these documents.

In fact, Avenol's vacillation reflected that of the Swiss authorities. As early as 1938 the Swiss had shown signs that the League's presence was an embarrassment and a threat to their neutrality. The League was, after all, closely associated with the enemies of Germany and Italy, Switzerland's immediate neighbours, and the Swiss Government was afraid that any conspicuous League activity could lead to military action by the Axis forces. On the other hand, they wanted to avoid forcing the League to leave suddenly, which might have set in motion a wave of panic in its own population signalling that a German invasion was imminent. As it became evident that the Germans were going to achieve a victory over France, Avenol began to think in terms of a future that corresponded to the military situation.

As for the Genevan authorities themselves, they let it be known that they found the presence of foreign diplomats on their soil a subject of unease. As the number of permanent delegations in Geneva declined, the city authorities also informed the League of Nations that if the organization ever left the Palais des Nations the premises would be taken over by the Canton of Geneva, which would then place the buildings at the disposition of any new body that corresponded to the present political situation in Europe. However, the League's Legal Department confirmed that this proposition was entirely erroneous. The League owned the buildings and grounds, having purchased the land outright in 1928 and paid for the construction which was completed in 1936.

As we know, Lester had already arranged for his wife and three daughters to remain in the comparative safety of Ireland where they had a car, a house in Dublin and a holiday residence on the remote Connemara coast. Lester's wife had come from Dublin to Geneva by train and ferry at the end of April for a short visit and decided to return to Ireland on 12 or 13 May. When the Lesters learned with great alarm that the German attack had taken place on 10 May and that there was the likelihood of being cut off in Geneva, his wife set off by train for Dieppe on the evening of Saturday, 11 May. Crossing France, the train was bombed and machine-gunned, but she reached London four days later—much to Lester's relief. His relief was short lived, however, when the thought crossed his mind that the German armed forces could easily invade undefended Ireland and establish a base for their aircraft and submarines as a way of attacking England on its unprotected western flank. With a regular force of only slightly over 7,000 men at the start of the war, and with limited supplies of modern weapons, the Irish Army would have been quickly overwhelmed by invasion from either side in the conflict. Although plans were drawn up for the invasion of Ireland—Operation Green—the German High Command came to the conclusion that the action would never succeed due to the strength of the British Navy. Furthermore, the whole purpose of the Second World War had been for the Germans to conquer "living space" in Eastern Europe, thus the invasion of Ireland and even the United Kingdom did not correspond to this ambition.

Lester was soon deprived of the assistance of the other Deputy Secretary-General, Frank Walters, who left for London on 28 May in spite of an annoyed letter from Avenol to the British Foreign Secretary saying he was needed in Geneva. Walters, who was Lester's next-door neighbour in Geneva, was hoping to obtain a post in the Foreign Office in Whitehall. Three days before his departure Walters came to see Lester as he was having a cup of morning coffee in bed and asked him what he was going to do. Lester explained to Walters: "I have spent the early part of my life working for what seemed a lost case and perhaps I was fated to spend my later years following another but . . . I [am] convinced my place lay here."

Secretary-General Avenol then conceived the idea that he was about to be kidnapped by the so-called "Fifth Column" and, to Lester's disgust, fled with his immediate staff to the French town of Nantua some 60 kilometres away. A few days later Avenol came back to Geneva but, rather than showing remorse for having deserted his post, declared his disapproval of Lester for letting a staff member with two small children leave in search of safety. At this point Lester was consumed by a burning anger and hit the table with his fist! He wrote to a colleague that he had two ambitions: to endeavour to retain his personal dignity and to attempt to look after the staff who had remained faithful to their posts. Among the Secretariat there was naturally great anxiety: people from occupied and unoccupied countries simply wanting to get home, others wanting to enlist in the armed forces, and others in a cruel dilemma.

Throughout the spring of 1940 it was clear that there was tension between Alex Loveday, the Head of the Economic and Financial Organisation, and Avenol about the future of the League. Furthermore, Avenol's behaviour became increasingly erratic and unpredictable, adding to the sentiment of demoralization and danger. On 14 June, the day the Germans marched into Paris, Avenol told Loveday, that he would resign, but then called in Under-Secretary-General Thanassis Aghnides[1] and announced: "That's it! It is done!" When Aghnides asked what Avenol meant, he was stunned by the Secretary-General's reply: "We must work hand-in-hand with Hitler in order to achieve the unity of Europe and expel England." Despite Hitler's and Mussolini's constant violation of international law, in the following weeks Avenol praised them and denounced the United Kingdom and the United States. He described "a new France, which was to be given a new soul to work in collaboration with Germany and Italy and keep the British out of Europe." He called the senior staff together and declared, to their astonishment, that he had discovered the virtues of Hitler and Mussolini. He had reached the bewildering conclusion that the German Chancellor's ambitions did not necessarily conflict with those of the League of Nations! With Europe under the military control of the Axis Powers, could Hitler see the League of Nations playing a role in creating a new European Confederation? Avenol made the unethical observation that "he did not yet know what Hitler and Mussolini would want as regards the League". Lester told Avenol that it was certainly not the League's task to anticipate such appalling scenarios on the part of non-member states. At this stage Lester was considering that the only solution for the League was "dissolution with dignity".

For some months Under-Secretary-General Aghnides had been ignored by Avenol but, to everyone's surprise, he now became the "court favourite". Avenol hinted vaguely that Aghnides was wanted for some kind of "new circumstance". Although Aghnides became Avenol's confidant, he remained loyal to Lester and Jacklin informing them of his increasingly absurd conversations with the Secretary-General.

As demoralization spread, Lester lost all respect for Avenol. When German troops reached the Swiss/French frontier about three kilometres from the Palais des Nations, Avenol announced solemnly his intention of remaining in Geneva. Lester almost burst into laughter as, in fact, he had very little choice! Avenol also declared pompously that it was important that the Secretary-General should not fall into German hands and that Lester should be prepared to take over if he (Avenol) had to go into hiding. Once again, Lester found this preposterous. After his adventures in Danzig, Lester's own fate if he were captured by the nazis can very easily be imagined.

A period of the deepest confusion followed. Avenol asked Aghnides and then the Argentine permanent delegate, Carlos Pardo, to make contact with the German consul-general in Geneva, Wolfgang Krauel;[2] both refused. He tried, again without success, to induce the Italian former Deputy Secretary-General, Pietro Stoppani, to establish a connection with Mussolini in Rome. Only a few weeks beforehand Avenol had been condemning Stoppani with extreme violence. Stoppani now found that he was in the presence of a born-again totalitarian who praised "the greatness of Herr Hitler". Avenol then made a hurried trip to Berne, where Lester and many of his colleagues were convinced he met the German and Italian ambassadors to offer to hand over the League to them, although Avenol later denied it. When Avenol first discussed this matter with Lester it resulted in some heated exchanges and the two men hardly spoke to each other ever again. Avenol asked for Lester's resignation, but the latter refused saying he would not be "used". Similarly, the League's Treasurer, Seymour Jacklin,[3] believed to be indispensable, was told that he was free to go whenever he wished, to which Jacklin replied that he would leave when his "job was finished" (i.e. never). Lester learned from Avenol's mistress, Vera Lever, that the Secretary-General intended replacing Jacklin with Charron who was, according to some, "of little more account than an office-boy". The German consul Krauel was not a nazi and was not contacted about Avenol's overtures at this stage. Lester described him later as a "humane" person.

Lester felt that, as Switzerland was now almost completely isolated, there was no reason for German troops to enter the country, but the problem of Swiss nervousness remained. On 16 July Avenol suggested that the League could make its presence less conspicuous by moving the remaining staff into the library wing of the Palais des Nations. He gave the clear impression that it was the Swiss authorities who had asked him to do this, but Édouard de Haller,[4] a Swiss member of staff, said that this was untrue and there had been no request of any kind from Berne. There did not seem to be any reason why Avenol felt obliged to lie in order to justify this perfectly reasonable proposal. It had now become a habit.

The first and most obvious difficulty for the organization to continue to function was the question of communications. With the German occupation of northern France and the Italian declaration of war on France and the United Kingdom on 10 June, Geneva's access to the outside world was limited to a complicated route through unoccupied southern France, across the Pyrenees to Spain and on to Portugal, which could at any moment be interrupted. Mail and telephone communications were equally affected. It was obviously impossible for committees to meet under these circumstances, while information, such as statistics, could not be collected. During these months a number of countries either withdrew from the League or, having been occupied, were no longer in a position to take part. Financial contributions declined sharply with the great bulk of finance now coming from the British Commonwealth.

One of the staff members who had already left Geneva was the American Arthur Sweetser,[5] former Director of the League's Public Information Section, who returned to New York by trans-Atlantic liner in May with his family. He was going to play a key role in the fate of the League of Nations in the coming months. Sweetser, a journalist who had covered the battlegrounds of the First World War and who subsequently became a staff member for the League of Nations, had been associated closely with the visionaries who sought peace among nations in 1919. Another recurring theme throughout his life was international education, most notably with the establishment of the International School of Geneva and the United Nations International School in New York. He believed that the ideals first promulgated by the League of Nations would take many generations to mature.

At the beginning of June 1940 Sweetser proposed that the League's technical units should be transferred to the United States so that they could avoid either isolation or dispersal, and continue to conduct their work in satisfactory conditions: first the Economic and Financial Organisation, then the Health Section, then particularly the Opium unit, and maybe others. He claimed that this was not, in fact, his own idea, but had rather originated with Winfield W. Riefler,[6] Professor of Economics and Politics in the Institute for Advanced Study at Princeton University. Nevertheless, it is clear from the correspondence that Sweetser had already discussed this matter with Loveday in Geneva before leaving. Other people, such as the British politicians Lord Halifax and R.A. Butler,[7] had been thinking along the same lines.

Sweetser had contacts with the Rockefeller Foundation and with the National Board of the League of Nations Association in New York, as well as with senior advisers to the government in Washington. He believed that a home could be found for the League's technical departments in the Institute for Advanced Study in New Jersey. Frank Aydelotte,[8] the Director of the Institute, was in favour of the proposition and so was the Director of the Rockefeller Institute for Medical Research. If the Institute or Princeton University itself extended an invitation to the League of Nations to transfer its technical departments and the Rockefeller Foundation provided the necessary material support, it would avoid the embarrassing situation of the government of a non-member state (i.e. the United States) issuing an official invitation. An invitation by the United States Government was unlikely since it would almost certainly involve consulting Congress during an election year.[9]

A request for the technical services of the League of Nations to come to the United States was drawn up by the Rockefeller Foundation, the Institute for Advanced Studies and Princeton University and shown to American Secretary of State Cordell Hull.[10] Hull had no objections and the invitation arrived in Geneva on 13 June signed by Harold W. Dodds,[11] President of Princeton University. The invitation could not have come at a worse time for Avenol as news of the fall of Paris came on the following day. It immediately resulted in a violent quarrel between Loveday and Avenol. As Loveday was to a certain extent behind the invitation, he felt very strongly that the technical units should be relocated where they would be most useful in gathering and distributing information—in the United States. Avenol said that he was opposed to the move to Princeton, and furthermore intended giving Loveday the sack in a general move to get rid of all British members of staff. Conversations with the Secretary-General now quickly deteriorated into shouting matches. He seemed to be thrown into the depths of despair and confusion, making a number of incoherent declarations to his assistant Aghnides. On 15 June Avenol replied to the Americans that he could not accept the invitation because it was not in his power to move the headquarters of the organization unless the initiative came from a member state. The invitation from Princeton had only mentioned the transfer of some technical units.

Aydelotte had given a copy of the invitation to his good friend the British Ambassador in Washington, Lord Lothian,[12] asking him to forward it to the Foreign Office in London. Two weeks later, on 27 June, the British Minister in Berne, David Kelly,[13] visited the Palais des Nations and informed the Secretary-General that the invitation from Princeton should be considered as an official proposition by the British Government and that it should be accepted. Avenol was strangely evasive in his replies to the British Minister for, having already replied negatively to the invitation, he was obliged to find a very good reason for having done so. Kelly said that, if Avenol had already turned down the invitation, he should revoke the refusal. In the minutes of the meeting it can be read that Avenol lied to Kelly: ". . . it could certainly not be said that he had refused the invitation." Avenol now expressed concern about legal difficulties over the status of international civil servants suggesting that the staff would not be able to carry out their work properly and independently in the United States. He stated that, to safeguard the international status of the League's officials, Washington had to authorize the invitation—not knowing that this was already the case. Kelly also raised questions about the way the British members of staff were being treated; once more Avenol prevaricated although, in his previous outbursts with Aghnides, he had declared that he was determined to remove all British members of staff from the organization as soon as possible.

The question of transferring offices to the United States also involved the International Labour Organization (ILO). At this time, the Director-General of the ILO was the American John Winant.[14] Despite both Lester and Phelan having misgivings about Winant's fitness for the post of Director-General, he would successfully transfer the entire organization to the other side of the Atlantic for the duration of the Second World War. This project was, in theory, facilitated by the fact that the United States was actually a member of the ILO and Winant was an American politician with contacts in Washington. On behalf of the ILO Winant appealed, without success, to the State Department for an invitation to the United States. After this refusal, the ILO did in fact move to Montreal, Canada, where it was accommodated at McGill University. Winant's foresight probably saved the organization and the lives of many ILO personnel whose home countries had been invaded by the German Army. One of the solutions envisaged by the League of Nations to save its technical units was to transfer them temporarily to the ILO during the move across the Atlantic, since it was believed that the ILO was more likely to succeed in this endeavour.

After the visit of Kelly, the British Minister, it was the American representative in Geneva, Harold H. Tittmann,[15] who tried to persuade Avenol to accept the Princeton invitation. During this meeting, the Secretary-General gave a completely different story saying that he had no intention of accepting the offer since it was merely an idea emanating from Arthur Sweetser (whom he didn't like). He repeated that he was concerned about the attitude of the State Department to the status of international civil servants in the United States. In any event, even if the State Department gave a satisfactory reply, he said that he would have to consult the member states. The situation changed when the Norwegian Government (i.e. Hambro) urged him to accept and reminded him that the British Government and its Dominions were also in favour of the transfer. Hambro added that sending some technical units to the United States was not the same thing as moving the headquarters of the organization to Princeton. He believed that the move was an effective way of keeping the League alive. David Kelly made a second trip to the Palais des Nations in company with the British consul-general in Geneva, Henry Livingston,[16] telling Avenol to withdraw his refusal, and requesting at the same time that there should be no further reductions in staff. If British members of staff lost their international status and then had to make a perilous journey back to the United Kingdom, they would be exposed to great risk. Throughout this interview, Avenol adopted an astonishingly hostile attitude to the British representatives, even though they embodied the only major power still a member of the League.

As respect for the maverick Avenol declined, Lester found himself assuming more and more responsibility and surrounding himself with colleagues who shared his ideals, such as Aghnides, Jacklin, Loveday, Renborg[17] and Skylstad,[18] as well as Phelan and Viple[19] of the ILO. On 17 July Lester wrote: "I am, I think, the core of the resistance."

During May, Lester had started to prepare a report proposing a reduced organization and budget for 1941, which would need to be approved by the League's Supervisory Commission. Jacklin, the League's Treasurer, had rejected it saying that there should be no illusions about 1941 as it would be impossible to pay the salaries of more than 130 staff—and probably less. Therefore, it was necessary to present the Supervisory Commission with a concrete plan establishing the likely income and the corresponding number of staff who could be paid. A meeting was held with the directors on 6 July to draw up lists for cutting down staff. When Lester suggested that a proper budget should be drawn up for 1941, Avenol quibbled saying it could not be done without a meeting of the Supervisory Commission—which was unlikely because he had no intention of preparing the budget or of communicating with Hambro, its chairman. At the time of this staff meeting, only one member of the Supervisory Commission had announced the likelihood of being able to attend. As Jacklin pointed out, if there was no approved budget for 1941, nobody would be able to spend any money or do any work. Lester's opinion was that they were not required to anticipate what would happen to the world in 1941 but rather simply to carry out their duty in ensuring the League's survival. The Supervisory Commission was, in the absence of the Assembly and the Council, the only alternative source of authority for the Secretary-General, but its members were now scattered. Sir Cecil Kisch,[20] the British member, was in London; Carl Hambro, the Norwegian Chairman, had just escaped to London and then gone to the United States; and the French (Boisanger), Belgian (Carton de Wiart), Dutch (Colijn), Finnish (Holma) and Argentine (Pardo) members were all likely to be faced with travel restrictions. League affairs, naturally enough, seemed unimportant in London locked in the Battle of Britain, while in Geneva there was an atmosphere of despair. The senior staff saw a meeting of the Supervisory Commission as the only way of stopping the deliberate destruction of the organization by its Secretary-General, and it was for this very same reason that Avenol wanted to avoid calling such a meeting.

During the latter half of June Lester had had a number of serious disputes with Avenol, particularly about the staff's safety. One day Avenol would lose his temper, the next day he would be polite and calm. Faced with the Secretary-General's temperamental storms, Lester wondered if he was "unbalanced" or that he was under the influence of some kind of "artificial aids". On 25 June Avenol summoned Lester to his office and declared angrily that the Princeton offer was a conspiracy concocted between Sweetser and Lester. While this was true of Sweetser and Loveday, Lester was in fact entirely blameless. After he had calmed Avenol down, Lester said his opinion was that the technical services could quite easily be moved to another country to avoid the risks of the war zone, while the political activities remained in Geneva. Several international economic experts, both on the League's staff and in the United States, felt that the Economic and Financial Organisation should be saved at all costs. The possibilities of being able to live and work in a suitable manner in Europe were disappearing fast. Meanwhile, the core of the Secretariat could stay in Geneva "to face physical dangers or discomforts". Lester also asked Avenol to send a message to the remaining British members of staff saying that he would try to get them out of Geneva with "every possible facility".

However, the memo that was distributed following this meeting was not at all what had been agreed, ending with "virtually an order to all members of the Secretariat to sign a formula of resignation"—this was without the agreement of Lester and the directors of sections. Avenol's idea was that the majority of officials should be asked to choose at once between suspension of their contracts and resignation. All those who did not resign immediately would not benefit from favourable terms of separation. Only a few staff members resigned, so that a new memorandum was issued on 4 July saying that, if people did not leave of their own accord, action would be taken within four days to dismiss them. Lester reminded Avenol that it was important to maintain the international character of the Secretariat. Avenol started dismissing staff who, in the opinion of his colleagues, included some of the best technical officers in the Drugs and Health Sections.

In the meantime, Avenol made discrete approaches to a number of individuals who were not hierarchical staff members but connected with the organization about the formation of a small committee of three—called a "Directoire"—that would take over the leadership of the League of Nations. The members of the Directoire would be Avenol, Treasurer Jacklin and a third person hand-picked by Avenol, meaning that Jacklin would be outvoted at every turn. With the move to dismiss staff and the formation of a Directoire, it was obvious that Avenol intended to reduce the League to a tiny core and create a situation where he could take decisions and spend money as he wished. In what was supposed to be a democratic institution he seemed about to assume dictatorial powers.

On 3 July the British Royal Navy had attacked and damaged several French warships moored at the naval base of Mers-el-Kébir on the coast of what was then French Algeria. The British Government, fearing that the French fleet would fall into German hands, was determined to put these ships out of action. The attack created much rancour between the United Kingdom and France, and seems to have turned the mind of Secretary-General Avenol definitively against the Anglo-Saxon world. His next step was a further anti-British campaign consisting of removing or hastening the departure of every British member of staff. Lester believed that this was a way of making the Secretariat more attractive to Hitler so that it could play its part in the new (nazi) Europe. If he could not achieve this ambition, Avenol was prepared to see the League reduced to the point that it was in danger of collapse—such as by not preparing a budget for 1941. His fantasy was that the United Kingdom would soon be invaded and defeated, while France (he believed) would receive decent and generous conditions from Hitler allowing it to form part of a block with Spain and Italy to counter-balance German power.

A few days later, Avenol had a meeting with Marius Viple, Assistant Director-General of the ILO, and described his new vision of France cooperating with Germany. Viple, a Frenchman, was shocked by his words and replied that nobody in France would seriously consider such a proposal. He reminded Avenol that he should be faithful to the trust placed in him by the international community and should not denigrate himself or France by making such foolish and dishonourable statements. On this same day Avenol made a second attempt to contact the German consul in Geneva.

During the early part of 1940, the Secretary-General had frequently threatened to resign, but with the German occupation of France he announced that he would definitely stay on. Again, in mid-July, Avenol suddenly announced that he was determined to resign "with a clean sheet" and, just as suddenly, decided that he could not possibly do so as he had been appointed by the unanimous votes of fifty States "including Germany and Italy". The intrigues continued. In consultations with Aghnides and Skylstad, Avenol proposed drastic reductions in the technical sections—but Aghnides suggested once again that nothing should be done without consulting the departmental directors. On 16 July Avenol planned a series of sweeping changes: Aghnides would become Acting Secretary-General (he refused); Lester and Skylstad would be sent away on permanent leave (they refused); Loveday would go on a six-month mission to the United States (he refused); Charron (Loveday's principal assistant) would take charge of the technical services. Avenol also declared falsely that Treasurer Jacklin agreed with these measures. He told Aghnides henceforth to sign documents as "Acting Secretary-General", to which Agnides immediately replied: "If I am Acting-Secretary-General, who is Secretary-General?" Avenol proposed to retire to his official residence and "manage" the League's financial reserves. During an intense conversation, Avenol tried to persuade Aghnides to accept this new arrangement, but Aghnides would not accept. "[I] would have all the responsibilities and no privileges," Aghnides told Avenol, "[while you] would have all the privileges and no responsibility." Both Aghnides and Avenol were very distressed by this conversation; Aghnides tendered his resignation and left for the mountains—it was the holiday season. Before leaving, Aghnides declared to Lester: "Avenol is a crook". When he returned from his holidays, he refused to see Avenol again. What complicates this scenario is that, due to previous bitter confrontations, Treasurer Jacklin totally refused to work under or with Aghnides. For reasons that are not clear, Avenol did not accept Aghnides' resignation, while Lester never forgot the way Aghnides had behaved: "you have conducted yourself as a man of honour" he wrote to him four years later. Aghnides himself was forced to admit: "[I have] never witnessed such [a] senseless and furious desire of destruction." From this moment, Avenol severed all relations with Aghnides.

By now, with open resistance from the senior staff, nobody took any notice of Avenol's "decisions". It seemed as if he had progressed from incompetence to treachery and was determined to bring the League of Nations to collapse. During one meeting Avenol announced in the middle of the discussions: "There are turncoats in this building." Lester looked at him completely astonished at such a remark and commented: "Well, you are the one who should know!" In reply to another request from the Secretary-General that he should step down while benefiting from tempting incentives, Lester replied to Avenol that, while the idea of going away on paid, unlimited leave was very attractive to him personally, he was determined not to leave as long as he felt "convinced there [was] a duty to be done." Lester was intrigued that the suggestion of sending people away on unlimited paid holidays did not bring any economies to the organization which was desperately searching for ways to save money.

By the middle of July rumours began to circulate that the French Government in Vichy had decided to remain a member of the League since it had received no indication from Berlin to the contrary. Avenol sent Charron to Vichy to pledge his allegiance, but before Charron returned the news reached Geneva that the French regime was not as anti-British as anticipated. They found it politically inconvenient to have a French Secretary-General. They wanted Avenol to resign and to be succeeded by Lester. This move was designed to indicate that Vichy did not intend to play an active role in international affairs. Although Avenol attempted to conceal this information from the other staff members, the ground had been cut from under his feet. He contacted Marshal Pétain[21] again to affirm his loyalty to the Vichy Government, ignoring the fact that he had been asked to resign and to do so as soon as possible. He found it hard to give up his position and thought about applying for Swiss citizenship so that he did not have to follow Vichy's instructions. It needed renewed pressure by the Vichy government through the acting Council President Adolfo Costa du Rels and a visit by Avenol to Vichy on 21 August to convince him that the game was up. For this trip, Avenol was accompanied by Charron and two other colleagues and was received by Prime Minister Pétain and Foreign Minister Baudouin[22] "very coldly". Despite two formal requests, he did not meet Minister of State Laval and General Weygand.[23] Surprisingly, when he returned, Avenol told two officials of the International Labour Organization that "left-wing organizations like the ILO are finished" and Europe "would be governed by Hitler, Mussolini and. . . ." His sentence trailed off and both of the ILO officials were certain Avenol was about to add "myself"! Costa du Rels brought the news from Vichy that the French regime considered Lester as Avenol's successor.

A second invitation had been received from Princeton University on 16 July, also extending hospitality to the Health, Social and Opium Sections of the League. Hambro telegraphed Avenol and urged him not to refuse it. The question of the international status of the League's officials had been overcome by the State Department declaring that their presence in Princeton was a temporary wartime measure that permitted them to keep their international status, after which the personnel would return to Geneva. As a delaying tactic, Avenol suggested sending Lester, Loveday and Skylstad to the United States to negotiate but without their staff—he would be glad to see the back of these troublesome people whom he had already tried, and failed, to get rid of. They saw through the ruse. A week later the British Government sent a telegram to Avenol saying that they expected the League to send as many people from the technical sections as possible to the United States. Avenol, whose position was now considerably weakened, accepted the invitation on 26 July, and President Dodds of Princeton University was informed that Loveday and Skylstad of the Economic and Financial Organisation were to proceed with their staff to Princeton very soon. When asked by British Minister Kelly to transfer all the other departments to the United States, Avenol resisted saying that he could not do so at the request of a single member state.

Towards the end of July, Lester felt that the chaotic situation within the Secretariat had reached a crisis point and needed to be resolved. In London, the Permanent Under-Secretary at the Foreign Office, Sir Alexander Cadogan, perfectly aware of the situation in Geneva, was investigating ways of removing Avenol. On 22 July Avenol declared to a meeting of the directors that it would be constitutionally and legally impossible for the League to carry on if he resigned and therefore he would remain faithful to his post. Nevertheless, three days later, after internal League friction lasting many weeks, Avenol drafted a letter of resignation and asked staff member Felkin[24] to take it to Kelly in Berne. Felkin said he had no intention of going to Berne until the letter had been shown to Lester and Loveday. In a long rambling message to member states dated 25 July 1940, Avenol concluded with: "I ask them to relieve me of the task with which they have entrusted me." Lester felt that a letter of resignation was not the same thing as actually leaving; the resignation was meaningless unless it carried a date upon which it would come into effect. However, when Avenol handed a copy to American consul Tittmann, he stated that he would leave "at the end of August". In the following days, many member states replied that they accepted his resignation.[25] Avenol was invited to a farewell lunch in Berne. Despite what had happened previously and what would happen later, the federal counsellors displayed a "friendly attitude toward the League of Nations". The authorities in Vichy, on the other hand, found that his resignation did not take place with the swiftness that they had desired and expected.

Avenol's letter of resignation had been accompanied by proposals that he should be offered a large salary to remain in control of the League's finances, accompanied by full diplomatic privileges and immunities. Even after his letter of resignation, he continued to make plans for the future of the organization, although Lester felt strongly that he had no right to do so. Then, on 5 August Lester noted that Avenol was trying to get the League's gold reserves back into Switzerland from England and the United States for his personal use, but was being blocked by Jacklin. Up until this time Jacklin felt a sense of personal loyalty to Avenol and could not believe that he was capable of deliberate wrong-doing. Jacklin had previously focused on the day-to-day management, but he had now awoken to the danger of Avenol's intentions and gave Lester his full support. The British Foreign Office took control of the League's finances and prepared to block its accounts if Germany invaded Switzerland or if the Swiss threatened the League's existence. On 20 August the Foreign Office cabled Kelly in Berne saying that Avenol's behaviour made it most desirable that his resignation be regarded as effective and that he should have no further influence over League policy. All the senior staff agreed that they would stand together against the Secretary-General and Avenol retired to his official residence, leaving Lester in charge—in theory at least.

Lester summed up Avenol's manoeuvring as treachery and short-sighted self-interest. Both Lester and Viple of the ILO had appealed to the Secretary-General's personal sense of honour to respect the international trust placed in him by the member states, with the result that Avenol no longer spoke to them. Avenol named Aghnides as his successor, but Aghnides had refused to accept and remained loyal to Lester who should have inherited the position of Secretary-General. He had also vainly asked Aghnides to make contact with the German Consul in Geneva. Avenol had requested voluntary resignations, emphasizing that this applied particularly to the senior directorial staff, but none of them accepted to play this game, believing that there was a moral issue at stake.

As news of Avenol's resignation filtered through, Lester received messages of support and encouragement. The President of the Council, Costa du Rels, informed Avenol that he had officially taken note of his resignation and accepted that Lester would take over as Acting Secretary-General. However, unaware of recent events, President of the Assembly and the Supervisory Commission Hambro had sent a long telegram to Avenol on 27 July urging him not to resign. Lester felt it was a pity Hambro was not better informed, particularly since Avenol was fiercely opposed to him and had for some time done everything possible to avoid consulting him. Later telegrams, however, showed that Hambro regretted his hasty and overgenerous attitude, having learned the true state of affairs from the Director-General of the ILO, Winant, who was also in New York finalizing the transfer of the ILO to Canada. On 27 August, Hambro confirmed that it was "essential that Avenol's resignation should become effective on 31 August". He stated that Lester would take over and that the member states should be officially informed of this event.

Lester was now the senior official and one of the very few with constructive ideas for the future. Only the British could save the League and, once they had decided it was worth saving in some form, they saw Lester, with whom they had contacts going back a decade, as a caretaker of the organization. For tactical reasons, however Lester's personal takeover would not be stressed, rather the automatic succession of Avenol's deputy. Before accepting the post of Acting Secretary-General, Lester asked if he would benefit from the support of the member states; he was assured that he would have the backing of both the member states and the staff.

The end was now in sight and Avenol turned to sordid and illegal financial bargaining—wanting his arrears to the Pension Fund to be cancelled, claiming a year's salary on full pay. He was still hoping to be appointed chairman—with a large salary—of a special trustee committee to oversee the League's finances. He requested that, upon his resignation, he should be provided with two secretaries, receive a special payment and be allowed to stay in his official residence, the upkeep of which would be assumed by the League. When he discovered that Lester had only granted him one month to complete his work, Avenol was livid and declared that he was doing the most important work of his life. Jacklin suggested to him that, if this work was indeed so important, why didn't he explain to Lester what he was doing—Lester was after all the Acting Secretary-General. Avenol refused. Lester threatened to bring the matter to the attention of the Supervisory Commission and observed in his diary that the whole situation had become comic—he was doing both his own and Avenol's work with just one secretary. Finally, Avenol announced self-importantly that it was his ambition to become a mediator between the British and French Governments, at which point Lester could no longer contain his laughter.

Avenol returned from Vichy to Geneva on 28 August with the intention of taking over again for the last three days of the month, but that day Lester had mustered a meeting which included Costa du Rels (President of the Council), Pardo (the Argentine member of the Supervisory Committee), Guerrero[26] (the President of the Permanent Court of International Justice), Julio López Oliván[27] (Registrar of the same)—who had escaped from the Netherlands and taken refuge in Geneva—and Aghnides. This powerful group agreed that Avenol was only making trouble and could not resume his functions without notifying member states—whom he himself had told a week previously that Lester was acting for him and had already been doing so since 26 July. Confronted by such united opposition, with no allies and with his home government anxious for his withdrawal, Avenol had little choice but to accept defeat.

On the same day Lester wrote a troubled memorandum to Avenol in an attempt to clarify the situation. He was able to point out anomalies in the functioning of the Secretariat that could all be attributed to Avenol and his equivocal actions. The first point was that, on two occasions, Avenol had informed the member states of his own resignation but had never discussed this matter with any of his immediate colleagues. He had officially sent messages to the member states saying that Lester had been the deputy acting on his behalf since 26 July, but had never shared this information with Lester and had in the meantime continued to take action on important issues without consulting anybody.

On his last three days in office Avenol undertook a number of spiteful initiatives to belittle the image of the League of Nations and to cause as much chaos as possible, but Lester, Jacklin and Costa du Rels were able to stifle them. On 30 August there was a rather bitter farewell luncheon at which Lester met Avenol for the first time since July. Avenol officially resigned on 31 August 1940 and two days later Lester was sworn into the office of Acting Secretary-General—Avenol ("the rascal") did not attend the ceremony even though it had been arranged at a time to suit him. Lester remained Acting Secretary-General in Geneva until 1946, after which he was retroactively appointed to Secretary-General back-dated to 1 September 1940.[28]

Lester describes Avenol's last day in office:

> Up to the last moment (and I mean 1 o'clock on the 31st), he (Avenol) gave trouble and made difficulties in every possible way. He has gone out ignominiously, without grace or dignity or any other saving virtue. . . . the delay of the past month has, as was intended, created great difficulties.

Amidst a general sigh of relief, a British newspaper printed the following: "Personally a perfectly agreeable character, M. Avenol has been little less than a disaster as Secretary-General." By December, and despite some sharp words on the part of his mistress Vera Lever, he was finally evicted from "La Pelouse", his official residence, and Lester moved in. Despite wonderful declarations about the value of his work, Avenol had merely been using "La Pelouse" as a base to conduct shameful actions intended to tarnish the League. Even Krauel, the German consul in Geneva, had a very poor opinion of him. Later Avenol settled with Vera Lever in the Haute-Savoie village of Marin.

In May 1942, shutting himself away in a Geneva hotel, Avenol wrote a memorandum summing up the war situation as he saw it. The document came to the same tired conclusions that he had held two years earlier: that Germany had already won the war and the future of France lay in collaboration with the nazis. Even though, with the entry of the United States into the conflict, there could be no further doubt about the outcome, he did not contemplate the possibility of an Allied victory, or even that he, as the former head of an international organization defending peace, law and justice, had an important moral image to project to the world. The text was written in an emotional and non-objective tone, and could easily be understood as anti-British and anti-American. Fortunately, he showed a draft of the document to René Charron and asked his opinion. Charron was dumbfounded and quickly shared the text with other colleagues, including Lester. Avenol became very angry when his old colleagues pointed out to him the danger if such a document fell into the wrong hands. The Geneva newspapers heard that Avenol had made a number of anti-British declarations and was ready to sell the League to the Axis Powers. The former Secretary-General was indignant but the information they published was not far from the truth.

Warned about an upcoming arrest by the Germans, on New Year's Eve 1943 Avenol and Vera Lever fled from France back into Switzerland to avoid being deported by the Germans—to whom he had shown unswerving loyalty. He was awarded political asylum in Switzerland and lived in self-imposed exile in Geneva until his death in 1952 aged 73.

NOTES

1. Thanassis Aghnides (1889–1984) was a Greek lawyer and diplomat. He joined the League in 1919 and had been Director of the Disarmament Section and the Political Section before entering the Office of the Secretary-General. Ambassador to London for the Greek Government in exile, 1942–1947.

2. Wolfgang Krauel (1888–1977) was a German diplomat. After military service in the First World War, he joined the Foreign Ministry in 1922. He was posted to Rio de Janeiro, 1925–1928, and then consul general in Geneva 1932–1943. He was a convinced anti-nazi and remained in Geneva when his period in office came to an end.

3. The South African Seymour Jacklin (1882–1971) had started work in the British Treasury. After serving as secretary to the Public Works Department in Pretoria, South Africa, he became Treasurer of the League in 1926, where he remained until 1946.

4. Édouard de Haller (1897–1982) was a Swiss politician and diplomat who worked for the League of Nations from 1926 to 1940, becoming Director of the Mandates Section. He joined the Red Cross in 1940 and was subsequently Ambassador to Norway, the USSR and the Netherlands.

5. Arthur Sweetser (1888–1968) was an international journalist and statesman present at the inception of the League of Nations. Sweetser joined the League's provisional Secretariat in London and became head of the Public Information Section in Geneva.

6. Winfield W. Riefler (1897–1974) earned a Croix de Guerre as an ambulance driver in the First World War. His career as an economist spanned four decades of prosperity, depression, war and reconstruction. In 1937 became an alternate member of the League of Nations' Finance Committee and director of the Foreign Policy Association in 1938.

7. Richard Austen "Rab" Butler, Baron Butler of Saffron Walden (1902–1982) was a British Conservative politician. Although he served in three of the four Great Offices of State (Chancellor of the Exchequer, Home Secretary and Foreign Secretary), he was twice passed over as Prime Minister.

8. Franklin Ridgeway Aydelotte (1880–1956) was an American educator. He is known as the director of the Institute for Advanced Study from 1939 until 1947, during which time the institute had many notable faculty, including Albert Einstein.

9. Clavin, P. *Securing the World Economy,* pp. 258–66. Oxford, UK: Oxford University Press, 2013.

10. Cordell Hull (1871–1955) was an American politician from Tennessee. He is the longest serving Secretary of State, holding the position from 1933 to 1944 in the administration of President Roosevelt. Hull received the Nobel Peace Prize in 1945 and was referred to by Roosevelt as the "Father of the United Nations".

11. Harold Willis Dodds (1889–1980) was the very popular fifteenth President of Princeton University from 1933 to 1957. Dodds had served in the U.S. Food Administration during the First World War. He became an expert on electoral law in Latin American nations.

12. Philip Henry Kerr, eleventh Marquis of Lothian (1882–1940), was a British politician, diplomat and newspaper editor. He was private secretary to Lloyd George between 1916 and 1921. After succeeding to his title in 1930, he held minor posts in the British Government. From 1939 he was Ambassador to the United States, where he died aged 58, having as a Christian Scientist refused medical treatment.

13. After military service in the First World War, Sir David Victor Kelly (1891–1959) joined the British Diplomatic Service and served in Buenos Aires, Lisbon, Mexico, Brussels, Stockholm and Cairo. He was subsequently Minister to Switzerland and Ambassador to Argentina, Turkey and the USSR.

14. John G. Winant (1889–1947) was Director-General of the ILO, 1939–1941. Despite his shortcomings as an administrator, he was an effective leader with a magnetic personality. In 1941, Winant resigned in order to become American Ambassador to London. Overcome with severe depression and in debt, he took his own life on 3 November 1947.

15. Having been seriously wounded in the First World War, Harold H. Tittmann (1893–1981) became a career diplomat with the United States Foreign Service. During the Second World War he became Chargé d'Affaires in the Vatican City and later wrote an account of the actions of Pope Pius XII.

16. Henry Brockholst Livingston was the British consul general in Geneva. On 8 August 1942 he transmitted the first information to London about the extermination of the Jews during the Second World War. He was subsequently British consul in Los Angeles and San José.

17. Bertil Arne Renborg (1892–1980) was the Swedish Chief of the Drug Control Service and the Drug Supervisory Board of the League of Nations.

18. Rasmus Skylstad (1893–1972) was a Norwegian diplomat who had been from 1924 head of the League of Nations Department in the Norwegian Ministry of Foreign Affairs. He then became Director of the Minorities Section of the League of Nations. He served as Permanent Under-Secretary for Foreign Affairs from 1948 to 1958. Norwegian Ambassador to France from 1958.

19. Marius Viple (1892–1949) was a Frenchman who joined the ILO in 1920 and became Chef du cabinet for Albert Thomas, the Director-General, eventually becoming Deputy Director-General.

20. Sir Cecil Kisch (1884–1961) joined the Indian Civil Service in 1909. In 1921 he became secretary of the Indian finance department and established the Reserve Bank of India. He represented India at the monetary conference in Geneva in 1933 and later served on the finance committee of the League of Nations. A man of wide-ranging interests, he translated Russian poetry into English, published a book on central banking and wrote the story of a famous fraud.

21. Henri Philippe Benoni Omer Joseph Pétain (1856–1951), known as Philippe Pétain, was a French military hero of the First World War and Chief of State of Vichy France. Pétain, 84 years old in 1940, ranks as France's oldest head of state. In 1945 de Gaulle placed Pétain on trial for treason. He was sentenced to death but, due to his age and his military record, this was commuted to life imprisonment.

22. Paul Baudouin (1894–1964) was a French banker in Indo-China who became a politician. He was appointed Minister of Foreign Affairs in Pétain's cabinet, and requested an armistice with Germany. Between 1941 and 1944 he returned to banking. After the war he was charged with collaborating with Germany and sentenced to five years hard labour. The sentence was commuted in 1949.

23. Maxime Weygand (1867–1965) was a French military commander in the First and Second World Wars. After the invasion of France in 1940, he collaborated with the Germans as

part of the Vichy regime. Appointed Minister for National Defence and then Delegate-General to the North African colonies. In November 1942, following the Allied invasion of North Africa, he was arrested by the Germans and imprisoned until May 1945.

24. Arthur Elliott Felkin (1892–1968), a British pacifist, worked as an interpreter in prison camps during the First World War. He became personal assistant to Lord Salter, General Secretary of the Reparation Commission in Paris. He was appointed head of the Economics Section of the League of Nations Secretariat and later Secretary to the League's Permanent Central Opium Board.

25. League of Nations, boxes R5807/R5808. Geneva, Switzerland: Archives of the League of Nations.

26. José Gustavo Guerrero (1876–1958) from El Salvador was a judge at the Permanent Court of International Justice in The Hague, 1931–1946, president from 1937 to 1946, and then president of the new International Court of Justice, 1946–1955.

27. Julio López Oliván (1891–1964) was a Spanish diplomat. When the Spanish Civil War broke out he was Ambassador to the United Kingdom. From 1936 to 1946, he was Secretary-General of the International Court of Justice in The Hague, holding the same post for the United Nations from 1953 to 1960.

28. League of Nations, box R5808. Geneva, Switzerland. Archives of the League of Nations.

Chapter Seventeen

Becoming Secretary-General

On 6 August 1940 eight League of Nations officials from Loveday's section and their families, a total of forty people, set off from Geneva by bus for Lisbon on the first leg of their journey to Princeton. Given that Avenol had only accepted the Princeton invitation on 26 July, it is remarkable that Loveday and his colleagues were ready to leave twelve days later. It would seem probable that they had concluded that their departure was inevitable and had been preparing to leave for some time. The journey would involve crossing Unoccupied France, the Pyrenees and Spain to reach Lisbon in Portugal. The next day Lester heard that Loveday's bus had been involved in a collision with a tram near Grenoble and had ended up in a ditch, but this proved less serious than feared. Seventeen passengers received minor injuries and another three were more seriously hurt, but everyone was able to continue the journey in another bus. The following day some thirty remaining staff members of the International Labour Organization (ILO) left Geneva on an exactly similar journey. There were still at the Palais des Nations about 100 officials and maintenance personnel, including a skeleton staff in the Economic, Financial and Transit Section containing William Hill and René Charron. Similarly, at the ILO a number of staff members stayed behind including Assistant Director-General Viple. Lester remarked some weeks later that he had been to a cinema in Geneva and to his dismay saw a newsreel of the departure announcing "The last of the League of Nations officials leaving Geneva!".

One of the staff members setting off from the ILO was Lester's friend Edward Phelan, who would make the journey to Lisbon by private car with another Irishman, Ronald Mortished.[1] They drove with a few jerry cans of petrol and reached the Spanish frontier on 15 August, unaware that General Franco had closed the border to League and ILO staff two days earlier.

Anticipating trouble, Phelan motored along a secondary road to a minor customs post and pointed to the word "Diplomatic" on his unfamiliar passport written in Irish Gaelic; the guards waved him through probably thinking he must be the Irish Minister to Madrid. As things turned out, Phelan and Mortished were to be among the last members of the Secretariat to cross the Spanish frontier that year. Further transfers would require lifting of the Spanish embargo. It was only on 18 August that the ILO announced publicly that it was moving its staff to Canada. When the Germans learned about it, they required the Government of Vichy to prevent French members of staff from travelling across their territory—although by this time it was far too late.

After an eventful journey through France, Spain and Portugal, Loveday flew the twenty-five hour voyage from Lisbon to New York via Bermuda on a "Yankee Clipper" flying boat with his wife and two children, while the rest of his party slummed it on board the *S.S. Exeter*. Upon arrival in New York on 25 August Loveday was met by a delegation including Arthur Sweetser and his wife. There was a great deal of interest as to whether other departments of the League could be transferred to the United States, particularly the Opium and Health Sections, where they would be cordially received, but Avenol had already refused to do this in July. As Lester was to discover himself, the closure of the Spanish frontier would also present an unsurmountable obstacle. Loveday, who had written to Lester both from Lisbon and on his arrival in the United States with advice for future travellers, wrote again from Princeton on 10 September describing his new offices.

The transfer of most of Loveday's unit to the United States was believed to be a wise move but, in view of the cost of living in Princeton or, to put it more accurately, the way the local housing market for rented property was structured, higher salaries were also needed. The League of Nations had had a pavilion at the New York World's Fair in 1939, the furniture of which had been stored in a warehouse. To equip his offices in Princeton, Loveday emptied the warehouse of its contents. Of all sections of the Secretariat, the Economic and Financial Organisation was to achieve the most during the war years. Loveday was not an easy person to work with but was an enthusiastic and industrious officer. The intellectual capacity of Loveday's unit and the series of studies published by his team materially assisted the future United Nations Specialized Agencies.[2]

Apart from the Economic and Financial Organisation and subsequently the Health and Opium Sections transferred to the United States, the units that survived the budgetary reductions were the Information, Communications, Mandates and Minorities Sections. Of the other technical sections, those dealing with Social questions and Intellectual Cooperation disappeared, most of the Refugee Section and the Treasury staff was transferred to London, while the once-famous Health Section, now greatly reduced, was actually divided between Geneva and the Washington, D.C. Officials were concerned with administrative tasks, such as collecting and publishing statistics, maintaining records and answering inquiries on such matters as international treaties.

The transfer of the Opium Section to Washington was not completed until October 1941. The staff prepared the statistics and estimates needed by the Drug Supervision Body and the Permanent Central Opium Board. Unfortunately, the personnel were divided between those who wanted to stay in Geneva and those who wanted to go to the United States, and before he resigned Avenol caused further confusion by holding the view that all member states must agree to the transfer. Originally, the American former staff members of the League had intended simply to help Jewish officials escape to the United States. Lester wanted to avoid dispersal of staff in different countries and therefore insisted on the whole group going if they went at all, so what started out as a small project gradually became more complex.

Having now heard at first-hand about the intrigues in Geneva during the summer of 1940, the American contingent sympathized with Lester carrying on in a situation in which he would become more and more isolated. As one correspondent observed, Lester now found himself as the "captain of a waterlogged boat". It became increasingly difficult to maintain the technical services in Geneva. Communication by mail was very slow and telegraphic communication haphazard.

Bigger than the Château of Versailles, the Palais des Nations stood in its own grounds on the outskirts of Geneva, a grand gaunt relic of a bygone glory. Compared to the feverish activity of 1938, the hubbub of delegates talking in the immense corridors had ceased. The incessant clatter of typewriters in its 500 offices had also fallen silent. The coffee bar was deserted and the restaurant with its fabulous view of Mont Blanc closed. The once busy courtyard thronging with diplomatic chauffeur-driven limousines was vacant. The only thing that had not changed were the few peacocks strutting under the cedar trees. Former colleague Arthur Sweetser referred to it as "the deserted palace", but Lester was quick to reprimand him saying that he should do everything in his power to oppose the dissemination of such ideas. Attention should not be drawn to the reductions, the economies and the feeling of abandonment, but rather to the maintenance of quiet, steady work, the continuation of services and readiness for the future. Lester kept himself intensely busy. The Secretariat's technical departments continued to furnish governments with useful information about hygiene, nutrition, housing, the protection of young people, assistance to refugees and the struggle against drug abuse.

Beyond the question of Avenol's state of mind, Lester's main preoccupation during August 1940 had been that a meeting should be held of the Supervisory Commission to establish the League's budget for 1941. Without an approved budget, the League of Nations would not be able to request contributions and spend money, which was equivalent to it ceasing to exist. With some commission members in Geneva, some in London and some in New York—and some who had been swallowed up in war-torn Europe—it was at first proposed that the Supervisory Commission should attempt to meet in August at Princeton. Avenol immediately informed the members of the commission that he would not travel to the United States due to the strong possibility that he would not be able to return to Geneva. The League's Legal Department stated that, if the Secretary-General could not attend, Lester, his second-in-command, could take his place. Everybody travelling from Geneva asked themselves the same question: would they be able to get back again? As things turned out, this was the least of their worries.

Because of prior commitments and the difficulty of the members actually reaching any particular place—in wartime—it was provisionally agreed that the meeting of the Supervisory Commission would take place in September 1940 and Lisbon seemed to be the most appropriate venue. The commission's decisions would have no authority unless there was a quorum of four members. Was it possible for four members to reach Lisbon? At one stage Lester envisaged that, if he and his colleagues from the Secretariat could get as far as Barcelona, they could charter an aeroplane to fly them to Lisbon. The Finnish member Holma asked for the meeting to be held in the last week of September, allowing time for people to obtain visas and for Lester and Jacklin to prepare a budget. Finally, it appeared that Hambro (from Middle America), Kisch (from London), Holma (from Vichy) and Pardo (from Washington, D.C.) could meet in Lisbon on 28 September, where Phelan representing the ILO was already waiting. As this situation did not become clear until 12 September, there was a mad rush after this date to obtain visas for the journey. Finally, at 12.30 on Saturday, 21 September, Lester, Jacklin, Bieler (Canadian, from treasury) and da Silva (a Portuguese-speaking member of staff), accompanied by Guerrero (President of the International Court of Justice) together with one English and one French typist, left the Palais des Nations by mini-bus. The plan was that they would pick up the Acting President of the Council, Costa du Rels, en route, but he was delayed and had to travel separately. This small detail was to be the salvation of the meeting.

Lester and his colleagues reached the frontier between France and Spain at Le Perthus on the following day, but the Spanish officer in charge explained rather apologetically that he had an order dating from 13 August forbidding any League official or anyone connected with the League of Nations from passing. Lester asked that the matter should be referred to the regional governor and then to the government in Madrid, but on Tuesday 23 September the final answer was still "no". Lester then suggested to Guerrero that he should go on alone carrying some vital papers but, even though he carried a diplomatic passport, he was also refused entry.

While they were waiting at the frontier, the Norwegian delegation from Vichy arrived and Lester was able discretely to give them some papers for the meeting as they passed through. In fact, the Norwegian delegation was being expelled from France. They also saw Harri Holma, the Finnish delegate from Vichy, and his wife, who managed to pass the frontier by pretending that they were on holiday. At this point, there was nothing more for Lester and his humiliated party to do than to get back in the mini-bus and return forlornly to Geneva. To rub salt into the wound, Avenol was delighted at their misfortune. The British Foreign Secretary, Lord Halifax, communicated his regrets, while Kisch telephoned from Lisbon to express complete confidence in Lester and Jacklin.

Avenol had asked Jacklin to carry two letters to Lisbon, one addressed to Carl Hambro and the other to Sir Cecil Kisch. While they had been travelling across France, Jacklin had shown the letters to Lester. The letter to Hambro was a restrained and dignified communication explaining that Avenol had been prevented from writing some useful reports because Lester had refused to provide him with a special allowance. The handwritten letter to Kisch expressed profound admiration for the way the British were defending "all of us in the world" against German aggression. Lester shared with Loveday in the United States his complete astonishment that Avenol had suddenly become anglophile.[3]

Not long after they returned from their abortive mission, da Silva expressed the desire to leave the League and go home to Portugal. Lester felt that this could be potentially embarrassing for relations between the League and the Portuguese Government, and was careful to avoid any possible grounds for the Portuguese authorities to react badly to da Silva's departure. Another problem was that Pardo, the Argentinian delegate, found himself in financial difficulties due to the chaotic international situation. Although Lester was able to create a fairly generous financial grant in his favour, Pardo appeared to be neither grateful nor satisfied.

The eighty-eighth meeting of the Supervisory Commission still held some surprises. There were so many refugees in the hotels of Lisbon that the meeting had to take place in Estoril, the seaside resort just outside the city. Due to bad weather in the Atlantic Ocean, Hambro was unable to reach Lisbon and had to "participate" by telegraph. Not surprisingly, the French, Belgian and Dutch members also failed to arrive. This meant that those present were only Kisch and Pardo, as well as Holma who finally had to be persuaded to join them since Finland found itself in a very delicate political triangle with Germany and the USSR. The meeting would therefore not have had a quorum had it not been for Costa du Rels, who had managed to cross the French/Spanish border on his own reaching Lisbon in time to be co-opted on to the Supervisory Commission.[4] The Secretariat was represented by Phelan of the ILO and López Oliván of the International Court of Justice. By early October the commission had adopted a budget for 1941 and agreed that the transfer of Loveday's unit to Princeton and the ILO to Montreal was in the best interests of the League. One hour after the meeting closed, Pardo, Phelan and Mortished sailed for the United States on board the *S.S. Excambion*.

On his way back from Lisbon, López Oliván visited Madrid in an attempt to ascertain why Lester's group had been refused passage across Spain. His contacts at the Ministry of Foreign Affairs did not know that the Ministry of the Interior had forbidden entry to League officials. Foreign Affairs, on the other hand, was aware of Lester's party leaving Geneva and had informed the frontier police by telegram that they were expected to cross the border at Le Perthus on 22 September, and specifically mentioned that Guerrero was a member of the group. Thus, the Ministry of Foreign Affairs had given one order and the Ministry of the Interior a counter-order, with the result that the former's telegram had no effect. Costa du Rels, who as well as being President of the Council was Bolivian Ambassador to Spain, had also tried to obtain permission in Madrid for Lester's party to cross the border, but to no avail. The Nationalist regime had received very negative treatment during the Spanish Civil War at the hands of the League of Nations and this resulted in the Franco Government considering it as an adversary. The specific reason given for the blocking of the frontier at this particular moment had been very colourful reports published in the American press about Loveday's and the ILO people's passage across Spain. League of Nation's staff were henceforth awarded no diplomatic immunity. Costa du Rels summed up the situation in the following words: "We live at a time when respect for the law has become a favour."

Beyond Jacklin's financial competence, Lester paid tribute to the Treasurer's integrity, outspokenness and courage. On the other hand, Lester observed that Jacklin suffered from an inferiority complex, had no political skills and his sensibilities had to be "nursed". He also suffered from gout and rheumatism, which made him very irritable. A Geneva bank manager mentioned discreetly to Lester that Jacklin even feared that he was being followed around the streets by the Gestapo! Nevertheless, for the time being, Lester treated Jacklin as his principal associate and shared all correspondence with him. Although at first it was thought that the Secretary-General and the Treasurer should stick together, it was eventually decided that the League needed someone outside Geneva to supervise its financial affairs. As early as June 1940 part of the Treasury Section had been transferred to the United Kingdom, where it was considered easier to collect contributions from member states. For this reason, Jacklin was invited by the British Foreign Office to work from London, where his family resided. But there was another logic behind his departure. Although he possessed South African nationality, he had begun his career in the British Treasury and the prospect of ending his career there appealed to him. How he was to reach London was another story!

Upon hearing reports that German troops were about to occupy the remainder of Southern France, Jacklin set off from Geneva on 21 December 1940 by heading first for Marseilles. There he boarded a small cargo boat calling at Oran in French Algeria and Casablanca in Morocco. There was no legal way of reaching Gibraltar, so he decided to cross the Atlantic to Martinique in the West Indies. Six weeks after leaving he reached Port of Spain in Trinidad, from where he sent a telegram saying "this route is not recommended"! He did eventually reach London, but Lester's confidence in him quickly collapsed because, upon reaching safety, he made some rather wild statements about the Axis Powers that could have made Lester's isolated position extremely uncomfortable. The attitude of the Spanish Government about League of Nations staff crossing its territory had relaxed and, a month after his departure, the Spanish consul in Geneva granted Jacklin permission to cross Spain on route for Portugal. Furthermore, the rumours that the German Army would occupy Southern France proved unfounded; this event did not take place until two years later in November 1942.

The year 1940 had been remarkable for major historical events in the world and crises within the Palais des Nations. Since December 1939 the League had lost sixteen member states, most, but not all, through the actions of the German Army. Even though the League had weathered the storm, Lester found himself without his family and without his great circle of diplomatic friends and colleagues, and was subject to periods of loneliness and melancholy. His life was filled with administrative problems and difficulties. Cremins, the League's former Irish representative, had been transferred to Berne as Chargé d'Affaires. Except for a visit to Cremins, Lester spent Christmas 1940 and the New Year on his own. His principal remaining acquaintances were Henry Livingston, the British consul in Geneva, Aghnides and Charron, as well as Carl Burckhardt, who now worked for the Red Cross in negotiations with nazi Germany about prisoners-of-war. Lester did, however, continue to hold official lunches and dinners with a wide range of visiting personalities.

In letters to his friends and colleagues, he took stock of the situation at the end of 1940. One year previously, countries believed themselves strong and well-protected, with enough food and wealth for their population and armies to defend them— and now some of them no longer existed. The League of Nations had been betrayed and belittled by all the Great Powers without exception, and the result was war. Lester was now found himself the guardian of a tiny flickering light, all that remained of the once flaming torch of great hopes and ideals. The Covenant of the League of Nations, a system to prevent war, had been repudiated, while the liberty of aggressors to go to war with impunity and invade their peaceful neighbours was assumed to be their sovereign right. In September 1943, Winston Churchill had this to say in an address given at Harvard University in the United States: "It is said that the League of Nations failed. If so, that is largely because it was abandoned and, later on, betrayed."

Lester was confident, however, that it was quite impossible for the nazi regime to survive for long or to dominate the world, even if in the first surge of its military power it had temporarily overwhelmed a number of countries. The human misery caused throughout Europe by nazi persecution and the total breakdown of economies and communications were no advertisement for Hitler's policies. The advent of a so-called new civilization under the self-styled master race was enough to show that might, after all, could not be right—the world could no longer be ruled by force. Hitler claimed that he was misunderstood and with amazing effrontery talked about his "good neighbour" policy. However, an American press release in 1941 made it clear that Hitler had made solemn promises about the territorial integrity of Austria, Czechoslovakia, Denmark, the Netherlands, Norway and Poland, and in each case he had robbed these countries of their freedom.

On 22 June 1941 Hitler's forces attacked Stalin's USSR in what was the greatest military operation of the Second World War. Lester noted in his diary that the USSR had been warned by the British Government of the impending attack but this information had been dismissed by the Soviets. On the very day of the invasion Russian newspapers denounced the rumours of a possible attack as British propaganda.

In April 1941 the head of the Vichy Government, Admiral François Darlan,[5] sent a telegram to Geneva notifying the intention of France to withdraw from the League of Nations. When the subject had first been raised in the summer of 1940, the departure of Avenol as Secretary-General had been sufficient to defuse the situation. Given that many of the League's policies since its inception were inspired by Paris—collective security, disarmament control, joint economic action—the gesture of leaving only made sense in the context of the German occupation of France. Lester took comfort in the fact that few people had any respect for Darlan due to his collaboration with the nazis, while the policies of the Vichy Government did not reflect what the vast majority of French people wanted. Given the swiftness with which Darlan had acted, Lester at first believed that some kind of deal had been struck with the German occupying force. Eventually, however, Lester came to the conclusion that the Vichy Government had given notice to the League of Nations as an act of housekeeping in order to tidy up its image in the eyes of Hitler. Vichy French forces at this time were occupying Syria and Lester believed that the Germans would before long demand to use this country as a base for their army and air force.

Lester's principal concern was that the departure of France would further undermine Switzerland's attitude towards the League, which was already cool on the part of the Government in Berne. The Swiss policy was not to collaborate with the League and this process might steadily worsen or even accelerate. The League operated a radio station on Swiss soil managed by Swiss officials. Lester was now officially informed that the radio station would be closed down. Furthermore, the League would no longer be able to use postage stamps bearing the image of the Palais des Nations, while the Swiss financial contribution would terminate. Lester could understand the delicate position of Switzerland, but pointed out bitterly in his diary that the League of Nations was still paying into the Swiss economy three times the Swiss contribution.

The League of Nations was fighting for its existence. The remaining staff numbered no more than a fraction of what it had been in 1939 but, even so, finding the money to pay them was a challenging task, not to mention maintaining the vast empty building of the Palais des Nations, a property valued at 40 million Swiss francs. The League did possess financial reserves, but these were not sufficient to ensure its survival for more than a few months. The remaining officials had agreed to forego a percentage of their salaries, with the senior staff accepting a reduction of 26%. On the contrary, the cost of living rose steeply in Geneva during the early part of the war and by June 1943 had increased by 46% compared to what it had been in 1939. The Supervisory Commission was obliged to agree to salary increases, particularly for the lower grades. However, thought Lester, the most important issue was that the headquarters of the organization survived intact as a rallying point. He noted that politicians who had managed to escape from occupied Europe considered the League of Nations as a "lifeboat" to which they clung. Roger Makins[6] of the British Foreign Office wrote that "there is nothing that would suit the enemies of the League better than to see the collapse of the organisation of the League at Geneva."

In June and July 1941, Lester discovered letters addressed to him from colleagues in the United States that had not actually been opened but had attached to them slips of paper from British censors located in Bermuda noting that this was the same Sean Lester who was on the "watch list". His initial reaction was one of amusement and it was in a jocular vein that he immediately shared this information with Henry Livingston, the British consul in Geneva. However, after a few days a deep feeling of outrage took possession of him. He felt it was a stupid insult to his position as Acting Secretary-General of the League of Nations and he was affronted that his mail should be tampered with by the last remaining Great Power that was a member state. He drafted an indignant letter to Anthony Eden, who could be counted among his close diplomatic acquaintances and who was at this time Secretary of State for Foreign Affairs in London. Before sending the letter he expressed his distress to Livingston, who shared his feelings and informed Kelly, the British Minister in Berne. Rather than send the letter, on 20 June

Lester sent Eden a telegram stating that, since he did not benefit from the unquestioned and complete confidence of the British Government, he had no alternative but to tender his resignation to Hambro, the Chairman of the Supervisory Commission. A week later the British Foreign Office admitted that a mistake had been made and communicated a personal apology from Anthony Eden, who reaffirmed the British Government's complete confidence in him. Sometime later, the Chief Censor in Bermuda also personally expressed his apologies to Lester for a clumsy gaffe. In these circumstances, he was content to remain at his post.

By the middle of 1941, the British Government was looking towards the League's budget for 1942. It was decided that the Supervisory Commission should meet in Montreal in July to give its approval. Among the delegates who would obviously be there were Hambro, the chairman, but it was suggested by Alexander Cadogan, the Permanent Under-Secretary at the Foreign Office, and Roger Makins, the contact person for the League in Whitehall, that Jacklin should attend and Lester should not. They believed that it was Lester's business to be present but their concern was that if he ever left Geneva there was a great risk that he would never be able to return or, more precisely, that he would be deliberately prevented from doing so. There was a strong argument that the Secretary-General would have had more impact if he had been located in the United States where he could have made his voice clearly heard to the free world and to occupied countries. Much as Lester wanted to travel to New York, Montreal and London (and particularly Dublin), he had to admit that doubts about his chances of returning to Geneva were well-grounded.

Both Lester and Loveday were also uneasy about Jacklin's state of physical and mental health. He appears to have been severely diminished by the journey from Geneva to London via Trinidad, but Loveday was able to report by September 1941 that he had regained his former abilities and judgement. The Supervisory Commission adopted the budget for 1942, although it was below the minimum that Lester considered desirable. Thanks to his vigilance, the League lived within its income. Nevertheless, he felt that the more the League managed to survive on the budget it was given, the greater were the grounds for reducing that income. At the same meeting the ILO was represented by fifty-seven staff members, in contrast to only one or two from each of the League's other sections. It was even suggested that the remnants of the League should move in with the ILO at McGill University to save money. Two months later the well-attended International Labour Conference was held in New York with a concluding session at the White House addressed by President Roosevelt. It was obvious that the ILO was competing successfully with the League and was likely to take over the best and most useful work of the Secretariat, particularly that of Loveday's section. Lester referred to this as the "disembowelling" of the League. It was also clear that, because the ILO was located in Canada and was conducting its affairs without hindrance, it was being favoured financially and was beginning to poach on the territory of the League in other fields, such as housing, nutrition and health. Since the ILO was only being asked to make economies two years after the League first began to save money, once again it started from an advantageous position. It was also particularly galling for Lester that his close friend Edward Phelan, who had now become Acting Director-General of the ILO at McGill University, had never wanted to transfer the organization to Canada in the first place. Now that it was located in the haven of Montreal, he was taking full advantage of the situation to the detriment of the League, even suggesting that the ILO should be authorized to collect its contributions from member States separately. Phelan was reported as saying that the ILO had escaped death by "creeping paralysis", while Lester drew the inference that the League had not been so lucky.[7]

The Supervisory Commission seemed to have concluded that, since the League's Headquarters in Geneva could no longer carry out any political activities, its budget should be reduced accordingly, but Lester pointed out that technical activities were still being undertaken there. To add to his sense of isolation, Lester did not receive the final report of the commission until three-and-a-half months after it had finished its work. However, it was agreed at this meeting to keep the League in existence at least until 1945.

Inevitably, with the dispersion of the League's technical departments and the ILO to the other side of the Atlantic Ocean, and the isolation of its headquarters in Geneva, Lester was beginning to feel his ability to make decisions about the League's policies weakened. Although the political symbol of maintaining the League's headquarters in the Palais des Nations had an impact, Lester noted that the final remnants of its prestige were slipping away. The critical time in the summer of 1940 when the "unspeakable" Joseph Avenol had been in charge had a lasting impact.

Lester recalled the enormous contributions that the League of Nations had made since its beginnings, even if they were restricted to matters of a moral and spiritual nature. But they went far beyond that, covering justice, economics, finance, trade, transport, public health, nutrition, drugs, refugees and the traffic in women and children. This far from exhaustive list was overshadowed by the responsibility that could be attributed to the League for post-war reconstruction. Even as the war continued, Lester was already thinking about how it would end. When the world decided that the time for peace had come, the League of Nations represented an enormous reservoir of experience and knowledge regarding such problems as disarmament, trade, currency and support for development. In the circumstances of 1941, it was essential to keep the League of Nations functioning as an organization. After the devastation of war would come a time for reconstruction. Post-war conditions would demand planning and effort on a global scale where international cooperation would be essential if chaos were to be avoided. In the aftermath of war it would be necessary to manage the demobilization of troops, the repatriation of prisoners-of-war, reconstruction, industrial imbalances, trade restrictions, the safeguarding of populations from epidemics, regulating the flow of refugees, the high price of essential commodities, and providing financial assistance to bankrupt economies. Only the machinery of the League of Nations had experience in these domains, so it was necessary to preserve it during a time of crisis. If a return to the law of the jungle were to be avoided, the League represented the best way of settling disputes through negotiation rather than slaughtering people by the lavish use of modern armaments.

Lester believed that, whatever international organization was created after the Second World War, it would inevitably follow the main lines of the Covenant of the League of Nations. The world needed a central agency for international cooperation based on law and justice. International action would be directed to the peaceful settlement of disputes and an improvement in the general standard of living through effective cooperation, trade and access to raw materials.

Two British politicians, Herbert Morrison and Anthony Eden, had each independently described the three main principles of a new international organization: it should represent all nations of the world without exception; it should have a unity of purpose; and it should have power sufficient to restrain those who would impede the maintenance of peace. Winston Churchill observed: "We have learned from hard experience that stronger, more efficient, more rigorous world institutions must be created to preserve peace and to forestall the causes of future wars". Any new international organization should also be attractive to smaller member states and should not involve them in risky situations due to the actions of more powerful nations. There had to be a balance between national sovereignty and communal interest. No post-war international organization could possibly guarantee world peace without the active and financial participation of the United States of America. And nothing would be possible without the victory of the Allies. The whole game plan changed in June 1941 when Germany invaded the USSR, and on 7 December when Japan declared war on the United Kingdom and the United States. Four days later, Italy and Germany also declared war against the United States.

NOTES

1. Ronald James Patrick Mortished (1891–1961), an Irish trade union official and long-term acquaintance of Lester, had been the editor of *Voice of Labour* (1922–1927) and later *The Irishman* (1927–1930), then adviser to the Irish delegation at the International Labour Conference from 1923 to 1926. He worked for the ILO from 1931 to 1956.

2. Clavin, P. *Securing the World Economy,* p. 267. Oxford, UK: Oxford University Press, 2013.

3. Gageby, D. *The Last Secretary-General: Sean Lester and the League of Nations*, p. 211. Dublin: Town House, 1999.

4. Ibid., p. 212.

5. Jean Louis Xavier François Darlan (1881–1942) was a French Admiral, commander in chief of the French Navy in 1939. After France capitulated in 1940, he served in the pro-German Vichy regime, becoming its deputy leader for a time. When the Allies invaded French North Africa in 1942, Darlan ordered French forces to cooperate with the Allies. Later he was assassinated.

6. Roger Mellor Makins (1904–1996) joined the British Diplomatic Service in 1928, eventually becoming Deputy Under-Secretary of State at the Foreign Office. In 1953 he was appointed Ambassador to the United States. He later became Chairman of the United Kingdom Atomic Energy Authority.

7. Clavin, p. 275.

Chapter Eighteen

The End of the League

For four long years Lester sat out the Second World War in Geneva. The separation from his wife and family was a great hardship, although he shared this fate with millions of other men and women scattered across the globe, many of whom found themselves in situations of great danger and deprivation. Communication with the outside world remained a problem since letters sometimes took months—even years—to arrive.

Although Switzerland was apparently no longer under direct threat of invasion by the Axis forces, the Government in Berne found the presence of the League inconvenient. In 1940 the Swiss withdrew their liaison officer and closed down the section dealing with the League within its political department. In the autumn, Switzerland decided that it would no longer pay its annual contribution and did not do so again until 1945. Upon taking up office, Lester wrote to the authorities in Berne to establish contact with them but had to wait six weeks for a verbal reply that was "so contradictory as to leave me in no doubt that no further approach was required." League of Nations' stamps were withdrawn from circulation in case their use would offend one of the belligerents. In the winter of 1940–1941, the supply of heating oil to the Palais des Nations was stopped, but was restored before catastrophic damage was done to the buildings. The Swiss Government also asked the national press not to publish any information about the League, although this directive was not strictly followed. Lester found these measures extremely annoying, particularly as half the posts in the Secretariat were occupied by Swiss people drawing a salary paid by the League. He felt that Switzerland had failed to meet its obligations as the host of the League.

The Supervisory Commission met again in Montreal in August 1942. There were two questions that appeared frequently in the correspondence between Lester and the Foreign Office in London: what was the purpose of maintaining the Secretary-General's presence in Geneva; and what would the role of international organizations be after the war? As regards the first question, Anthony Eden remarked that the moral and political value of flying the flag in Geneva would only be understood if the time came to haul it down. Roger Makins, who was the officer responsible for the affairs of the League of Nations in the Foreign Office, urged Lester to stay in Geneva and not attempt to attend any meetings of the Supervisory Commission. Whatever assurances Lester received concerning foreign travel, Makins believed, the Axis Powers would do everything in their power to prevent him from returning to Geneva. Many governments in exile had taken refuge in London, so the British felt a duty and commitment to keep the League of Nations alive in Europe. The British Government would be embarrassed if, for instance, the Secretary-General decided to take up residence in the United States. Even the exiled governments in London continued to make symbolic financial contributions to the League. This concerned Belgium, Czechoslovakia, France, Greece, the Netherlands, Norway and Poland, as well as some neutral nations such as Ireland and Portugal.[1]

As to the future existence of the League, it was not until 1944 that Lester learned that it would not continue after the Second World War. In March 1944, Hambro, as Chairman of the Supervisory Commission, told him that it had been decided not to re-establish the League "as it was before". Sir Alexander Cadogan, the Under-Secretary of State for Foreign Affairs in London, informed him in June 1944 that a new world organization would be created. Apart from the attitude of the United States, it was perfectly clear that the USSR, one of the major powers in the anticipated victory over Germany, would under no circumstances return due to the fact that it had been expelled from the organization in 1939. While all the planned new organizations were being provided with unlimited support, the League of Nations had become something of a political orphan.

In 1942 Lester's youngest daughter Ann was able to travel to Geneva using her neutral Irish passport and joined him until the Allied Forces reached the Swiss border.[2] Finally, during November 1944 the Allied advance across France allowed him to travel to Ireland for a holiday with his family. For a month in London he was warmly feted by illustrious names on the international scene, ambassadors and leading politicians. In the new year of 1945, it was the same story as he travelled to Paris and Geneva and then back to London.

The League of Nations was finally laid to rest in two stages. The first took place from April to June 1945, when forty-five nations met at the San Francisco Conference to set up the United Nations. Here, the League was humbled and, as Patricia Clavin writes: "Lester and Loveday were guests at their own funeral".[3] The second was a more dignified event when the Assembly met in Geneva for the first time since 1939 with Lester and Loveday taking centre stage.

So what happened in San Francisco? The sponsors of the conference were the four victorious nations that had been fighting Germany and Japan and had subscribed to the United Nations Declaration—China, the United Kingdom, the United States and the USSR. There were 850 delegates, while their advisers and staff together with the conference secretariat brought the number of people present to 3,500. In addition, there were more than 2,500 press, radio and newsreel representatives and observers from many societies and organizations. In all, the San Francisco Conference was one of largest international gatherings ever to have taken place. The heads of the delegations of the sponsoring countries took turns as chairman of the plenary meetings: Soong of China; Eden of the United Kingdom; Stettinius of the United States; and Molotov of the USSR.

Twelve days before it opened, the United States Ambassador in London, Lester's old acquaintance from the ILO John Winant, belatedly invited the League of Nations to be "unofficially represented" and to be ready for "informal consultation relating to matters that might arise". Lester was informed that, due to accommodation problems, the League's delegation should not exceed two or three people. Due to the late arrival of the invitation and the offhand manner in which it was communicated, Lester wondered whether the presence of the League was actually desired at all. Was the League an embarrassing gatecrasher or was there a danger of it being relegated to the sidelines?

Since the League was still a substantial organization with more than forty member states and the possessor of considerable assets, the Supervisory Commission authorized representatives of the Secretariat to attend the conference. A meeting of the League's Assembly would take place afterwards to decide what to do next. When Lester and his three colleagues—Alexander Loveday, Seymour Jacklin and Manley Hudson[4] —reached San Francisco, they found that there were no arrangements for them to register, to obtain documents or to gain admission to the meeting rooms. They were lodged in a third-class hotel. During the opening ceremony the League was allocated one seat at the very back of the auditorium among the general public, which included children. Lester was prepared to attribute the lack of status shown to the League to the general state of confusion, but Loveday was not so sure. At times Lester had to acknowledge that the presence of the League was obviously a mortification for the organizers and this was just another occasion when he had to accept humiliation on behalf of the organization.

When the end of the Second World War came the USSR was in an ebullient mood and wanted absolutely nothing to do with the League of Nations. Furthermore, Molotov, the head of the Russian delegation, carried away by the jubilation of the victorious nations, protested that the delegations of intergovernmental organizations should not be headed by people from neutral nations. This affected a lot of people, but particularly Lester of the League, Phelan of the ILO and Guerrero of the International Court of Justice. The situation of neutral nations had been spectacularly damaged by Éamon de Valera who had insisted, for reasons known only to himself, upon calling on the German ambassador in Dublin on 3 May 1945 to convey the condolences of the Irish Government upon the death of Adolf Hitler.[5] This event made headlines throughout the world with the *New York Herald Tribune* describing it as "Neutrality gone mad". On the same day, the swastika flag was observed flying at half-mast over the premises of the Irish delegation in Lisbon—although it was later established that this had nothing to do with the Irish representative to Portugal. He shared a building with a German intelligence organization.

Molotov was reminded by the conference organizers that he had agreed to the League and the ILO being invited to the San Francisco Conference beforehand without raising any objections. Upon receiving this information Molotov "looked sulky".[6] Hambro and Lester felt strongly that the status of an international civil servant should be accepted since these people were not representing their governments, and more particularly since the same argument was going to affect anyone who worked for the future United Nations. The Secretary-General of the conference, Alger Hiss,[7] reminded the League of Nations' delegates that it was a meeting of the victors of the war, and the participation of the League represented by someone from a neutral country intruded upon the celebration. Forty-four years later in 1989 Hiss denied that he had any intentions of snubbing the League and claimed that Lester's nationality did not justify such an act. Finally, it was agreed that representatives of inter-governmental organizations would be tolerated at the San Francisco Conference. Nevertheless, worse was to come. A new Polish Government had just been elected in Warsaw; nonetheless, Molotov informed the conference contemptuously that, while attempting to leave for San Francisco, its representatives had been arrested by the Russians. The Cold War had begun.

There was an unwritten but unmistakable message conveyed by the San Francisco Conference that, independent of the shortcomings of its member states, the League of Nations had failed. Following the Second World War the United States and the USSR were in charge of reconstructing the new world order; they wanted a new start. The Charter of the United Nations was signed in San Francisco on 26 June 1945. A meeting was arranged in London in September to launch the new organization, where it was proposed that the League's Supervisory Commission should also be present with the idea, no doubt, of winding up the League of Nations. However, the British Foreign Office insisted that the final Assembly of the League must be held in "the dignity and tranquillity" of its Headquarters in Geneva.

Thus, the twenty-first meeting of the Assembly of the League of Nations took place on 12 April 1946 in the Palais des Nations attended by delegates from thirty-four nations. For eleven days delegates reminisced about the noble sentiments of the League's beginnings, its prestigious days in the 1920s, and the shattering of its dreams in the 1930s. The League was wound up and its assets worth approximately US$22 million (including the Palais des Nations and the League's archives) transferred to the UN. Other financial reserves were returned to the nations that had supplied them, and the League's debts settled. Lester was thanked for having maintained the organization during the war and was formally nominated as the third and last Secretary-General backdated to 1 September 1940. The motion dissolving the League was then passed unanimously. The President of the Assembly, Hambro declared "the twenty-first and last session of the General Assembly of the League of Nations closed". The League of Nations ceased to exist on 19 April 1946 although the liquidation of its assets kept Lester busy until the autumn of 1947.

In December 1945, Lester had received the Woodrow Wilson Foundation award recognizing that, during the Second World War, he had upheld "the ideals, traditions and mechanism of international co-operation for peace". In 1947 he was conferred an honorary doctorate in laws by Trinity College, Dublin, and in 1948 he received an honorary doctorate from the National University of Ireland, also in Dublin.

In conversations about his future with the Department of External Affairs in Dublin, Lester said that that he did not want to accept a post abroad, and this included the United Nations. After eighteen years away, he was approaching his fifty-ninth birthday and inclined to retire and settle in Ireland. While Ireland could have benefited from his long international experience, he was not appointed as a senator or to any other governmental or political position. Moreover, he was not attracted to any of the posts that the government was prepared to offer him. As his daughter Ann wickedly noted on part of the correspondence: "It was the fishing season!"

After six years of living in Wicklow, to the south of Dublin, the Lesters moved to their house at Recess in Connemara. Here they had access to miles of first-class fishing on trout streams. A few weeks before the sea trout made their way up the rivers and lakes a few yards from his home in the spring of 1959, Lester died of a stroke on 13 June aged 70 and is buried in the Protestant Church of Ireland graveyard at Clifden, Galway. After her husband's death, Elsie Lester built a house in Dublin and another holiday home on the west coast of Ireland. She subsequently moved several times. She outlived her husband by fifteen years and is buried alongside him.

When Lester returned home to Ireland, he brought with him much written material covering his eighteen years of service abroad: a diary in various forms, as well as correspondence, texts of talks he had given, reports and documents, and a vast number of press cuttings. His intention had been to write a book about his experiences, particularly as High Commissioner in Danzig during a crucial historical period, and as the last Secretary-General of the League of Nations—but he never did.

After Lester died in 1959 and his wife's subsequent moves, his papers became scattered. However, in the 1980s, all the papers were found, filed chronologically and assembled into a collection, the only exception being his bound diary, which is available separately. A full set of the collection is with the League of Nations Archives in Geneva and is available for consultation by researchers. The collection was donated to the Archives by Lester's daughters: Dorothy Mary Gageby, Patricia Kilroy and Ann Gorski.

During the ceremony to wind up the League in Geneva, Philip Noel-Baker, the principal British delegate, paid the following tribute to Sean Lester in April 1946:

> The words of Seneca come to mind: 'with nothing to hope for, he despaired of nothing'.[8]

NOTES

1. Gageby, D. *The Last Secretary-General: Sean Lester and the League of Nations*, p. 255. Dublin: Town House, 1999.
2. Ibid., p. 213.
3. Clavin, P. *Securing the World Economy*, p. 341. Oxford, UK: Oxford University Press, 2013.
4. Manley Ottmer Hudson (1886–1960) was a U.S. lawyer. He was a judge at the Permanent Court of International Justice, a member of the International Law Commission, and a mediator in international conflicts. The American Society of International Law named a medal after him; as did Harvard University with a professorship. He was nominated twice for the Nobel Peace Prize.
5. Gageby, p. 244.
6. Ibid., p. 243.
7. Alger Hiss (1904–1996) was an American lawyer, government official, author and lecturer. He worked for the United States State Department and as a United Nations official. He was accused of being a Soviet spy in 1948 and convicted of perjury in 1950. The circumstances of his trial led to endless controversy and he was subsequently rehabilitated.
8. Gageby, p. 251.

Bibliography

Azcárate, P. de, ed. *William Martin: Un Grand Journaliste à Genève*. Geneva, Switzerland: Centre européen de la Dotation Carnegie pour la paix internationale, 1970.
Barros, J. *Betrayal from within: Joseph Avenol, Secretary-General of the League of Nations*. New Haven/London: Yale University Press, 1969.
Barros, J. *Office without Power: Secretary General Sir Eric Drummond, 1919–1933*. Oxford, UK: Clarendon Press, 1979.
Clavin, P. *Securing the World Economy*. Oxford, UK: Oxford University Press, 2013.
Ellis, C.H., ed. *The Origin, Structure and Working of the League of Nations*. London: Allen & Unwin, 1928.
Epstein, C. *Model Nazi: Arthur Greiser and the Occupation of Western Poland*. Oxford, UK: Oxford University Press, 2010.
Fosdick, R.B. *The League and the United Nations after Fifty Years: The Six Secretaries-General*. Newtown, CT: 1972.
Fox, J.; Fosse, M. *The League of Nations: From Collective Security to Global Rearmament*. New York: United Nations, 2012.
Gageby, D. *The Last Secretary-General: Sean Lester and the League of Nations*. Dublin: Town House, 1999.
Gerbet, P. *Société des Nations et Organisation des Nations Unies*. Paris: Éditions Richelieu, 1973.
Gibson, H. *The Road to Foreign Policy*. Garden City, NY: Doubleday, Doran, 1944.
League of Nations. *Essential Facts about the League of Nations*. Geneva, Switzerland: League of Nations, 1936.
McNamara, P. *Sean Lester, Poland and the Nazi takeover of Danzig*. Dublin/Portland, OR: Irish Academic Press, 2009.
Myers, D.P. *Handbook of the League of Nations since 1920*. Boston, MA: World Peace Foundation, 1930.
Salter, J.A. *Geneva and the League of Nations*. London: Faber & Faber, 1961.
Van Ginneken, A.H.M. *Historical Dictionary of the League of Nations*. Lanham, MD: The Scarecrow Press, 2006.
Yearwood, P. *Guarantee of Peace: The League of Nations in British Policy, 1914–1924*. Oxford, UK: Oxford University Press, 2009.

Index

Abbey Theatre, 9n5, 16n2
Abyssinia. *See* Ethiopia
Acts of Union, 5
Addis Ababa, 142
Admiral Scheer Incident, 109–110
Afghanistan, 53
Aghnides, Thanassis, 168, 175–176, 178–179, 182, 185–186, 197
Albania, 61, 65, 163, 167–168
Algeria, 181, 197
Allied Powers, 20, 75
Allies/Allied, 74, 136, 188, 202, 206
Aloisi, Baron Pompeo, 140, 142
Alsace-Lorraine, 78
Amazon River, 39–40
American Consulate, 161
Anglo-Irish Agreement, 155
Anglo-Irish Treaty, 13
Appeasement, 21, 70, 119, 150
Argentina, 38
Argentine Government, 39
Asia, 29
Asquith, Herbert H., 6, 58
Australia, 24, 153
Austria, 61, 65, 151, 153, 167, 198
Austro-Hungarian Empire, 65, 73
Avenol, Joseph, 15–16, 27, 51, 59–62, 80, 82, 108–109, 119, 122–123, 131–132, 140, 143–144, 147–149, 151, 153–155, 159–162, 164, 166–168, 172–176, 178–182, 184–188, 191–195, 198, 201

Axis Powers, 15, 49, 144, 150, 166, 173, 175, 183, 188, 197, 205–206
Aydelotte, Frank, 177–178
Azcárate, Pablo de, 57, 131, 147–149

Balfour, Arthur, 58, 75
Baltic Sea, 73, 75
Bank of China, 162
Bank of Danzig, 108
Bank of International Settlements, 45, 108
Barros, James, 153
Battle of Britain, 180
Baudouin, Paul, 183
Beck, Józef, 78, 81, 82, 98, 122, 127, 128, 129, 130, 131, 132, 133, 134, 165
Belgium, 45, 65, 78, 144, 150, 171, 173, 206
Benavides, Óscar, 41
Beneš, Édvard, 38, 47, 48, 151
Bérenger, Henry, 23, 70
Berlin, 15, 69, 87–88, 92, 97, 104, 109–110, 112, 121, 125–127, 129–130, 132–133, 135, 144, 151–152, 161, 165, 183
Bermuda, 192, 200
Berne, 184–185, 197, 199, 205
Bernsdorff, Johann Heinrich Graf von, 45
Black and Tans, 8, 13
Blum, Léon, 161
Blythe, Ernest, 11–13
Boisanger, Yves-Bréart de, 180

213

Bolivia, 38–40
Bolivia/Paraguay Dispute, 38
Bonnet, Georges-Étienne, 161
Böttcher, Viktor, 103–104, 107, 112, 117, 120
Brazil, 38–40
Briand, Aristide, 23, 30, 78, 123
British Army, 6
British Commonwealth, 8, 80–82, 177
British Consul General in Danzig, 111, 113
British Consul General in Geneva, 179
British Dominions, 81, 179
British Empire, 8
British Foreign Office, 59, 80–81, 120, 140, 159, 168, 178, 184–185, 196, 199–200, 205–206, 208
British Foreign Secretary, 23, 58, 113, 120, 126, 133, 141, 150, 152, 160, 162, 174, 195, 199
British Government, 5–8, 13–14, 33, 47, 60, 107, 111, 113–114, 120–121, 123, 139, 150, 154, 160–164, 178–179, 181, 184, 186, 198, 200, 206
British Minister in Berne, 178–179, 199
British Navy, 174, 181
British Parliament, 5–6, 24
British Prime Minister, 150–151, 164
Brost, Erich, 92, 104, 130, 132
Bruce Committee, 167
Bruce Report, 155, 167
Bruce, Stanley, 153, 167
Brussels, 51
Bulgaria, 41, 61, 65
Burckhardt, Carl, 117–118, 133–134, 136, 153, 156, 197
Butler, Harold B., 59
Butler, R.A., 177

Caballero de Bedoya, Ramón, 38
Cadogan, Sir Alexander, 59, 184, 200, 206
Cambon Commission, 74
Canada, 24, 192, 201
Carr, Edward H., 81
Carson, Sir Edward, 6
Carton de Wiart, Count Henri, 180
Casement, Sir Roger, 6, 7
Castillo Nájera, Francisco, 38
Catholic Centre Party, 92, 102–104, 123, 128

Catholic Nationalists, 5, 12
Catholic Press Agency, 94
Cecil, Lord Robert, 33, 45, 171
Central Committee for Economic and Social Questions, 167
Chaco Boreal War, 37–38, 147
Chamberlain, Neville, 150–152, 164
Charron, René, 108, 176, 182–183, 188, 191, 197
Chiang Kai-Shek, 28, 34
Chile, 38, 150
China, 27–34, 43, 45, 47, 61, 154–155, 159–160, 162, 207; Republic of, 29
Chinese Army, 31
Chinese Government, 27–29, 31, 33–155, 162
Chinese National Economic Council, 28
Churchill, Winston, 3, 119, 152, 198, 202
Ciano, Gian Galeazzo, 144
Clemenceau, Georges, 58
Cold War, 162, 208
Colijn, Hendrik, 180
Collins, Michael, 7–8
Colombia, 37, 39–41
Colombian Government, 40
Committee on Technical Collaboration, 155
Communist(s), 96, 104–105, 160, 162
Communist Party, 92, 123
Conference for the Reduction and the Limitation of Armaments. *See* Disarmament Conference
Cooper, Lady Diana, 130
Cosgrave, W.T., 8, 13–15
Cosgrave Government, 85
Costa du Rels, Adolfo, 38, 40, 183, 185–187, 194, 195–196
Coyne, Thomas J., 24
Cremins, Frank, 85, 155, 197
Curzon, George, 58
Czechoslovak Army, 151
Czechoslovak Government, 151
Czechoslovakia, 38, 47–48, 61, 65, 67, 78, 134, 151–152, 163, 165, 167–168, 198, 206

Dáil Éireann, 7, 13, 155
Daladier, Édouard, 151, 161

Danzig, Free City of, 1, 15, 21, 24–25, 44, 47, 61, 73–77, 80, 83, 85–86, 91–92, 94, 96, 98, 99–100, 101–102, 104–106, 108–110, 112, 117–125, 127–136, 139, 143, 147–148, 151, 153, 155, 163–164, 168, 175; Constitution of the, 75–76, 80, 86–88, 92–93, 95–99, 102–107, 113, 122–124, 131; High Commissioner of the, 25, 44, 62, 75, 76, 77–82, 84, 91–92, 131, 147; Mandate of the, 131; Senate of the, 76, 78, 83–84, 86–87, 91–93, 95–99, 101–103, 105–106, 108, 110–112, 117–120, 122–128, 130, 132, 156; *Volkstag* of the, 92, 113
Danzig Government, 74, 86, 98–99, 102, 107, 110, 119
Danzig High Court, 106
Danzig opposition, 111, 113
Danzig Supreme Court, 106, 119
Danzig-West Prussia, 135
Darlan, Admiral François, 198
De Bono, Marshall Emilio, 140
De Brouckère, Louis, 45
De Haller, Édouard, 176
De Madariaga, Salvador, 23, 38, 82
De Valera, Éamon, 7–8, 13, 15, 24, 43, 155; as *Taoiseach*, 8, 15, 37, 85, 155, 208; as President of Ireland, 8; as President of the Council, 38; as President of the Assembly, 155
De Valera Government, 85
Debré, Robert, 162
Declaration of Irish Independence, 7
Denmark, 173, 198
Directoire, 181
Disarmament, 22, 167
Disarmament Conference, 24, 31, 44–45, 47–50, 82; Preparatory Commission for the, 45–46
Dodds, Harold W., 178, 184
Doig, Henry, 13
Doumer, Paul, 44
Drug Supervision Body, 193
Drummond, Sir Eric, 14, 27, 31, 51, 57–58, 60–62, 75, 149, 173
Dublin, 6–7, 12–15, 21, 24, 84, 109, 149, 156, 174, 200, 209
Duff Cooper, Alfred, 130

Dungannon Clubs, 12

East Prussia, 75, 92, 135, 164
Easter Monday 1916, 7, 13
Eastern Europe, 174
Economic and Financial Organisation, 51–52, 156, 166–167, 175, 177, 180, 184, 192
Ecuador, 39, 53
Eden, Anthony, 23, 102–103, 110, 112, 120–121, 126, 131–132, 150, 160, 168, 199–200, 202, 206–207
EFO. *See* Economic and Financial Organisation
Egypt, 53, 140, 144
Eire, 5, 8
Emmett, Robert, 5
Emperor of Ethiopia, 142
Enabling Act, 69
England, 33, 152, 168, 174–175, 185
Eritrea, 139
Erskine William, 83
Estonia, 61, 65
Ethiopia, 61, 107, 113, 123, 126–127, 139–144, 150, 153, 160, 168
Ethiopian Conflict, 53, 111, 127
Ethiopian Government, 144
Europe, 28, 39, 51, 65, 121, 141, 143–144, 150–151, 163, 168, 173, 175, 180–181, 183, 198–199, 206

Fascist/fascism, 52, 152, 154, 159–160
Felkin, Arthur E., 184
Fianna Fáil, 8
Fifth Column, 172, 174
Finland, 167–168, 195
First World War, 6–7, 19–20, 23, 27, 45, 51, 65, 68, 73–75, 77, 92, 102, 119, 134, 177
Fitzgerald, Desmond, 13
Fitzmaurice, Lord Edmond, 58
Forster, Albert, 86–87, 93–95, 99, 101, 104–105, 107–109, 111–112, 117–121, 122–126, 128, 129, 133–136
Fourteen Points, 73–74
Fourth Committee, 22, 53, 60
France, 29–30, 33, 43, 45, 47–49, 52, 58–59, 65–66, 74–75, 78, 81–82, 99, 119, 131, 139–143, 149–152, 157, 160,

162, 164–168, 171, 173–176, 181–182, 187, 192, 194–195, 198, 206; Third Republic of, 23, 150
Franco, General Francisco, 154, 191
Franco Government, 196
Franco-Italian Agreement, 140
French Foreign Minister, 152
French Government, 107, 111, 113–114, 120, 123, 139, 150, 154, 159–161, 164, 186
Führer. See Hitler, Adolf

Gaelic League, 12
Gaelic Revival, 12
Gageby, Dorothy Mary, 2, 13, 210
García Calderon, Francisco, 40
Gdańsk, 25, 136
Gdynia, 77, 107–109, 127, 164
General Post Office, 7
Geneva, 1, 11, 14–16, 21–24, 32, 38, 43, 53, 60, 62, 69, 76, 82–83, 85, 91, 94, 96, 101–103, 108, 110, 112–113, 117, 119–120, 123, 126–127, 129–131, 133, 142–143, 147, 152–153, 155–156, 161–162, 168, 171–177, 179–188, 191–201, 205–208, 210
George V, 24, 120
George VI, 165
German Air Force, 108
German Army, 102, 108, 123, 150, 172, 179, 197
German Consul General in Danzig, 98, 103, 124–125
German Empire, 65
German Foreign Minister, 129, 134, 150, 163
German Foreign Ministry, 101, 125, 135
German Government, 6, 45, 69, 74, 87, 92, 110, 112, 127, 133, 150, 161
German National People's Party, 92
German-Polish Convention, 68
German-Polish Non-Aggression Pact, 79
Germany, 6, 23, 29–30, 45, 47–49, 52–53, 58–59, 61–62, 65–68, 70, 73–82, 84, 88, 93, 96, 98, 99, 101–102, 111, 119–120, 123, 125, 127, 129, 131, 133–136, 143–144, 151, 159–165, 167–168, 172–173, 175, 182, 185, 195, 202, 207; Nazi, 25, 48–49, 91, 107, 139, 150, 152–154, 187, 197, 206; Third Reich, 25, 68, 87, 134
Gestapo, 62, 114n1, 129, 134, 196
Gibraltar, 197
Gibson, Hugh, 45, 49
Giustiniani, Enrico, 92, 104
Goebbels, Joseph, 70, 104, 113
Göring, Hermann, 79, 101, 104, 120, 125–127, 129–130, 133, 151
Gorski, Ann, 2, 13, 136, 206, 209–210
Government of Ireland Act, 8
Gran Chaco, 38, 40
Grandi, Dino, 140
Gravina, Count Manfredi, 79, 95
Great Britain, 12
Great Famine, 5–6, 44
Great Power(s), 14, 21, 23, 25, 32–34, 48, 50, 58–59, 78, 80–82, 91–92, 143, 147–148, 150–151, 165–166, 171, 197, 201
Greece, 41, 61, 65, 141, 164, 206
Gregory, Lady Augusta, 6
Greiser, Albert, 87–88, 94, 99, 101–105, 107–109, 111–112, 117–133, 135–136
Grey, Sir Edward, 58
Griffith, Arthur, 6
Guatemala, 38
Guerrero, José G., 186, 194, 196, 208
Gwiadowski, Tadeusz, 15

Haas, Robert, 27
Haile Selassie, 61, 142–143
Haking, General Sir Richard, 75–76
Halifax, Lord (Viscount), 150, 162, 177, 195
Hambro, Carl, 22, 57, 60, 134, 148–149, 179–180, 184–185, 194–195, 200, 206, 208–209
Health, 22
Heinlein, Konrad, 151
Henderson, Arthur, 45, 46, 50
Herriot, Édouard, 47, 161
Hess, Rudolf, 104
Hesselgren, Kerstin, 142
Heydrich, Reinhardt, 133
High Commissioner for Danzig. *See* Danzig, Free City of
High Commissioner for Refugees, 2
Hill, William, 168, 191

Himmler, Heinrich, 133
Hiss, Alger, 208
Hitler, Adolf, 1, 3, 15, 25, 49, 61–62, 67, 69, 78–79, 86–88, 93, 96, 99, 101, 107–109, 112, 114, 118–121, 123, 125–134, 136, 139, 150–152, 162–165, 175–176, 181, 183, 198, 208
Hitler Youth, 94
Hoare, Samuel, 113, 120, 141
Hoare-Laval Pact, 61, 113
Hoden, Marcel, 160–161
Holma, Harri, 180, 194–195
Holocaust, 89n27, 137n14
Holy See, 165
Home Rule, 6
Hoover, Herbert, 47, 52, 162
Hudson, Manley, 207
Hull, Cordell, 177
Hungary, 61, 65, 163, 167
Hutchinson, Ernest, 29

ILO. *See* International Labour Organization
Institute for Advanced Study, 177
Intellectual Cooperation, 22
International Children's Center, 162
International Committee of the Red Cross, 19, 197
International Financial Conference, 51
International Health Office, 2
International Labour Conference, 200
International Labour Office, 2, 22
International Labour Organization, 22, 25n5, 44, 59, 77, 166–167, 171–172, 178–179, 182–183, 185, 191, 194–196, 200–201, 208; Director-General of the, 44, 185
International School of Geneva, 177
Iraq, 44, 53, 65
Ireland, 3, 5–9, 12, 14–15, 21, 24, 33, 37, 43–44, 67, 84–85, 120, 129, 132, 136, 154–156, 164–165, 168, 174, 206, 209; Republic of, 5
Irish Army, 174
Irish Constitution, 155
Irish Free State, 8, 13–14, 20–21, 24, 33, 37–38, 43, 46, 67, 81, 85
Irish Gaelic, 5, 7, 12, 192
Irish Government, 24, 122, 156, 165, 208

Irish independence, 6, 8, 11
Irish language, 11
Irish League of Nations Society, 85
Irish Nationalist Party, 13
Irish Parliament, 5
Irish Potato Famine. *See* Great Famine
Irish Provisional Government, 8
Irish Republic, Provisional Government of the, 7
Irish Republican Army, 7, 13
Irish Republican Brotherhood, 6, 12
Irish Volunteers, 13
Irish War of Independence, 7, 13
Italian-Ethiopian Treaty of Amity, Conciliation and Arbitration, 140
Italian Government, 69, 144, 161
Italian Somaliland, 139
Italo-Ethiopian Crisis, 139
Italy, 30, 43, 47–49, 52–53, 59, 61–62, 65–66, 69, 80–81, 107, 113, 126–127, 139–141, 143–144, 148, 150–151, 153–154, 159–162, 167–168, 173, 175, 181–182, 202
Iwane, General Matsui, 32

Jacklin, Seymour, 166, 175–176, 179–182, 185–187, 194–197, 200, 207
Japan, 28–34, 43, 45, 47, 53, 61, 67, 143, 150, 153, 154, 159–160, 168, 202, 207
Japanese Army, 29, 30
Japanese Government, 32
Jew(s)/Jewish, 62n5, 68, 70, 78–79, 86, 89n25, 96, 105–106, 108, 110, 127–128, 133, 136, 137n8, 137n13, 145n2, 152–153, 160, 169n3, 189n16, 193
Jewish Party, 123

Kellogg-Briand Pact, 165
Kelly, David, 178–179, 184–185, 199
Kennard, Howard, 108, 111
Kilroy, Patricia, 2, 13, 210
Kingdom of Ireland, 7
Kisch, Sir Cecil, 180, 194–195
Knox, Sir Geoffrey, 102
Krabbe, Ludwig, 103
Krauel, Wolfgang, 176, 187
Kuomintang, 29, 33, 34n3, 159

218   *Index*

Lange, Christian, 23
Latin America, 25, 27, 37, 39
Latvia, 65, 135
Laval, Pierre, 120, 140–142, 183
League of Nations, 1, 2, 11, 13–16, 19–21, 23–24, 28–34, 37–41, 44–45, 49, 51–53, 58, 61–62, 65–70, 73, 78, 82, 84–85, 88, 91, 97–100, 101, 104–105, 107, 109, 111, 112–114, 118–123, 126–128, 130–131, 134, 139–144, 147–150, 152–155, 157, 159–162, 164–168, 171–173, 175–177, 179–181, 183–188, 191–201, 205–207, 208–209; Archives, 1, 210; Assembly of the, 16, 21, 22, 30–33, 38–39, 41, 43–44, 58, 60, 66, 70, 120, 126, 129, 143–144, 148, 152–153, 155, 160–161, 166–168, 171, 180, 206–209; Committee of Jurists, 107, 110; Committee of Three, 38–40, 131; Communications Section, 192; Council of the, 20–24, 28–34, 37–41, 43–45, 57–60, 66–67, 71, 75–78, 80–81, 83–86, 93, 95–96, 98, 101–103, 106–108, 110–114, 117–121, 123–127, 130–132, 142, 147–148, 150, 167, 180, 202; Covenant of the, 14, 19–20, 25, 29, 32, 34, 37, 39, 44, 66, 68, 94, 140, 142–143, 148, 150, 160, 165–166, 197, 202; Department of External Affairs, 85; Deputy Secretary-General of the, 44, 57, 60, 131, 162, 174, 176; Economic, Financial and Transit Section, 191; Economic Relations Section, 28; Health Section, 27–28, 159, 177, 181, 183, 192; High Commissioner for Danzig, 94–96, 107–113, 117, 120–122, 124, 127, 129–133, 136, 139, 143, 153, 162; Intellectual Cooperation, 192; Legal Department, 173, 194; Mandates Section, 102, 192; Minorities Section, 79–80, 148, 192; Opium Section, 177, 181, 183, 192, 193; President of the Assembly of the, 185; President of the Council of the, 23, 37, 42n4, 185–186, 194, 196; Public Information Section, 177, 192; Rapporteur for Danzig, 81, 83, 102, 110, 121; Refugee Section, 192; Secretariat of the, 15, 22, 24–25, 27, 41, 57–61, 75, 79–81, 83–85, 101, 103, 147–149, 155, 157, 159–161, 166–167, 172, 174, 180–181, 184, 187, 192–195, 200, 205, 207; Secretary-General of the, 14, 39, 57–61, 75, 84, 95, 108–109, 119, 122–123, 125, 131, 140, 147, 153, 160–161, 166–167, 172, 178, 180, 183, 185, 188, 194, 196, 198, 206; Social Section, 183, 192; Treasury Section, 192, 196; Under Secretary-General of the, 44, 57
Leipzig Incident, 125, 127, 129
Lester, Elsie, 13, 84, 128, 147, 156, 164, 174, 209
Lester, Sean, 2, 3, 11–12, 20, 62, 85, 87, 156, 210; as Acting President of the Council, 40–41, 65; as Acting Secretary-General of the League of Nations, 16, 185–188, 191–201, 205–208; as Deputy Secretary-General of the League of Nations, 15, 58, 85, 147–151, 154–155, 157, 160–166, 168, 171–174, 176, 178–187, 194; as Director of Publicity, 14; as Government Press Officer, 13; as High Commissioner for Danzig, 12, 15, 67, 74, 80–88, 91, 92, 94, 96–100, 102–103, 105–114, 117–134, 136, 147, 156, 210; as Irish Representative to the League of Nations, 15, 22–24, 32–33, 37–38, 43–44, 46–50, 53, 57, 60, 67, 70, 95, 101, 148; as John Ernest Lester, 11; as Rapporteur on Minorities, 67–69; as Rapporteur to the Assembly, 53; as Rapporteur to the Council, 155; as Sean Mac Leastair, 11; as Secretary-General of the League of Nations, 1, 16, 187, 209–210
Leticia, 39, 41, 85
Leticia Dispute, 37–38, 40, 147
Leticia Trapeze, 41
Lever, Vera Blanche, 60, 176, 187–188
Liberia, 139
Lipski, Jósef, 79, 130
Lisbon, 191–192, 194–195, 208
Lithuania, 65, 132, 135, 163
Livingston, Henry, 179, 197, 199
Lloyd George, David, 8, 74
Locarno Pact, 45, 78, 123

Index

London, 14, 23–24, 59–60, 80, 84, 102, 109, 113, 121, 131, 135, 161–162, 168, 174, 178, 180, 184, 192, 194, 196–197, 199–200, 206–208
López Olivan, Julio, 186, 195–196
López Pumajero, Alfonso, 41
Lothian, Lord, 178
Loudon, Jonkheer, 45
Loveday, Alexander, 51, 156, 167, 175, 177–180, 182, 184, 191–192, 195–196, 200, 206–207
Lower Silesia, 68
Lubieński, Michal, 127
Luxembourg, 171, 173
Lytton Commission, 30, 31
Lytton, Earl of, 30
Lytton Report, 30, 32

McCarthyists, 162
MacDonald, Ramsay, 48, 140
McDonnell, Mervyn S., 76
McGill University, 179, 200–201
McGilligan, Patrick, 14
MacNeill, Eoin, 13
MacWhite, Michael, 14, 21
Madrid, 196
Makins, Roger, 199–200, 206
Manchukuo, 29–32
Manchuria, 28–32, 34, 37, 85, 153, 168
Manchurian Affair, 29
Manchurian Crisis, 24, 31–34, 58, 127, 160
Mandates, 22
Mandel, Georges, 161
Marseilles, 197
Martinique, 197
Matos, José, 38
Matsuoka, Yosuke, 32
Mediterranean, 140
Memel, 163, 168
Mexico, 38, 53
Middle East, 140
Minorities, 22, 65–68, 73, 92. *See also* League of Nations Minorities Section
Molotov, Vyacheslav M., 207–208
Monnet, Jean, 51, 60, 147, 162
Montreal, 179, 196, 200–201
Morocco, 197
Morrison, Herbert, 202
Mortishead, Ronald, 191–192, 196

Motta, Guiseppe, 46
Mukden Incident, 30
Munich Agreement, 61, 134, 151–152, 159–161, 164
Mussolini, Benito, 1, 3, 61–62, 120, 139–142, 150–151, 153, 160, 162–163, 175–176, 183

National Board of the League of Nations Association, 177
National Socialist German Workers' Party, 86, 93, 107
National Socialist Government, 101
National University of Ireland, 16, 209
Nazi(s)/nazism, 15, 52, 69–70, 77, 86, 92–94, 96–99, 102–105, 107, 110–114, 118, 119–126, 128, 130–133, 136, 147, 150–153, 163, 166, 175, 181, 198
Nazi Germany. *See* Germany, Nazi
Nazi Party, 61, 75, 80, 86–88, 92–96, 99, 102, 104–107, 109–110, 112, 114, 119, 124, 126, 133, 150
Netherlands, 45, 107, 150, 165, 171, 173, 186, 198, 206
New York, 177, 192, 194, 200
New York World's Fair, 192
New Zealand, 24
Nobel Prize: for Literature, 9n5; for Peace, 26n12, 35n11, 50, 54n9, 54n16, 88n9, 145n10, 189n10
Noel-Baker, Philip, 50, 210
Northern Ireland, 5, 8–9, 12, 67
Northern Irish Protestants, 6, 11, 67
Norway, 173, 198, 206
Norwegian Government, 179
NSDAP. *See* National Socialist German Workers' Party

O'Connell, Daniel, 5
O'Donavan, Declan, 136
Olaya, Enrique, 39
Olympic Games 1936, 129
Opium, 19, 22, 154
Organisation for Communications and Transport, 28
Organisation for Intellectual Collaboration, 28
Ormsby-Gore, William, 70

O'Rourke, Count Edvard, 94, 114, 128, 132
Ottoman Empire, 65

Palais des Nations, 131, 153, 155, 168, 171–172, 175–176, 178–179, 191, 193–194, 197, 199, 201, 205, 209
Panama Canal, 40
Pan-American Union, 37
Papée, Kazimierz, 98, 104, 107, 111, 122, 124, 127–128, 130, 134
Paraguay, 38, 39
Pardo, Carlos, 166, 176, 180, 186, 194, 196
Paris, 135, 147, 161–162, 195, 198, 206
Paris Convention, 73
Paris Peace Conference, 58, 74
Parnell, Charles Stewart, 6
Paul-Boncour, Joseph, 45, 68–69
Permanent Central Opium Board, 193
Permanent Court of International Justice, 2, 22, 59, 77–78, 110, 167, 171, 186, 194, 195, 208
Persia, 44
Peru, 37–41
Peruvian Government, 39–41
Pétain, Marshall Philippe, 183
Phelan, Edward, 22, 166, 178–179, 191–196, 201, 208
Phoney War, 168
Pilotti, Massimo, 44, 57, 147–149, 162
Piłsudski, Józef, 78, 134
Plunkett, Joseph, 6
Poland, 14–15, 25, 27, 45, 62, 65, 67–69, 73–84, 91, 95, 98, 99, 101–109, 111, 113–114, 119, 121–123, 127–131, 133–136, 144, 153, 162–165, 198, 206
Polish Army, 124
Polish Consul General, 104, 107, 111, 125, 128, 130
Polish Corridor, 25, 73, 75
Polish/Danzig Pact, 124
Polish Government, 74–75, 77, 82–83, 92, 98, 111, 114, 121–122, 126, 130, 132, 151, 162, 164–165, 208
Polish Party, 92, 106
Polish-Soviet War, 77
Portugal, 131, 176, 192, 195, 197, 206
Portuguese Government, 195

Princeton University, 52, 177–180, 183–184, 191–192, 194, 196
Prisoners-of-war, 19, 58, 197
Protestant, 5, 9, 12, 67–68, 149, 156, 209
Protestant Unionists, 12
Prussia, 73

Rajchman, Ludwik, 27, 155, 159–162
Rauschning, Anna, 94
Rauschning, Hermann, 86–87, 91, 93, 95, 97–99, 101, 105, 109, 112, 132, 163
Red Army, 136
Refugees, 19, 58
Renborg, Bertil A., 179
Reynaud, Paul, 161
Rhineland, 78, 123, 168
Ribbentrop-Molotov Non-Aggression Pact, 164
Riefler, Winfield W., 177
Rio de Janeiro Protocol, 41
Robinson, L.M., 111, 120
Rockefeller Foundation, 177
Rockefeller Institute for Medical Research, 177
Roman Catholic(s), 5–6, 9, 12, 24, 60, 67–68, 79, 93, 101, 105, 132
Romania, 65, 67, 163–164
Rome, 62, 140, 144, 161
Roosevelt, Franklin Delano, 3, 52, 167, 200
Rosting, Helmer, 79–80, 82–83, 93, 95
Royal Institute of International Affairs, 33
Russia, 66, 73
Russian Empire, 65

Saar Commission, 102
Saar Plebiscite, 102, 104
Saarland, 73, 75, 85, 102
Saavedra Lamas, Carlos, 143
Salomón-Lozano Treaty, 39, 41
Salter, Sir Arthur, 51
San Francisco Conference, 206–208
Sánchez, Luis Miguel, 39, 41
Santos, Eduardo, 40
Sarajevo Incident, 57
Scandinavia, 130
Schober, Johannes, 39
Schuschnigg, Kurt, 150

Second World War, 15, 22–23, 27, 38, 48–49, 52, 61–62, 68, 117–118, 134–135, 142, 156, 162–165, 167, 171, 177–178, 198, 202, 205–209
Secretary of State for Foreign Affairs. *See* British Foreign Secretary
Shanghai Ceasefire Agreement, 32
Shanghai Incident, 31
Shaw, George Bernard, 50
Silesia. *See* Upper/Lower Silesia
Silesian Minorities Treaty, 68
Simon, Sir John, 81–83
Sinn Féin, 6–7, 12–13
Sino-Japanese Conflict, 33
Skylstad, Rasmus, 179, 182, 184
Smuts, General Jan Christiaan, 19
Social Democratic Party, 92, 99, 104, 123, 130
Sokoline, Vladimir, 168
Somalia, 139
Soong, Tse-ven, 207
South America, 25, 37
Southern Ireland, 8
Spain, 38, 57, 59, 61, 148, 154, 176, 181, 192, 194, 196
Spanish Civil War, 61, 127, 144, 154, 196
Spanish Government, 197
Stalin, Joseph, 3, 140, 164, 198
Statute of Westminster, 24
Stettinius, Edward, 207
Stimson Doctrine, 32
Stoppani, Pietro, 51, 176
Stresa Front, 140
Stresemann, Gustav, 78, 123
Strutt, Lieutenant-Colonel Edward L., 76
Sudetenland, 61, 134, 151
Suez Canal, 141
Supervisory Commission, 148, 166, 179–180, 185–186, 193–195, 199–201, 205–208
Sweden, 107, 131, 135
Sweetser, Arthur, 177, 179–180, 192–193
Swiss Government, 142, 172–173, 205
Switzerland, 23, 107, 135, 144, 154, 163, 166, 172, 176, 185, 188, 198–199, 205
Syria, 198
Szembek, Jan, 129

Te Water, Charles T., 85

Temperley, Major-General A.C., 84
Teschen, 134
Thomas, Albert, 44, 59
Tittmann, Harold H., 179, 184
Tone, Wolf, 5
Tower, Sir Reginald, 76, 83
Treaty of Versailles. *See* Versailles, Treaty of
Trendelenburg, Ernst, 57
Trinidad, 197, 200
Trinity College, Dublin, 16, 209
Turkey, 44, 53, 65
Tyrrell, Elizabeth Ruth. *See* Lester, Elsie

Ulster, 5, 8, 12
Ulster Unionists, 6
Union of Soviet Socialist Republics. *See* USSR
Unionists, 5
United Kingdom, 5, 8, 24, 29–30, 33, 43–45, 48–49, 52, 65–66, 80–83, 85, 111, 119–120, 127, 131, 139–142, 149–150, 155, 164–165, 167–168, 171, 174–176, 179, 181, 196, 202, 207
United Nations, 155, 167, 206, 208–209; Charter of the, 208
United Nations Children's Emergency Fund, 162
United Nations Declaration, 207
United Nations International school, 177
United Nations Library, Geneva, 2
United Nations Relief and Rehabilitation Administration, 162
United Nations Specialized Agencies, 192
United States Government, 177
United States of America, 14, 28, 30, 33, 37, 39, 44–45, 48–49, 52, 58, 141, 155, 162, 166–168, 175, 177–180, 184–185, 187, 192–193, 195–196, 198–200, 202, 206–207; President of the, 20, 47, 52, 167, 194; State Department, 179, 184
Upper Silesia, 24, 67–68, 69–70, 97, 106
USSR, 28, 45, 53, 140, 152, 154, 164–165, 167–168, 195, 198, 206–207

Van Eysinga, Willem Jan Marie, 59
Vansittart, Sir Robert, 119
Vásquez Cobo, General Alfredo, 39
Venezuela, 150

Venizelos, Eleftherios, 58
Versailles, 78, 91; Treaty of, 15, 25n5, 44–45, 47, 49, 73–76, 78, 87, 91–92, 123, 129, 132, 163, 165; Peace Conference, 22, 48, 67, 151
Vichy, 166, 173, 183, 186, 194–195
Vichy Government, 183–184, 192, 198
Vichy Regime, 142
Victor Emanuel III, 142
Vigier, Eugène, 168
Viple, Marius, 179, 182, 185, 191
Vistula River, 77
Von Keller, Friedrich, 69
Von Moltke, Hans-Adolf, 111
Von Neurath, Konstantin, 82, 101, 112, 121, 150
Von Radowicz, Otto, 103, 124–125
Von Ribbentrop, Joachim, 129, 133–134, 150, 163
Von Weizsäcker, Ernst, 135

Wall Street Collapse, 93
Walters, Francis P., 60, 122, 148, 149, 162, 168, 174

Wal-Wal Incident, 139–140
Washington Commission of Neutrals, 37–38
Washington D.C., 177–179, 192–194
Warsaw, 15, 83, 108, 109, 111–113, 121, 130, 132, 208
Warsaw Convention, 74
Weimar Germany, 92
Western Europe, 171, 172
Westerplatte, 77, 79, 93, 134, 136
Westerplatte Incident, 44
Weygand, General Maxime, 183
Williams, Yen Wei-Ching, 29
Wilson, Woodrow, 20, 58, 73–74
Winant, John, 178–179, 185, 207
Wiskemann, Elizabeth, 129–130
Woodrow Wilson Foundation, 16, 52, 209

Yalta Conference, 136
Yeats, William Butler, 6
Yugoslavia, 65

Zilliacus, Konni, 50–51

www.ingramcontent.com/pod-product-compliance
Lightning Source LLC
Chambersburg PA
CBHW022011300426
44117CB00005B/137